Teaching English as a Foreign or Second Language

Teaching English as a Foreign or Second Language

A Self-development and Methodology Guide

Jerry G. Gebhard

Ann Arbor

THE UNIVERSITY OF MICHIGAN PRESS

Copyright © by the University of Michigan 1996
All rights reserved
Published in the United States of America by
The University of Michigan Press
Manufactured in the United States of America
⊚ Printed on acid-free paper

1999   1998   1997   1996   4   3   2   1

A CIP catalog record for this book is available from the British Library.

Library of Congress Cataloging-in-Publication Data

Gebhard, Jerry Greer.
    Teaching English as a foreign or second language : a self-
development and methodology guide / Jerry G. Gebhard.
        p.   cm.
    Includes bibliographical references (p.   ) and index.
    ISBN 0-472-08231-0 (pbk. : acid-free paper)
    1. English language—Study and teaching—Foreign speakers.
2. English teachers—Training of.   I. Title.
PE1128.A2G38   1996
428'.007—dc20   96-9952
                                                        CIP

This book is dedicated to my mother, Margaret Gebhard, who understood the importance of patience, loving kindness, and self-respect.

Acknowledgments

I sincerely thank Maria Saryuz Szarska, Dong Xu, and Tim Conrad for assisting me with research during the development of this book. I thank John Fanselow, Thomas Farrell, Pamela Friedman, Barbara Hill Hudson, Joe O'Connor, Judi Moy, and Lilia Savova for reading and commenting on this book at different stages in its development. I thank the administration at the American Language Institute (ALI) at the Indiana University of Pennsylvania (IUP) for their consent to observe and photograph classes; Mary Beth Mahler, Zubeyde Tezel, and Trikartikaningsih for inviting me into their classes; the students in their ALI classes for being so very cooperative; and Takahiko Hara for developing the photographs in this book.

I also thank the numerous graduate students in the Ph.D. Rhetoric and Linguistics and M.A. TESOL programs at IUP who read and commented on chapters from this book as a part of their course experiences in Cross-cultural Communication, TESL/TEFL Methodology, ESL Materials and Media, and Introduction to TESOL; Ali Aghbar and Dan Tannacito for their support; and my wife, Yoko Gebhard, for doing some of the sketches in this book and for encouraging me to write the book.

Contents

Introduction: A Self-development Guide

I'm an English Teacher!?

—Remark made by an unprepared teacher

The Audience for This Book

This book is a teacher development and methodology guide. It can be used by those of you who are learning to teach English as a foreign language (EFL) and English as a second language (ESL) as a part of your preservice teacher education program. It can also be used as a teacher development text in in-service teacher development programs, as a source for experienced EFL/ESL teachers who would like to refresh their knowledge and continue to work on the development of their teaching. In addition, this book can act as an exploratory text for those of you who are simply curious about teaching EFL/ESL or by those of you who have accepted an EFL/ESL teaching position without the benefit of a formal teacher education program and find yourselves unprepared to take on the responsibilities of being a teacher.

The Purpose and Content of This Book

This book provides ways for you to work on the development of your teaching beliefs and classroom practices. It includes how you, as an EFL or ESL teacher, can develop your teaching through a process of exploration. This book also provides you with discussion, examples, and illustrations on how EFL/ESL can be taught as interaction among people, how classrooms can be managed, how teachers and students can make use of authentic teaching materials and media, and the significance of culture for both students and teachers. In addition, this book shows how EFL/ESL teachers teach students to comprehend spoken English, to converse in English, to read for meaning, and to process writing.

This book is based on questions EFL/ESL teachers, including myself, have asked about teaching and learning over a number of years, and each chapter begins with a set of questions related to the content of that chapter. As such, one way to use this book as a part of your development is as a reference for ideas based on the questions posed at the beginning of each chapter and answered within it. This book also has a list of recommended sources at the end of each chapter and includes references to professional books and articles as well as EFL/ESL textbooks. The appendixes contain information on publishing companies and academic and practical journals on teaching EFL/ESL. These additional sources provide you with a way to work further on your own development as an EFL/ESL teacher.

The end of each chapter includes a set of self-development tasks that are an integral part of this book. The purpose of these tasks is to provide you with opportunities to work on your development as an EFL/ESL teacher by observing, talking about, and writing about teaching, and I encourage you to spend time on these tasks. I realize that finding the time to do these tasks is not necessarily easy, especially for those of you with busy teaching schedules. However, I encourage you to keep an open mind and to find the time to systematically reflect on your teaching in new ways and stretch your imaginations through the teacher development tasks.

Teaching EFL versus ESL

Throughout this book I discuss how you can develop your abilities to teach EFL and ESL. By EFL I mean English as studied by people who live in places where English is not the first language of the people who live in the country, such as in Italy, Saudi Arabia, and Korea. By ESL I mean English as studied by people who speak other languages as their first language—such as Spanish, Arabic, Chinese, or Swahili—but live in places where English is the first language, such as in Australia, New Zealand, Canada, the United States, and the United Kingdom.

It is important to point out that there are obvious differences between teaching and learning English in EFL and ESL settings.

Although I am at risk of overgeneralizing, it is possible to point out a few of these differences.[1] To begin with, student populations differ. In many EFL contexts, the population is homogeneous in many ways; for example, all the students might share a similar history of being Korean, German, or Egyptian. Even if there are cultural differences—for example, being a Christian or a Muslim in Malaysia—there is still a common bond through the larger cultural identity. However, with the exception of special programs for specific groups of people (for example, a refugee program), many ESL settings are quite heterogeneous. Students from a great variety of countries can be found in the same ESL classroom. For example, I recently taught an ESL class with students from Bangladesh, Kenya, Germany, Italy, Costa Rica, Malaysia, Turkey, Pakistan, and Japan.

In addition, the goals of learning EFL and ESL are often quite different. In many countries where English is a foreign language, the primary goal for children studying in the educational system is to pass English entrance exams to enter good high schools and universities. As such, much of the teaching is directed at making students able to analyze and comprehend English so they can pass entrance examinations, not necessarily at preparing them to communicate in English. However, the goal is quite different for children studying ESL in America, Australia, and other countries where the medium of communication is English. In the ESL setting, the goal is often tied to literacy. The goal is for the child to use English as does a native speaker so he or she can assimilate into the mainstream English-speaking population. Of course, there are people in EFL settings who want and need to learn English to communicate effectively with others, including those interested in traveling, living abroad, doing international business, working as simultaneous translators, and working in the tourist industry. Likewise, there are those who study in ESL settings because they want to pass entrance exams—for example, students at language institutes who want to pass the Test of English as a Foreign Language (TOEFL) to gain admittance into an American university.

Teachers' concerns also differ. In EFL settings, teachers are consistently concerned with ways to get students to speak English in class, ways to use authentic language teaching materials, having to teach to test, having too little time with students, and getting students to take on more responsibility for their learning.[2] Of course, some ESL teachers have these same concerns, but they are not as magnified. A related concern is that in EFL settings there are fewer chances for students to apply what they study to communicative situations outside the classroom. Quite often the only comprehensible English some EFL students hear and read is in the classroom. In contrast, when ESL students leave the classroom, they can enter any number of situations in which they can use English.

Despite the differences, it is possible to discuss EFL and ESL teaching together, especially when discussion centers on how teachers can make more informed teaching decisions through observing, talking about, and writing about teaching. Likewise, it is possible to discuss EFL and ESL in relation to teaching English as interaction among people, how classroom interaction is managed, the kinds of materials and media available, culture as it relates to the lives of teachers and students, and teaching the skills of listening, speaking, reading, and writing.

Assumptions Underlying This Book

One assumption underlying this book is that being a competent teacher is not easy. It demands time, devotion, and opportunity to develop your teaching beliefs and practices. A closely related, second assumption is that you are willing to take on the responsibility for teaching EFL/ESL to students in your classes and that, to do this, you will use this book as a way to gain the kind of knowledge that you can use to be more accountable to the students and administrators in relation to increasing the possibilities for students' success.

A third assumption is that you recognize that self-development is an ongoing process. It is not just for expatriates new to teaching. Even very experienced teachers need to consistently work on their development through exploration of beliefs about teaching and teaching practices. Such exploration also requires you to be assertive, especially in gaining the cooperation of others. Through collaboration with others you, as teachers, will gain opportunities to explore teaching, and through such exploration you will see your own teaching differently and clearly as well as generate and implement creative new ways to teach.

A fourth assumption is that teaching can be learned. There are no born teachers. There are some people whose personalities, life experience, and natural ways of interacting are conducive to classroom teaching. But even so, without knowledge of how EFL/ESL teaching is accomplished, even the most talented person can lose teaching opportunities.

A fifth assumption is that there is no best way to teach in every setting. Teaching is basically an interactive process involving teacher, students, and task; and the way that teaching is accomplished in one setting may not work in another. As such, this book does not provide prescriptions about how you should teach. Rather, it provides a process through which you can explore your own teaching beliefs and practices, discussion on the basics of teaching EFL/ESL and ways skills can be taught, and teaching suggestions that can be adapted. As you are capable of creative thinking, some of the ideas in this book will hopefully stretch your imaginations.

A final assumption is that earning a professional degree in teaching English to speakers of other languages (TESOL) or a related field is very important, and although teachers can learn to be adequate teachers without a professional degree, this book is not meant to replace the kind of knowledge that can be gained in a professional degree program. Such a program is an initiation into the field and a way to gain a full understanding of the expectations of professionals in TESOL.

With the purpose and assumptions in mind, I invite you to discover and rediscover your teaching self through exploration of the basics of teaching and of ways to see your own teaching more clearly and differently.

Notes

1. I say I am at risk of overgeneralizing because "English teaching is an activity infused with social and political significance" (McKay 1992, ix). Even in different countries where EFL is taught, there are significant differences in regard to who studies English, why they study, who teaches them, and how they are taught.
2. I base my statements about teaching EFL on my own experience as an EFL teacher in Thailand, Japan, China, and Hungary, as well as on a survey by Nunan (1993).

Part 1

Self-development and Exploration

Chapter 1

The Self-developed Language Teacher

> Teachers themselves who, with their colleagues, must become the primary shapers of their own development.
>
> —Lieberman 1992, vi

- Does self-development make a difference?
- What factors are central to teacher self-development?

Does Self-development Make a Difference?

To emphasize the concept of self-development, I begin this book by illustrating its advantages. To do this, I invite you to enter two different EFL classrooms. The first is the classroom of a teacher (Yoshi) who has not had the opportunity to work on the development of his teaching. The second is that of a teacher (Kathy) who has taken on the responsibility for her own development. I emphasize that both teachers can gain much by paying ongoing attention to their development as teachers.

Yoshi's Class

After attending high school in the United States and earning bachelor's and master's degrees in geography from an American university, Yoshi accepted a position with a corporation in Japan, his home country, where he has been employed for the past six months. Because of his strong language skills, his job includes editing and translating letters, contracts, and other documents in English. A second part of his job is to teach English to two groups of businesspeople three mornings each week as part of an education program for company employees. Yoshi enjoys the editing and translating part of his job. However, he has become a little discouraged with his responsibilities as an EFL teacher. Let's take a look inside one of his classes.

Nine men and two women are there today and sit along the sides of a conference table. Yoshi begins by telling them to open their books to page 52. The text covers topics about contemporary world issues, such as world hunger, population control, and drug trafficking. The class is on chapter 4, which is about the plight of refugees around the world. Yoshi reads the introductory paragraphs aloud. After he finishes, he asks the students if they have any questions, and as usual, no one does. He then tells the students to listen to a tape that accompanies the text. It is a short lecture about the common problems refugees have.

When the lecture ends, Yoshi directs questions in English to the class about the content of the tape. He asks, "What's one of the problems refugees have in common?" A student gives the response, "They are hungry." Yoshi smiles and says, "Very good. What's another problem?" The students willingly answer his questions, all using English.

Next, Yoshi turns to a reading activity. He asks each student in turn to read from the text. As they do, Yoshi stops them to correct their pronunciation. After each student reads, Yoshi paraphrases and explains vocabulary words to them. Some students write down their understanding of the meaning in Japanese.

When they finish, Yoshi asks the students to answer the comprehension questions about the reading selection, and a few of the students answer his questions while the rest sit silently or look up words in their bilingual dictionaries. Yoshi expands on each of the answers, sometimes offering Japanese translation. At the end of the hour, he gives a homework assignment to memorize words in the "Expand your Vocabulary" section of their textbook.

After the students leave, Yoshi reflects on the class. He is happy that he uses English most of the time, and the majority of the students are willing to speak English with him and seem quite content with the class. However, he feels frustrated that the students do not prepare for class and do not ask questions. He also is disheartened because he ends up summarizing the content of the tapes and text, doing almost all of the talking in class. Except for a few golden moments, the only time students talk is when he introduces grammar and pronunciation drills or directly asks them questions. He realizes that his geography degrees have not prepared him to be a language teacher, and he wonders how he might change his way of teaching. As he leaves the classroom, he considers the idea of going to the bookstore to look for books on teaching English.

Kathy's Class

Kathy graduated from college with a bachelor's degree in history. Before going on to graduate school, she wanted to gain some life experience, contribute something of herself to others, and visit places she had read about in her history books. Kathy was lucky enough to be selected as a Peace Corps volunteer and was sent to Hungary to teach English. After her initial intensive training in aspects of cultural assimilation, language, and EFL teaching in Hungary, she was sent to teach EFL at a high school in an industrial town where she is presently the only volunteer.

The class we will consider here is titled Fourth Year English, and her lessons usually combine listening, speaking, reading, and writing. Kathy had raced to the classroom five minutes early to put pictures on the wall of people using exaggerated gestures and to put the following message on the board:

> Study the pictures on the wall. What do you think the gestures mean? Feel free to talk with your neighbor, but be sure to speak in English.

She purposely did this for two reasons. First, she is bothered by how long it takes to begin class. Second, she wants to explore how she can get students to speak English spontaneously with each other. Her objective on this day is to see if students would silently read the message on the blackboard, study the pictures, and start to talk in English.

As the students enter the classroom, they are chatting in Hungarian. But they soon see Kathy pointing to the message, and they silently read it. Before long the class fills with talk, but Kathy has mixed feelings. A few of the students are using English, but others continue to use Hungarian. Kathy gets their attention and points to a picture of a man with a wrinkled brow and wide eyes, his head tilted, shrugging his shoulders. She asks, "How about this picture? What does this gesture possibly mean?" One student volunteers, "It mean 'I don't know'?" Kathy accepts this and goes on to the next picture. After the students give their interpretations, Kathy tells the class they will spend the next few class periods considering their own and others' nonverbal behaviors—such as eye contact, gestures, and the use of space—as well as different ways to express meaning in different cultures.

Kathy then has students select pieces of hard candy from a bag, telling the students with the cherry flavor to form a group in the back, those with lemon to group to the right, those with grape in the front, and those with lime to the left. After the students settle, she gives each group a set of statements about nonverbal behavior and asks them to decide if they are true or false. The students are silent at first as they study such statements as this one: "During a conversation in Japan, the proper place to focus one's eyes is on the neck of one's conversation partner, while in Saudi Arabia it is proper to gaze directly into the person's eyes."

As they work on this task, Kathy circulates among the groups. She does not tell them the answers, even when they coax her. The room is full of laughter, but Kathy also notices that students are speaking more than the usual amount of Hungarian today. She also notices their language errors and wonders how she might give students more feedback on their language use.

Kathy next gets their attention and goes through the list of statements. Students ask her questions and react to each others' opinions. In the end, they discover that all the statements are true. One student whispers to her in jest, "You trick us!"

As planned, Kathy then hands out a short article on nonverbal behavior she learned about at a workshop for language teachers. She tells the students to read the first three paragraphs silently, after which she has a volunteer paraphrase the meaning. The article is about kinesics (the study of gestures, eye contact, and posture). She then passes out five small gold stars to each student and tells them to read the article twice, the second time pasting the stars next to ideas in the reading they find most interesting. Kathy tells the students that they cannot use a dictionary for this activity and that they should try to guess the meaning of an unfamiliar word from the context. She points out that if they are stumped, they can call on her, as she jokingly calls herself, a "walking dictionary."

As Kathy walks out of the class, she has mixed feelings about the lesson. Her exploration with the message and pictures seemed somewhat successful; she started the class quickly, and some of the students used English. The students also stayed on task during the class, and they appeared to enjoy it. But many of the students used Hungarian during group work. She was also concerned that she did not give them feedback on their language. "Perhaps if I gave them more feedback, they'd want to use more English," she murmured to herself.

Comparison between Yoshi's and Kathy's Teaching

There are some obvious differences between Yoshi's and Kathy's way of teaching. While Yoshi goes through his lessons in a more or less "lockstep" fashion, mostly following the text, Kathy designs her own lessons and brings innovative ideas into her teaching. Yoshi follows a course program in which he leads into a topic with a tape, followed by a reading selection, comprehension questions, another reading, and discussion questions. He rarely breaks from the step-by-step progression in the course text, even when he senses the students are not showing interest or comprehending the content. He does his best to explain the meaning of the text, but he does not break from it. Nor does he engage the students in negotiating the meaning of the text with him or each other. He feels secure in having the text to follow, and although at some level he senses that his lessons could be greatly different, he does not break away from his lockstep way of teaching.

In contrast, Kathy likes to break from a lockstep way of teaching. Rather than making herself the center of classroom interaction, she consciously pays attention to how she can provide opportunities for the class to be a community of learners in which students feel free to communicate with each other in English, ask her and classmates real questions, and take on some of the responsibility for their own learning.

Recognizing the differences between the way Yoshi and Kathy

approach teaching, it is worth asking why Kathy explores creative ways to teach while Yoshi does not. Probably part of the reason is because Kathy went through an intensive Peace Corps training program. But this training was relatively brief, and it was meant only to acquaint her with what EFL teachers do in the classroom. Perhaps cultural background has something to do with the difference. Kathy is a native speaker of English who comes from America, while Yoshi has the same native language and cultural background as the students. Although the students want Yoshi, a near-native speaker of English, to use English with them in class, they might be hesitant to speak up in English with someone who also shares the same native language and rules of their own culture. This could also be difficult for Yoshi, who, outside of class, likely speaks Japanese with these same people.

Perhaps the setting has something to do with it. Yoshi teaches in a corporate world, a setting where, in many cases, students' business responsibilities take precedence over English classes and homework assignments and where students are not required to attend the classes. Kathy teaches at a high school where many of the students are quite motivated to learn English (and other languages).

However, a significant reason for the difference is the way they approach their development as teachers. While Kathy is eager to take on the responsibility for her own development, Yoshi is now just realizing the need to do this. As such, it is worth asking what Kathy has done to work on her development, and in the next section I address what she has done. I also point out that although Kathy has made considerable progress in her development, she can learn more about how to explore her teaching. As I discuss in chapter 2, she could, for example, learn to more systematically reflect and act on her reflections through self-observation, observing others, keeping a teaching journal, and engaging others in talk about teaching.

What Factors Are Central to Teacher Self-development?

Several factors affect teacher self-development. First, there is no doubt that development takes time. It takes time to observe interaction in our own classrooms and to visit other teachers' classes, as well as to write in a journal and to talk to others about teaching. Preservice teachers have an advantage in that the time factor is built into the teacher education program. However, teachers in in-service teacher development programs or teachers working on their development on their own usually have less time. Nonetheless, if teachers believe that development is important, then they need to make a commitment to devote time to their development.

In addition, for teachers new to teaching, time is also needed for them to work through stages in their development.[1] Kathy, for example, allowed herself to work through these stages. She was not always confident or able to create and re-create relevant, interesting lessons for the students. The developmental stages of a teacher include going from being dependent on outside sources (such as supervisors and the textbook) and concerned with self-survival ("What do I do tomorrow in class!") and with what kinds of techniques to use, to being concerned with student learning and able to make informed teaching decisions.

Second, development requires an ongoing commitment. Development is not something that teachers do just while in a teacher education program or at the beginning of a teaching career. Rather, even the most experienced teacher can learn new things about teaching, and development is enhanced when the teacher makes a commitment to ongoing development. For example, although many would call Kathy's teaching skills developed, she continues to explore her teaching and its consequences on students.

Third, development is enhanced through problem solving. When teachers recognize problems and work at solving them, they can discover new things about teaching and about themselves as teachers. For example, Kathy's exploration into getting the class started quickly and her interest in getting students to use more English in class indicate that she continues to generate ways to solve perceived problems in her teaching.

Fourth, development is also enhanced through exploration for exploration's sake. Teachers can, indeed, discover much by exploring simply to explore, not to solve a problem. Such exploration can be based on pure interest—for example, trying the opposite simply to see what happens or trying out an idea simply because it sounds interesting.

Fifth, development is enhanced by paying attention to and

reviewing the basics of EFL/ESL teaching. For example, Kathy pays attention to the basics of teaching. Although her introduction to the basics began during her Peace Corps training, she has continued to study ways to provide chances for students to interact in English, ways to manage classroom behavior, materials and media used to teach EFL, and cultural concepts as they relate to language and herself as a teacher. In addition, she has undoubtedly considered ways to teach different skills, such as reading, writing, listening, and speaking.

Sixth, development is enhanced by searching out opportunities to develop. Kathy, for example, looks for opportunities to develop her teaching. She talks with other teachers about teaching, reads about teaching, attends teaching seminars and workshops, and participates in other activities that give her chances to reflect on her teaching and see new teaching possibilities. In other words, when we, as teachers, teach lessons in different settings, read about teaching, observe our own and others' teaching, write about teaching, and talk about teaching issues and problems, we are provided with opportunities to raise new questions about our teaching, as well as ways to search for answers to these questions. The more activities we experience related to teaching, and the more questions and answers we can come up with through this ongoing process, the more chances we have to develop our teaching beliefs and practices.[2]

Seventh, as Kathy also recognizes, self-development of teaching beliefs and practices requires the cooperation of others.[3] It takes others who are willing to observe, listen to, and talk with us. These people include administrators, students, other teachers, and friends. Without their cooperation, self-development is very difficult, as there is neither any source for feedback nor any stimulus for ideas.

Teacher Self-development Tasks

These tasks can be an integral part of your development as an EFL/ESL teacher. Although some can be done alone, it is to your advantage to gain the cooperation of others. If you are using this book as part of a preservice or in-service teacher education program, it will be easy to attain the support of other teachers. If you are reading this book on your own, I encourage you to seek out others who will read this book and work on the self-development tasks with you. If you are not yet teaching and are using this book as a way to learn about the field, it will not be possible to do all of the tasks. However, there will still be many you can do, and it is still possible to do them with others.

Talk Tasks

1. What does self-development mean to you? What kinds of things do you believe you can do to work on your development as a teacher? Find another EFL/ESL teacher. Ask her or him these questions. Discuss what self-development means and the kinds of things you can do to work on your own development.
2. Draw up a plan to work on your development as an EFL teacher. Here are a few questions to get you started.
   a) Are you ready to work on your teaching development? How strongly do you want to expand your knowledge of teaching and learn how to explore your teaching beliefs and practices?
   b) How much time are you willing to invest in your development as a language teacher? Can you make a tentative schedule of the time you can devote to this undertaking?
   c) Thumb through this book. Also study the table of contents and the list of questions at the beginning of each chapter. What areas of teaching are you interested in developing right now? What questions capture your interest?
   d) How will you read this book? Will you selectively read chapters? Use the index? Use the questions at the start of each chapter as a way to decide on what to read?
   e) How will you get others involved in your process of development?

Sit down with another EFL/ESL teacher who has made a plan. Compare your plans. Can you revise your plan based on this discussion?

Journal Writing Tasks

1. Purchase a notebook that you can easily carry around with you and that has ample space for writing.
2. Write freely about what self-development means to you based on your discussions with another teacher.
3. Create in writing a plan for working on your development. What kinds of things do you plan to do to work on your development as a teacher?

Recommended Teacher Resources

Task-based Teacher Development Books

Edge, J. 1992. *Cooperative Development.* Essex: Longman.

Fanselow, J. F. 1992. *Contrasting Conversations: Activities for Exploring Our Beliefs and Teaching Practices.* New York: Longman.

Parrott, M. 1993. *Tasks for Language Teachers: A Resource Book for Training and Development.* Cambridge: Cambridge University Press.

Richards, J. C., and C. Lockhart. 1994. *Language Teaching in Focus: Reflective Teaching in Second Language Classrooms.* New York: Cambridge University Press.

Shrum, J. L., and E. W. Glisan. 1994. *Teacher's Handbook: Contextualized Language Instruction.* Boston: Heinle and Heinle.

Professional Preparation Programs in TESOL

Kornblum, H., and E. Garshick. 1992. *Directory of Professional Preparation Programs in TESOL in the United States: 1992-1994.* Alexandria, Va.: TESOL.

Notes

1. Research by Bullough and Baughman (1993), Calderhead (1988), and Fuller and Brown (1975) shows that teachers need considerable time to develop their teaching abilities. Research by Fuller (1969) and Fuller

and Brown (1975) suggests that teachers move through stages from self-survival to making informed teaching decisions. Recent research in second language teaching points out how little we know about teachers' thinking in relation to their classroom practices during stages of their development. However, there is some effort (Johnson 1992; Nunan 1992) to discover more about the development of teachers' beliefs and thoughts in relation to their teaching decisions and practices.

2. My research into teacher development (Gebhard 1990b; Gebhard, Gaitan, and Oprandy 1987; Gebhard and Ueda-Motonaga 1992) shows that when teachers have opportunities to process their teaching through a variety of activities, they will explore and sometimes change their way of teaching.

3. Edge (1992) and Fanselow (1988, 1992) also point out that without the cooperation of others, self-development is difficult.

Chapter 2

Exploration of Teaching

As we explore, rather than seeking prescriptions and judgments from others, rules (can be) broken that say we teachers must seek alternatives from those in charge, rather than ourselves or our peers, and that we must work alone within our autonomous but isolated and lonely classrooms, rather than with colleagues.

—Fanselow 1987, 7

- How can teachers explore teaching through self-observation?
- How can teachers explore their own teaching through the observation of other teachers?
- How can teachers use talking and writing as a part of the exploration process?
- How does this book provide opportunities for EFL teachers to explore teaching?

How Can Teachers Explore Their Own Teaching?

As teachers, we can explore our own teaching through a cyclic process of reflecting and then acting on knowledge gained through reflection.[1] Here is how I see this process: The first step in the cycle is to collect descriptive samples of our teaching. This is followed by an analysis and appraisal of these samples. The next step is to consider how the same lesson could be taught differently and to draw up a teaching plan. Then, by implementing the new plan, the cycle returns to the collection of samples of teaching. Let's take a closer look at each stage in the cycle.

Collecting Samples of Teaching

The reason to collect samples of teaching is to have descriptions of what actually goes on in the classroom that focus attention on some aspect of our teaching. To give you an idea of areas of teach-

**Teach while collecting
samples of teaching**

audiotape
videotape

Analyze teaching

- Listen to or view the tape
  while doing one or more of
  the following tasks:

   Making short
   transcripts
   (Code)

   Tallying behaviors

   Taking notes

- Study interaction and look for
  patterns

Ask:

   What is going on?

   How is it going on?

   What behaviors do I see
   recurring?

**Decide on changes in
teaching behavior:**

Ask:

   What do I want to keep doing?

   What do I want to change?

   How can I break the pattern?

   How can I bring about new
   consequences?

Appraise Teaching

Ask interpretative questions:

   How are opportunities
   possibly provided for
   students to learn the second
   language?

   How are opportunities
   possibly hampered?

   Why do I teach the way I do?

   What are my beliefs about
   teaching and learning?

A cyclic process of exploration: self-observation

ing that can be described, see the chart on page 23 listing some of
the exploratory questions teachers have asked. On the left are initial descriptive questions. On the right are questions aimed at
understanding what happens when a change in teaching behavior
is initiated.

   To collect samples of teaching that address an area of classroom
behavior, as illustrated in the chart on exploratory questions, it is to
our advantage to audio- or videotape classroom interaction. To do

Exploratory Questions

Initial Descriptive Questions

- What kinds of questions do I ask? Yes-no? Either-or? Wh-?, Tag?
- What are the content of my questions? About study of language? People's lives in general? Students' personal lives? Procedures? Other?
- How long do I wait after asking a question to get a response?
- How much time do students stay on task? What do they do when off task? What triggers going off task?
- How do I give instructions? How much time does it take? Do students know what to do after given instructions?
- What are usual seat arrangements in my class?
- How often do students speak their native language in class? When? What do I do when they use it?
- How do I praise students? What words do I use? What nonverbal behaviors? What student behaviors do I praise? How often do I praise?

Questions: Further Exploration

- What happens when I ask only yes- no questions?
- What happens when I increase the number of questions I ask about students' personal lives?
- What happens when I increase wait time?
- What happens when I add a time limit? Decrease time given to finish a task? Give no time limit?
- What happens when I change the way I give instructions, such as give them as a dictation? Role play them? Have students paraphrase them? Project them on an overhead? Use a combination of these things?
- What happens when students sit in different seating arrangements?
- What happens when I require students to only speak English? When they cannot speak any English for ten minutes?
- What happens when I do not praise students? When I only praise specific accomplishments?

this, I suggest you use a small Walkman-type audio recorder or camcorder. The advantage of an audio recorder is that it is easy to use. However, some teachers prefer to videotape because of the visual aspect. It is easy to recognize who is talking and possible to study nonverbal behaviors.

At first the audio recorder or camcorder may seem a novelty, and some students will change their behavior because they are being taped. But it really does not take long before students accept it and act normally. I have audio- and videotaped many classes, and it is amazing how fast students accept the recorder, especially if it is treated as a natural part of the classroom setting.

How taping is done often depends on the goals of exploration. For example, if you are interested in the students' reactions to instructions or explanations, the audio recorder or video camera can be focused on the students. If you are interested in what happens during group work, it is logical to focus the audio recorder or camcorder on a group of students for a period of time. If the exploratory aim is to learn about the types of questions you ask, you might carry the audio recorder with you as you teach or set it nearby, or when using a camera, it can be focused on you, perhaps scanning the students from time to time. The idea is to think about the objective of your exploration and to consider how to best tape the class to obtain useful samples for later analysis. Although more complex, there is also value in using two cameras, one focused on the teacher and the other on the students. This provides a way to see what the teacher is doing in relation to the students and the reverse.

Analyzing the Samples of Teaching

The second stage is to analyze the collected samples of teaching, and analysis also depends on the objective of your exploration. The first step is to review your audiotape or videotape, and while listening, you can perform certain tasks that focus attention on the aspect of teaching you are interested in learning more about. For example, if you are interested in knowing about the number of questions you ask, you can listen to or view the tape and tally each question you ask, as well as jot down examples of actual questions.

You can do the same thing for the number of errors you treat, the number of times students speak English or their native language, and the seconds you wait for students to answer a question.

A second way to analyze the collection of teaching samples is to make short transcripts from the audio- or videotapes. Again, what you decide to transcribe depends mainly on the focus of your exploration. For example, if you are interested in learning about how you treat language errors, you might make and study short transcripts of the times errors are treated. If the interest is on learning about the accuracy of the students language during group work, you can transcribe and study short sections of interaction among students during group work activities. A further step you can take in analyzing interaction is to code a transcript with a category system. Although I do not directly discuss such systems in this book, I recommend two, one called Communicative Orientation of Language Teaching (COLT) and another called Foci on Communications Used in Settings (FOCUS).[2]

Appraising Teaching Based on the Analysis

The next step in the exploration process is to appraise teaching based on the analysis. Some teachers like to appraise their teaching as being good or bad. I prefer not to do this because we simply do not yet know enough about the relationship between teaching and learning to determine what good or bad teaching is in all settings.[3]

To me, a more important reason not to judge teaching as good or bad is that judgments get in the way of exploring. Judgments like "Oh! I'm not a very good teacher! I can't get these students to speak!" and "Wow! I'm really hot today. The students sounded like busy bees!" can get in the way of seeing our teaching clearly. We get so involved in the good feelings from our positive judgments and in the bad feelings from our negative judgments that we miss out on capturing descriptions that could be quite useful.

Rather than appraise teaching as good or bad, I recommend we ask interpretative questions, such as "How are opportunities possibly provided for students in my class to learn the language?" and "How are opportunities possibly hampered?" In relation to specific areas of exploration, these questions can be adjusted. For example, it is possible to ask, "Does my treatment of students' errors provide them with opportunities for feedback on their English?" or "Are my instructions clear enough for the students to know what to do?" I emphasize that we ask such questions because they allow us to stand back and consider our teaching behavior in relation to the kinds of opportunities we give to students to learn the language.

In addition, we can consider our reasoning behind our practices. For example, if your attention is focused on the way you treat students' language errors, you might ask, "Why do I treat errors the way I do? What do I believe is the relationship between the way I treat errors and student learning?"[4]

In relation to considering the reasoning that motivates our teaching practices, it is also possible to reflect on our own past learning experiences as they relate to our teaching. As teaching is often guided by past learning experiences,[5] which frequently affect our teaching without our awareness, reflecting on those experiences can free us to explore beyond preconceived notions of teaching. For example, while reflecting on my error treatment practices, I realized that I behaved as a teacher in much the same way as the teachers who taught me. After realizing this I was able to go beyond my usual ways when treating errors, as well as to consider my own beliefs about error treatment and language learning.

Deciding on Changes in Teaching Behavior

The next stage in the exploration cycle is to decide on changes we want to make in our teaching through such questions as "What do I want to continue to do?" and "What small changes do I want to make in my teaching behavior?" Here I agree with John Fanselow, who has observed that small changes can have big consequences.[6]

One reason to change the way we teach is because there is a problem to be solved: students do not talk; instructions are not clear; students speak their native language too much. However, it is also possible to explore teaching simply to explore, to see what happens. This could include doing the opposite of what we usually do or trying out something we have never tried before. For example, if you always give instructions orally, you could write them down and let students read them. If you always teach from the front of the room, you could teach from the back.

Based on the changes you decide to make, you can design the next lesson. The cycle continues as these changes are implemented, while you again collect samples of teaching through audio or video recordings.

What Teachers Have Done: Examples of the Reflective Process

Here are how some teachers have worked through the cyclic reflective process. The first example illustrates what an ESL teacher did to explore the way she gave instructions.[7] The teacher videotaped her teaching and made short transcripts focusing on how she gave instructions and on what the students did afterward. She discovered that her oral instructions took about two minutes and that many of the students did not understand her instructions. During the start of a group activity, for example, some students asked each other—some in their native language—what they were supposed to be doing. Two students finally asked her to explain the task again. She ended up going from group to group to explain the instructions, and it took five additional minutes before the students were all working on the task.

She reflected on her way of giving instructions and decided that she was not giving the students ample opportunity to comprehend her instructions and was taking up too much class time to make the instructions clear. However, she also saw some value in giving vague instructions; students were given chances to negotiate meaning with her, and to do this, they had to express their ideas in English. To explore different ways to give instructions, after talking with another teacher to gain ideas, she decided to try a few different things, each on different days, and she taped and analyzed what happened when she used these alternative techniques. One day she wrote the instructions on the board and presented them orally. On another day she gave the instructions as a dictation, and on the third day she had students paraphrase the instructions back to her. Through her analysis, she discovered that all three ways worked for this particular class. Although it took longer to give the instructions, students displayed less confusion and began the task soon after the instructions were given. In addition, she discovered that it was possible to turn instructions into a language-learning activity.

Another example is an EFL teacher who explored her praise behaviors with preteenage children.[8] After audiotaping, she listened to the tape while tallying the number of times she praised students and jotting down samples of language she used to praise them. She discovered that she verbalized "very good" quite often, and she identified her frequent use of "very good" as being ambiguous to the students. Because she praised them so often, and sometimes when they gave wrong responses, she wondered if students knew she was praising them or were accepting the praise as empty gestures. She also considered why she praised students and decided that praise was important for these children. She stated that praise, when genuine, can be a motivating factor. But if children cannot distinguish when and why she is praising them, it is useless. As such, she decided to implement small changes in her praising techniques. For example, she monitored her use of praise and verbally expressed it only when she was genuinely impressed. When students submitted written work, she put happy-face stickers on their work, but only when their work was considered outstanding.

After taping and analyzing her praise behaviors again, she knew that she used praise far less frequently and usually at times when students met her high expectations. She also analyzed the quality of the students written work, and she concluded, after two months, that their work was genuinely improving. Some students even told her that they try harder because they want to see a happy face on their written work.

The next example is from my own teaching. While teaching an American literature course in Hungary, I wondered about the way I used questions in class. To better understand my questioning behaviors, I designed a tally sheet. I audiotaped my class, and using the tally sheet, I kept track of the targets of my questions (e.g., to an individual student or the whole class) and the content of each question (e.g., about students' lives, about people and places in general, about language, or about the content of the reading selection). The following tally sheet records what I found.[9]

Tally Sheet: Content and Target of Teacher Questions

Content of Questions	To Individual	To Whole Class
Questions: Student lives	//	
Questions: People & places		///////////
Questions: Language	/	///////
Questions: Material Content		//////

During my analysis, I discovered that I asked twenty-eight questions during a twenty-five-minute time period, that most of my questions were addressed to the whole class, and that twelve of my questions were about general places and people, eight about language, and six directly about the content of the reading.

Upon reflection, I was not surprised that I asked mostly whole-class questions, as I often did this intentionally. However, I was surprised that I averaged over a question per minute. This discovery was very useful. First, it gave me the chance to reflect on my questioning behavior. As a part of my reflection, I thought about how discussions go on outside classrooms, how all the participants not only answer questions but also ask them and react to each others responses. Second, I was able to see that my questioning techniques dominated class discussion and prevented students from raising their own questions and reacting to responses. Third, I was able to systematically modify my questioning behavior. In the next seminar, while audiotaping, I consciously asked less questions and attempted to achieve more discussion based on a single question. Also, after a student responded to one of my questions, I remained silent or said, "uh-huh," in an encouraging way while looking at the other students. If no one reacted or asked a question, I paraphrased what was just said.

After audiotaping and analyzing this second seminar, I discovered that I asked less questions (twenty-six), that students asked each other questions (nine), and that students reacted to the responses of others many times. In short, I was able to achieve my objective, to have students discuss a reading selection in their foreign language.

The preceding examples illustrate how teachers have worked through problem areas in their teaching. A final example shows how a teacher explored her teaching simply to explore.[10] The teacher, a native Japanese speaker, was teaching an introductory class in Japanese as a foreign language to American university students. She was interested in exploring her teaching simply to discover patterns in her teaching behavior. So she audiotaped her class, transcribed short segments of the class, and studied them for recurring patterns of interaction.

She discovered certain patterns of interaction in her classes. She found that most of her teaching consisted of drills and that she followed a lockstep way of teaching. She asked all the questions, the students responded, and she reacted to these responses. She also reflected on the fact that she asked display questions (e.g., questions for which she already knew the answers) and that the content of the lessons mostly concerned the study of language (e.g., learning about language rather than using language for a communicative purpose).

Based on her knowledge about patterns of interaction reflected in her classroom, the teacher decided that students did not have ample opportunities to communicate in their foreign language in class. As such, she decided to make a small change in her teaching by doing the opposite of what she usually did. Instead of drilling students on language points, she planned to ask the students questions about their lives. She knew that some students were going on a trip to a nearby city, and she decided to ask them about their trip in the foreign language. As an afterthought, she decided to bring a map of the city to class. She audiotaped her teaching while posing these "life-personal" questions in Japanese, and then she transcribed parts of the class.

Classroom interaction changed dramatically. Students asked each other questions and reacted to each others' comments. The teacher and students asked questions that they did not know the answers to before asking them. Such query was not evident in the interaction in the earlier class.

What brought about this change in the interaction? The teacher's purpose was to do the opposite of what she normally did, to ask personal questions to see if the interaction would change in her class, and she did begin her lesson by asking personal questions about where a student went on spring break. According to the teacher's analysis, this change was most likely a part of the reason why student interactions changed. However, the teacher also had students show her exactly where they went by using the map. This map also had the apparent consequence (which the teacher was surprised to discover) of allowing the interaction to shift from asking and answering personal questions to studying the map itself. In short, the teacher interpreted the reason for the emergence of student questions and reactions to be the combination of asking personal questions and using the map. It is interesting that the teacher had not predicted that the map itself would contribute to this change in the pattern. This discovery was quite incidental, and such discoveries are one reason to explore teaching.

My purpose in giving these examples of self-observation has been to demonstrate how teachers can explore their own teaching. However, exploration does not have to be limited to looking at what goes on in one's own classroom. It is also possible to explore teaching by observing other teachers' classrooms, the topic of the next section.

How Can Teachers Explore Their Own Teaching through the Observation of Other Teachers?

At first the idea that we can explore our own teaching by observing other teachers may seem contradictory. However, as John Fanselow points out, as teachers, we can see our own teaching in the teaching of others.[11] When we observe others to gain knowledge of self, we have the chance to construct and reconstruct our own knowledge. Fanselow articulates this in another way: "I came to your class not only with a magnifying glass to look carefully at what was being done, but with a mirror so that I could see that what you were doing is a reflection of much of what I do."[12]

While observing other teachers, it is possible to collect samples of teaching in a variety of ways. We can take fast notes, draw sketches, tally behaviors, and jot down short transcript-like samples of interaction. As with collecting samples in our own classes, it is possible to audio- or videotape other teachers' classes and photograph interaction. These tapes can be used later to analyze classroom behaviors. I want to point out that I encourage observers and the observed teacher to get together to look at photos, listen to tapes, view videos, study short transcripts, and talk about the class. By doing so, exploration will be enhanced for all. The examples I give next and my later discussion on the value of talking about teaching should make this clear.

Observing Others to Explore One's Own Teaching: Some Examples

This first example of the value of exploring one's own teaching by observing that of others involves collaboration between myself and my teaching partner. My partner showed consistent interest in error treatment and wanted to gain more awareness of how she treated students' errors. As such, I audiotaped her class and transcribed short segments that centered on how she treated students' language errors. Here is one of these short transcripts:[13]

Student: I have only two sister.
Teacher: Uh-huh.
Student: I have no brother.
Teacher: Two sisters?
Student: Because my mother she dead when I was three years old.
Teacher: She *died* when you were three?
Student: Yes. She dead when I was three years old.

My partner and I later met to talk, and she was delighted (and a little surprised) to see the way she treated errors. She used rising intonation (e.g., when she said, "Two sisters?") or asked questions while emphasizing the word she was correcting (as in "She *died* when you were three?"). After appraising her treatment techniques, she decided that the students most likely did not know she was even treating their errors. Instead, they focused on meaning. As a part of our discussion, she also raised a concern over whether or not treating errors was useful. She had been reading Steven Krashen's ideas about how error treatment does not necessarily contribute to gains in the acquisition of the students' second language, and she expressed her confusion over the need to correct errors at all.[14] However, at the same time, students were asking her to treat their language errors, and she wanted to comply. As such, she decided that if she did treat the errors, she could at least do so in a way in which the students were aware of being corrected. She read about and discussed error treatment and subsequently designed and implemented alternative ways to treat errors.

My partner obviously gained awareness from more clearly seeing her way of treating errors, and through the process of observing (and talking) with my partner, I also had the chance to reflect on my own beliefs and techniques for treating errors. I was able to see my teaching in hers, and I realized that I often treated errors similarly, and that, most likely, students were not especially aware that I was treating specific language errors. By audiotaping and analyzing my teaching, I was able to reconfirm this reflection and develop new ways to treat students' errors.

A second example of the value of observing others teach involves a teacher in Japan who wanted to explore the use of photography as a way to observe teaching.[15] He was invited to observe a class at a private language school for young children, and he decided to take his camera. He was able to move freely around the classroom while the students and teacher went about their lesson, and as a second observer, I was impressed by the way he was able to fit into the natural flow of the classroom interaction in an unobtrusive way. Surprisingly, after the first few snapshots, the children hardly paid any attention to him.

Later, he created a photographic essay of the classroom interaction, and while looking at the photos with the teacher, he was able to reflect on his own teaching. For example, he noticed how spontaneously the children spoke up in English and wondered how he could get students in his high school EFL class to do this. As a second observer, I was also able to see my teaching in the teaching of the photographed teacher, and as I studied the photos, I was impressed by the great number of activities the teacher did with the students, each leading naturally into the next, and I wondered how I could design lessons to do this in my own classes.

How Can Teachers Use Talking and Writing as a Part of the Exploration Process?

Exploration can be enhanced through talking and writing about teaching. In this section, I briefly address how each of these can be used as a part of the exploration process.

Talking about Teaching

In addition to observing teaching, talking about teaching can offer chances to learn about and reflect on our own teaching. Talking can indeed be a useful thing to do. Unfortunately, talking about teaching is not something that normally goes on among EFL/ESL teachers, and when it does, it seems to take on a face-saving nature. As Paul Arcario points out,[16] the way conversations about teaching normally take place begins with the observer giving an opening evaluative remark, such as "I liked your class." This is followed by a three-step evaluative sequence. In the first step of the sequence a positive or negative evaluation is made, such as "I think the students are talking a lot" (positive) or "Maybe the students don't have enough chances to speak" (negative). These comments lead to a second step, justification (explanation of why the comment was made), and then onward to the third step, prescriptions about what should be done in the class to improve teaching, such as "You should do more group work." Arcario points out that this last prescriptive step is more obvious when a negative evaluation is made, because there is a perceived problem to be solved.

This usual way of talking about teaching is not especially productive. It is also not necessarily easy to change. But change can be made, especially if we take the time and effort to prepare for the discussions and follow agreed on rules that aim at nonjudgmental and nonprescriptive discussion. This was evident from a recent experience I had in Japan, where I had the pleasure of working with twelve experienced American, Canadian, and Japanese EFL teachers, all of whom taught in different settings (Japanese public and private schools, corporations, and language schools). We planned for and visited some of the teachers' classes in small groups of three or four. After observing, we talked about the classes over lunch or coffee.

We found both the observations and the discussions to be highly stimulating and informative, and part of the reason was our planning. Before each observation, the teacher whose class we were to visit gave us an aspect of teaching on which she or he wanted us to focus our attention. For example, one teacher wanted us to focus on how she treats students' oral errors, another on the times students speak their native language, another on the amount of time students stayed on task.

We also established rules about how to talk about the teaching we observed. We came to an agreement to stop ourselves from making judgments about our own and others' teaching, including positive and negative judgments. We made this agreement because, as mentioned earlier, judgments take attention away from description of and toward feelings about what is going on. We also agreed not to seek prescriptions about teaching, in other words, what we *should* do in the classroom. Rather, we worked at generating alternatives based on descriptions of teaching. We looked for possibilities to try out, not best ways to teach. The teachers and I found these two sets of rules to be very powerful. We gained lots of description of teaching, were able to generate lots of alternative ways to do things in the classroom, and, by the end of our experience together, became far less judgmental in our attitudes toward teaching.

As we did in Japan, I encourage you to talk to other teachers about teaching. To do this, I invite you to plan observation visits; meet to talk about your observations in nonprescriptive, nonjudgmental terms; and generate alternative ways to teach. However, I also encourage you to talk about issues in teaching, media and materials, technology, and mutual problems, such as problems with student motivation, unreasonable administrative demands, and working conditions.

Writing about Teaching

In addition to talking about teaching, we can explore teaching by writing in a journal or diary. The purpose of writing in a journal is

Teachers talking about the use of the Internet

to have a place to record our observations of what goes on in our own and other teachers' classrooms, write about our discussions, consider teaching ideas, and reflect on our teaching. However, journals are also a place for us to raise doubts, express frustrations, and raise questions.[17] The following is a list of what some teachers include in their journals.

- Quickly written descriptions of classroom interaction collected in their own and other teachers' classrooms, as well as analyses and interpretations of these descriptions
- Tally sheets, transcripts, sketches, and coding as a part of their description and analysis
- Photos (snapshots) and descriptions of what goes on in each photo
- Summaries and reflections on discussions with other teachers
- Lists of alternative ways to teach aspects of a lesson (e.g., different ways to give instructions)
- Stream-of-consciousness writing (to let ideas flow)

- Reflections on language-learning experiences
- Thoughts on their beliefs about teaching and learning
- Questions about teaching and learning
- Answers to their own questions
- Summaries and critiques of journal articles and books
- Lesson plans and teaching ideas

Those of us who have maintained teaching journals know how time-consuming it can be. As such, I suggest you only try to keep a journal from time to time. For me, two months a year seems just about right. I also encourage you to carry a journal with you and take the time to write down ideas when they emerge, even while walking down the street or over breakfast. Along with these inspired entries, I encourage you to write entries soon after teaching, while the experiences are fresh. Finally, at the end of a period of time (for instance, two months), I encourage you to take the time to read your entries thoughtfully, look for patterns in your teaching and thinking about teaching, and write an entry on this analysis.[18] Taking time to review past entries is important, as it is through this kind of reflection that we can see ourselves as teachers and view our teaching differently.

How Does This Book Provide Opportunities for Teachers to Explore Teaching?

Since observation, as a way to explore teaching, can be empowering, in this book I provide a number of opportunities for you to explore teaching through observation. This book contains descriptions of teaching based on my observations of lessons taught by EFL/ESL teachers and on my own self-observations. In a sense, by reading this book, you are considering a variety of different observation reports on what EFL/ESL teachers do in their classrooms.

In addition, in the "Teacher Self-development Tasks" section at the end of each chapter, I provide a variety of different observation tasks. The purpose of these tasks is to teach you a nonjudgmental process of looking at what goes on in your own and others' classrooms. Some of these tasks ask you to audio- and videotape teach-

A busy teacher reflecting during a free moment

ing, tally behaviors or make short transcripts, and analyze teaching. The goal of doing these observation tasks is for you to see your teaching differently. Through awareness of your own and others' teaching, it is possible for you to see new possibilities.

As you perform these observation tasks, I also encourage you to work through the reflective exploration cycle by collecting samples of your teaching, analyzing these samples, asking interpretative questions, deciding on small changes in the way you teach, and implementing these changes while again collecting samples of your teaching for analysis and continuation of the cycle. Through this cycle, I encourage you to explore to solve problems in your teaching, as well as to explore for exploration's sake, simply to see what happens.

Throughout the tasks in each chapter, I also provide chances for you to talk about teaching. For discussion with other teachers, I offer topics related to the content of each chapter, and I also provide chances for you to generate your own topics based on your interests and needs. I remind you that although talk about teaching may be done in a usual, evaluative, prescriptive way that is not especially productive, it may also be done in a nonjudgmental, descriptive way that is alternative generating.

Finally, at the end of each chapter I provide chances for you to write in a journal or diary about your teaching experiences, ideas, observations, and beliefs about teaching. Although I give a variety of writing tasks related to the content of each chapter, I also encourage you to go beyond my suggestions.

As I pointed out in chapter 1, it is through the combination of reading, observing, talking, and writing about teaching that you will gain the kind of knowledge that frees you to raise new questions and ideas about your teaching beliefs and practices, as well as to search for answers to your questions and discover and rediscover the teacher that lies within you.

Teacher Self-development Tasks

Talk Tasks

1. Answer the following questions:
   a) What is a judgment? What words indicate that a judgment is being made? Why do I suggest teachers avoid making judgments about the teaching they observe?
   b) What is a prescription? What are words that indicate a teaching prescription is being made? (For example, "You should . . ." indicates prescription.) Why do I think prescriptions of teaching are not very useful?
   c) What is an alternative? What is the value of generating alternative teaching ideas (over prescriptions)?
2. Talk about your experiences as a language learner. How did your past language teachers teach? What did you like or dislike about the way they taught? How do you think your language-learning experience has influenced you as a teacher?
3. Read the observation report at the end of this chapter. Notice that at the end of this report I offer two interpretations. The first is my optimistic interpretation, that because of the quick pace and various activities, students gained lots of opportunities to experience English, which possibly contributed to the development of their language skills. The second interpretation is the

opposite: students could easily fool the teacher into believing they were comprehending the content of the lesson, because the teacher did not really check their comprehension; she simply and swiftly went from one activity to another. Here are three questions for you to answer concerning my observation report:

a) Although the second interpretation is meant to be outlandish (or contrived), do you think this interpretation might have some validity?

b) What is the value of giving outlandish interpretations in our descriptions and analyses of teaching?

c) List alternative ways in which the teacher could teach this lesson, both in regard to the pace of the lesson and in regard to some of the activity procedures.

Observation and Talk Tasks

1. Arrange to visit a friend's class with at least one other teacher.
   a) Prepare to observe the class by asking the teacher what aspects of teaching he or she wants you to observe. (You might want to study the list of topics at the start of this chapter.) Also consider how you will go about collecting descriptions of teaching that will capture aspects of this teaching. (For example, will you write quick notes, draw sketches, jot down dialogue, tally behaviors, audio- or videotape, photograph?)
   b) Observe the class.
   c) Meet after the class over coffee or lunch to talk about the class. As I discussed earlier in this chapter, monitor your way of talking about the class so that your conversations about teaching are nonjudgmental and nonprescriptive. During your conversation, generate a list of alternative ways the teacher could teach aspects of the same lesson differently.
2. Tape-record or videotape interaction in your class. Listen to or view the tape. From the tape, select interaction that interests you. Make short transcriptions of the interaction in dialogue form (using a new line when the speaker changes). Then meet with another teacher. Together, study and talk about the transcripts by working through the following steps:

a) Analyze the interaction. What is going on? Is there anything in the interaction that captures your attention? What?

b) Interpret the teaching. Are opportunities provided for students to learn English? Are opportunities possibly blocked?

c) Decide on a small change. What are alternative ways to teach? Which would you like to try?

d) Design a new lesson that includes a small change. Implement this change while taping, and again analyze what happened.

Journal Writing Tasks

1. Write about your experiences as a language learner. How did your past language teachers teach? What did you like or dislike about the way they taught? How do you think your language-learning experience has influenced you as a teacher?

2. Write about your observation and conversation experiences (from doing the observation and talk tasks). Take time to reflect on the experience. What did you learn about teaching? What ideas do you now have about your own teaching? What did you learn about observation and about talking about teaching in a nonjudgmental, descriptive way?

3. Carry your journal around with you. When a teaching idea or reflection comes to you, write it down.

4. The idea of this task is to experience writing about a class over a period of time. Pick one of your classes. Make sure you have a break soon after the class. Just after the class, each time you have taught it, take fifteen minutes to write about this class. Use a stream-of-consciousness approach to your writing. In other words, just let the ideas flow. Feel free to add sketches—anything that works for you. After a few weeks, read all your entries. Then take time to write about what you have learned about yourself as a teacher and about how you teach.

Recommended Teacher Resources

Allwright, D., and K. M. Bailey. 1991. *Focus on the Language Classroom: An Introduction to Classroom Research for Language Teachers.* Cambridge: Cambridge University Press.

Bailey, K. M. 1990. "Diary Studies in Teacher Education Programs." In *Second Language Teacher Education,* ed. J. C. Richards and D. Nunan, 215–26. New York: Cambridge University Press.

Bartlett, L. 1990. "Teacher Development through Reflective Teaching." In *Second Language Teacher Education,* ed. J. C. Richards and D. Nunan, 202–14. New York: Cambridge University Press.

Day, R. R. 1990. "Teacher Observation in Second Language Teacher Education." In *Second Language Teacher Education,* ed. J. C. Richards and D. Nunan, 43–61. New York: Cambridge University Press.

Fanselow, J. F. 1987. *Breaking Rules: Generating and Exploring Alternatives in Language Teaching.* White Plains, New York: Longman.

———. 1988. " 'Let's See': Contrasting Conversations about Teaching." *TESOL Quarterly* 22:113–20.

Gebhard, J. G. 1992. "Awareness of Teaching: Approaches, Benefits, Tasks. *English Teaching Forum* 30 (4): 2–7.

Gebhard, J. G., and A. Ueda-Motonaga. 1992. "The Power of Observation: 'Make a Wish, Make a Dream, Imagine All the Possibilities.'" In *Collaborative Language Learning and Teaching,* ed. D. Nunan, 179–91. Cambridge: Cambridge University Press.

Hubbard, R. S., and B. M. Power. 1993. *The Art of Classroom Inquiry.* Portsmouth, N.H.: Heinemann.

Schon, D. A. 1983. *The Reflective Practitioner: How Professionals Think in Action.* New York: Basic Books.

An Observation Report

Teacher: American, twenty-six years old
Class: fourteen advanced-level students
Observation: The lesson began by the teacher telling the students she would be right back. She left the classroom, coming back dressed in a full-length black dress with a black veil. She sat down and held up a series of signs that read: "How does my presence make you feel?" "What do you notice and what are you thinking about?" "What do you think I am?" and "Take one minute to freewrite." During the entire time, the teacher and students were silent.

The teacher then took off her veil and asked, "How did my presence make you feel?" As students responded, she listed their ideas on the board: scary, startled, uncomfortable, grim reaper, anticipation, trembling, silence. The teacher then related all their words to one concept—death—and she explained that the lesson would be on their perceptions of death.

From this point on the teacher took the class through a series of quick-paced activities that centered their attention on the topic of death. She passed out blank paper and a basket of crayons and asked the class to draw a picture that represents death. Then she had them discuss their pictures in pairs and write down words that came to mind concerning death. After this, she elicited from the class words that they used to describe death (change, God, scary, nature, forgiveness, vague, strength, empty, confusing), and she wrote them on the board.

The teacher followed this activity by handing out newspaper clippings (death notices) to half the class and sympathy cards to the other half. She had students work in pairs, discussing the meaning of the short verse in the cards and the meaning of the newspaper death notices. She then had volunteers read the greeting card verses, and she answered their questions about the meaning of specific words. She also asked students a series of questions, such as "When do you think Americans send these cards?" and "Do people in your country use such cards?" She then did the same thing for newspaper death notices, having students read a few notices aloud, as well as discussing cultural differences between American culture and some of the students' cultures.

At the end of the lesson, the teacher instructed the class to write about the experience in their journals. The purpose was for the students to reflect on the activity, writing about what they learned. The teacher joined the students by also writing in her journal. As they wrote, the teacher played an audiotape of Rachmaninoff's classical death march.

The teacher asked me to pay particular attention to the structure and pace of the lesson. Here is an account of the steps in the lesson and the time it took for each.

- Starting the lesson: four minutes
- Holding up signs/silence: six minutes

- Eliciting feelings/words: seven minutes
- Drawing pictures that represent death: seven minutes
- Pairs discussing their pictures and listing death words: eleven minutes
- Pairs discussing cards and newspaper death notices: twelve minutes
- Groups reading greeting cards and class discussion: fourteen minutes
- Reading newspaper death notices and class discussion: eight minutes
- Journal writing about the experience: seventeen minutes
- Teacher distributing homework (song verse): two minutes

My analysis of the lesson shows that the teacher included ten different activities (if starting the lesson is included), each taking anywhere from four to seventeen minutes. The activities varied in the skill required of the students, including reading, writing, and speaking. The combined time that the students spent doing these activities was eighty-eight minutes out of the ninety-minute class period.

As for my interpretation of the lesson, I believe that both the varied activity types and the quick pace kept students interested and alert. At no time did I see students yawn or look bored. They focused their attention on the task at hand and seemed to enjoy each step of the lesson. The only time some students looked puzzled was at the end of the lesson, when the teacher gave out the homework. Perhaps some students did not know what to do. I also believe that the quick pace and varied activities of this class offered opportunities for students to learn English used to talk about death, as well as something about how American society responds to death as a social phenomenon.

However, there are other possible interpretations. One is that the students were confused by so much information given to them so quickly. The only way the teacher checked their comprehension was by eliciting single words and phrases about her behavior and by viewing the students' pictures. In short, to please the teacher, the students simply went from one activity to another looking as if they were following and enjoying the lesson. The varied activities and quick pace made this easier. Students could easily fool the teacher into thinking that they understood, as there was not enough time for the teacher to fully check the students' comprehension, and as she was quite happy with the fact that they were talking, especially in groups.

Notes

1. Those who study teaching as taking action based on reflection see the process as being cyclic and include Bartlett (1990), Fanselow (1987), Gebhard (1990a, 1992), Gebhard and Ueda-Motonaga (1992), Richards and Lockhart (1994), and Wallace (1991).
2. COLT was created by Allen, Frohlick, and Spada (1984); FOCUS by Fanselow (1977a, 1987).
3. Chaudron (1988), Fanselow (1987, 1992), Nunan (1991), and Richards (1987) also state that the relationship between teaching and learning is complex.
4. Freeman and Richards (1993) point out that teachers classify conceptions about teaching into three main categories. Some see teaching as a science based on research; some see it as an art or craft; some see it as a theory or philosophy. When thinking about why we teach the way we do—for example, the way we treat errors—we can consider whether or not our actions in the classroom are based on science/research, art/craft, theory/philosophy, or a combination of these.
5. This idea comes from Lortie 1975.
6. See Fanselow 1987.
7. This project was done by Barbara Duncan, at the time an ESL instructor at the American Language Institute and a graduate student in the M.A. TESOL program at the Indiana University of Pennsylvania.
8. At the time of this exploration into her praise behaviors, the teacher, Miharu Hiyoshi, a near-native speaker of English, was a student in the M.A. TESOL program at Teachers College, Columbia University (Tokyo), and an EFL teacher at the Yokohama YMCA.
9. This tally sheet was first published in Gebhard 1991.
10. A more detailed account can be found in Gebhard and Ueda-Motonaga 1992.
11. See Fanselow 1988, 1992.
12. See Fanselow 1992, 2.

13. This transcript was originally published in Gebhard 1990b.
14. Specifically, the teacher was reading Krashen 1982.
15. The observer-photographer was Yutaka Yamauchi, at the time a student in the M.A. TESOL program at Teachers College, Columbia University (Tokyo) and a high school EFL teacher.
16. See Arcario 1994.
17. Here I agree with Bailey (1990) that teachers need room to express their frustrations, anger, and opinions.
18. Bailey (1990) emphasizes that reviewing entries and looking for salient features in teaching is crucial to a journaling experience.

Part 2

Principles of EFL/ESL Teaching and Learning

Chapter 3

Teaching Language as Interaction among People

Language learning and teaching can be an exciting and refreshing interval in the day for students and teacher. There are so many possible ways of stimulating communicative interaction, yet, all over the world, one still finds classrooms where language learning is a tedious, dry-as-dust process, devoid of contact with the real world in which language use is as natural as breathing.

—Rivers 1987, 14

- How do EFL/ESL teachers provide opportunities for students to interact in English?
- What makes an interactive classroom interactive?
- What experiences do EFL/ESL students bring to the interactive classroom?
- What roles are native and near-native English-speaking EFL/ESL teachers expected to play?
- What problems do some EFL/ESL teachers face when teaching English as interaction among people?

How Do EFL/ESL Teachers Provide Opportunities for Students to Interact in English?

Some EFL/ESL classes are taught in a fairly teacher-centered fashion. Interaction is dominated by the teacher who, for example, gives lengthy explanations and lectures, drills repetitively, asks the majority of the questions, and makes judgments about the students' answers. However, other EFL/ESL teachers see value in getting students involved in interacting in English, and in this section, based on a framework provided by Littlewood,[1] I discuss how this can be done.

Some teachers who aim at having an interactive classroom begin lessons with what Littlewood calls "precommunicative activities." Used primarily with beginner and intermediate level students, the purpose of precommunicative activities is for the teacher to isolate specific elements of knowledge or skill that comprise communicative ability, giving students opportunities to practice them without having to fully engage in communicating meaning. Littlewood discusses two types of precommunicative activities: structural and quasi-communicative. Structural activities focus on the grammar and lexicon (vocabulary) of English, while quasi-communicative activities focus on how the language is used to communicate meaning. Quasi-communicative activities are often in the form of dialogues or relatively simple activities in which students interact under highly controlled conditions.

Allow me to illustrate these two types of precommunicative activities by describing a beginning-level class I observed in Hungary. The teacher's goal was to teach students how to ask about food likes and dislikes. The teacher first taught a grammatical item, the use of the auxiliary verb *do* when used in a yes-no question (a structural activity). She began by giving several examples, such as this one:

Statement: You like (to eat) cake.
Question: Do you like (to eat) cake?

She then did a vocabulary-building activity (another structural activity) in which she put large pictures of food items on the wall and matched them with the names of food items she had written in big bold letters on separate pieces of paper. She gave students chances to read the names of food items, say them aloud as a whole class, and copy the names while drawing their own pictures of each item.

In order to further build up to a communicative activity, the teacher gave students the sample precommunicative activity handout shown on page 51.

Then the teacher held up a picture of each item (e.g., of a piece of cake), and as she did this, she asked the whole class, "Do you like to eat cake?" The students then shouted out "Yes!" or "No!" depending on their own preference. There was lots of laughter, especially when she asked, "Do you like to eat toilet paper?"

Do you like (to eat) cake?
bananas?
fish?
ice cream?
apples?
toilet paper?
pie?

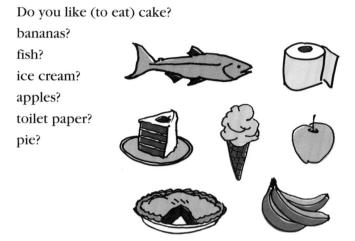

A precommunicative activity handout

The teacher then handed out a dialogue that combined grammatical and vocabulary items and added a little new language:

A: Do you like cake?
B: Yes, I do.
A: Do you like bananas?
B: Yes. Very much.
A: How about fish? Do you like fish?
B: I don't know. Maybe.

The teacher read the dialogue out loud, had students repeat it after her, and had students practice it in pairs.

Next, the teacher divided students into pairs and placed a set of pictures of different food items face down on their desks. The students took turns picking a picture from a pile, then using the picture as a cue, asking each other about their likes and dislikes. The teacher included a few comical items, such as a picture of soap, and a few students made up their own comical items, such as "chicken ice cream."

Some teachers follow up precommunicative activities with what Littlewood calls "communicative activities." As a way to illustrate what communicative activities are and how they can follow precommunicative activities, let's return to my observation on food items and preferences. After doing structural and quasi-communicative activities with the students, the teacher had the students write letters to students in one of her other classes. Although the teacher encouraged the students to ask about what food they liked, she also encouraged them to express themselves freely.

There are many other possible examples of precommunicative and communicative activities teachers can have students do in classrooms, and I provide more examples in this book in part 3 on teaching language skills. The point here is that as teachers, we can create lessons that aim at getting students involved in communicating with the teacher and each other in meaningful ways in English. As I illustrated through my observations, this can be done with students just starting to learn English. We do not have to wait until students have mastered the grammar of English to give students chances to communicate. We can focus on what it is that students already know and are now studying, as well as on creating communicative activities that allow students to make use of this knowledge.

It is also possible to omit precommunicative activities, especially if we are teaching students beyond a basic level. Instead, we can challenge the students by using communicative activities. Students can begin with a task, such as writing and producing their own play, giving oral and written presentations on topics they researched through interviewing and library research, and solving problems in small groups. As students work on these tasks, their attention will sometimes shift to language use—for example, they might ask the meaning of a word or how to express an idea—but the thrust of the lesson is for students to communicate with the teacher and each other in meaningful ways.

What Makes an Interactive Classroom Interactive?

There are at least five closely related factors that can contribute to making interactive classrooms interactive. One is reducing the central (and traditional) position of the teacher.[2] This does not mean that we teachers have to give up control of the class. As I discuss in greater detail in chapter 4 on classroom management, the teacher can maintain control of what goes on in the classroom while still giving freedom to students to initiate interaction among themselves and with the teacher.[3]

Factors contributing to making classrooms interactive include

- Reduction in the centrality of the teacher
- An appreciation for the uniqueness of individuals
- Chances for students to express themselves in meaningful ways
- Opportunities for students to negotiate meaning with each other and the teacher
- Choices, both in relation to what students say and how they say it

Genuine communicative interaction is enhanced if there is an appreciation for the uniqueness of individuals in the class.[4] Each student brings to the classroom unique language-learning and life experiences (both successful and unsuccessful), as well as feelings about these experiences (including joy, anxiety, and fear). As teachers, we need to be sensitive to each individual's background and affective state. To create a classroom atmosphere conducive to interaction, we need to understand and accept each student as he or she is, which sometimes can require considerable effort.

Also, providing chances for the students to express themselves in meaningful ways potentially contributes to creating an interactive classroom. Students need chances to listen to each other, express their ideas in speech and writing, and read each others' writing. Negotiation of meaning needs to become the norm, and while negotiating, students need chances to ask for and receive clarification, confirm their understanding, generally ask questions, respond to questions, and react to responses. If true negotiation of meaning is going on, students will be fully engaged in using English to understand the meaning intended by others, as well as to express their own meaning as clearly as possible. Negotiation of meaning also implies that students have choices as to what they want to say, to whom they want to say it, and how they want to say it.

What Experiences Do EFL/ESL Students Bring to the Interactive Classroom?

Although approaches to teaching English are changing, it is safe to say that many students' language-learning experiences are relatively traditional in nature. In some schools, English is treated like an academic subject, like history or geography, and considerable emphasis is placed on learning to read and translate. During class, students read orally, repeat after the teacher, do grammar drills, listen to grammar explanations given in the teacher's native language, and generally study about language, often oblivious to the use this language has to communicate meaning.

Some students experience a functional curriculum in which they study about and practice the functions of language—for example, how to make a request, ask for permission, ask for information, make a suggestion, complain about something, agree/disagree, and so on. Usually, the class follows a text, and with some teachers, students practice using the functions of language to express themselves through dialogue practice, role plays, and other activities. However, generally most of the students who enter our classrooms do not have much experience interacting with native speakers of English or much ability in communicating in English.

It is fairly easy to accept ESL students as having diverse backgrounds and interests, because students in our classes tend to come from multiple cultural backgrounds. However, when considering EFL students, we need to remind ourselves not to overgeneralize. As students usually are homogeneous, such as all Russian or Japanese or Italian or Chinese or Costa Rican, it is easy to assume that students are fairly much alike. However, we need to remind ourselves that these students have different personal interests. Some students like kick boxing, others cooking. Some prefer science, others history or art or psychology. Some want to travel or read novels in English; others are interested in hotel management or folk dancing.

Likewise, both ESL and EFL students enter our classes with different attitudes. Some are enthusiastic about having the chance to interact in English; others are shy and find it very difficult. Some have had teachers who have been responsive to their emotional needs. Such teachers have recognized that learning a language can be a threatening experience, and they have worked with the students to create a nondefensive and secure classroom atmosphere. However, other students have experienced teachers who have unintentionally intimidated them, resulting in students being defensive and recoiling to a half-in, half-out engagement.

Likewise, students' learning-style preferences can be quite different.[5] Language students' learning channels can be grouped into four basic perceptual modalities. They can use visual learning (reading, studying charts), auditory learning (listening to lectures, audiotapes), kinesthetic learning (total physical involvement with a learning situation), and tactile learning (hands-on learning, such as building models). Although some nationalities of students exhibit a certain learning-style preference over another (e.g., Indonesian students favor auditory and kinesthetic), it is also obvious that students from a single culture vary in their learning-style preferences. For example, Japanese, Arab, Chinese, and Korean students appear to have multiple learning-style preferences.

What Roles Are Native and Near-native English-speaking EFL/ESL Teachers Expected to Play?

Here is a sample of roles EFL/ESL teachers take on:[6] Drama coach, puppet maker, creative-writing specialist, folksinger, mime, photographer, cross-cultural trainer, public speaker, counselor, film critic, poet, storyteller, discussion leader, team builder, grammarian, jazz chanter, reading specialist, error analyst, gaming specialist, values clarifier, computer program specialist, materials developer, curriculum planner, curriculum evaluator, interviewer, friend, language authority, interaction manager, cultural informant, needs assessor, language model, joke teller, disciplinarian, language tester, text adapter, parent, strategy trainer, artist.

As the following list shows, teaching is multifaceted, and much of the complexity involves how to assume roles that capitalize on our abilities in English while we at the same time take on roles that contribute to creating interaction in the classroom that is meaningful for both teacher and students. In this section I address these two sets of roles.

Use of English Language Abilities
- Language authority
- Cultural informant
- Model English speaker

Use of Ability to Create Meaningful Interaction
- Needs assessor
- Classroom manager
- Text adaptor
- Entertainer

Roles Related to English Language Abilities

One role we are expected to take on is that of language authority. We are sometimes expected to explain complex rules of English grammar, such as the difference between static and dynamic verbs or how adjectives and adverbs differ. However, our role as language authority is consonant with our native or near-native intuitive ability to explain the nuances of English, such as how emphatic stress changes the meaning of a sentence, as in "I went *there*," "I *went* there," and "*I* went there." Likewise, we are asked to explain the rules of speaking—for example, when a speaker of English would say "I'm sorry" as opposed to "Excuse me," or what native speakers say and do during social situations, such as at a dinner party or when scheduling an appointment with a doctor on the phone. Sometimes we are also expected to explain the fine nuances of meaning in readings as well as the rules of writing—for example, how to write a good paragraph, use transitions to connect paragraphs and ideas, and use punctuation.

Students also expect us to speak English with them and to model how it is used to express meaning. For example, some students are curious about our use of humor (or lack of it) and its appropriate use, as well as how we display nonverbal behaviors. In addition, some students also expect us to use samples of our speech and writing as a model text for them to study. For example, students sometimes ask me to pronounce a word or sentence as they attempt to approximate the pronunciation.

As native or near-native speakers, we also are expected to take on the role of cultural informant. Students ask questions not only about language behaviors ("What is a normal distance to stand from a stranger in Ireland?" "What do you say when you greet someone for the first time?" "How do you let a friend know you are angry with her?") but also about cultural values, beliefs, and assumptions ("Why do Americans say they value equality but then discriminate against each other?" "What is traditional about Australia?").

Students also ask questions about socialization—for example, as it takes place in education, family life, and friendships ("What's dating like in New Zealand?" "Could you explain what goes on in a typical Australian family?" "What do best friends do together in your country?")—and even about technology ("Could you explain the New York City subway system to me?" "Which computer company sells the most programs in your country?").

For native English speakers, the reason answering such questions is not easy is because most of us are never asked such questions in our own countries. We unconsciously acquire the rules of our native cultures through experiences as participators in them. Not having had the opportunity to think about our own experiences beyond the normal expectations of those around us in our home countries, it can be quite perplexing to be asked questions related to our cultures. However, time, thought, experience, and a little research can make answering such questions easier.

Roles Related to Creating Meaningful Interaction

A number of educators encourage language teachers to take on the role of needs assessor. Doing so includes learning about students language-learning history, goals, interests, study habits, learning strategies, and language-learning styles. They suggest we interview students, have them complete questionnaires, and generally observe what they do and say.[7]

With small classes, I personally like to use dialogue journals to learn about the students. As I use them, dialogue journals are like informal letters being written back and forth between the student and myself, the teacher. The purpose of the journal entries is to give students chances to communicate ideas in writing, and as a result, it is possible to learn about what each student is interested in and cares about. Dialogue journals can be a way to discover what really bothers students or to discuss topics that are personal in nature—for example, why a student is not doing his or her home-work or how a student can work at overcoming the excessive anx-iety she or he feels when asked to speak English.

The teacher can also take on the role of text adapter. Quite often, the textbook and the teacher's manual become the teacher's main resource, but the text does not necessarily provide enough ways to promote the kind of interaction the teacher wants to have in the classroom. To foster interaction, we teachers can go beyond the text by adapting materials and activities to the lessons in the text or introducing new activities unrelated to the text. We can add such things as role plays, games, movies, TV shows, songs, read-ings, news programs, and more. Likewise, we can have birthday parties, plan trips, tell stories, interview guest speakers, and under-take other activities that promote genuine interaction. Because I discuss the uses of materials and media in chapter 5 and a variety of activities to teach language skills in chapters 7 through 10, I do not go into detail here. However, I point out the importance for teach-ers to go beyond the text, to adapt to their classroom lessons authentic materials and media and creative activities that address the needs and interests of the students and engage them in mean-ingful interaction.

Another role the teacher can take on to promote interaction is that of classroom manager. Since I devote chapter 4 to this topic, I will not go into detail here. I will simply show the complexity of classroom management by listing some of the things that we, as teachers, need to be able to do as skilled classroom managers. To manage classrooms, we need to be able to

- Engineer the amount of classroom talk we do
- Manipulate our questioning behaviors
- Control the way we give instructions
- Orchestrate group and pair work
- Keep learners on task
- Make language comprehensible to students
- Handle affective variables of classroom life

We are sometimes asked to take on the role of entertainer, and I have included this role because it is controversial. Some students

A birthday party in an ESL class

can be very good at getting us to tell stories about ourselves and others, tell jokes, and even sing. EFL/ESL students can be a great audience. Many will laugh at jokes, attentively listen, and encourage us to continue, and when this happens, some of us will strongly argue that our job is not to entertain.

However, some of us see value in the teacher's role as entertainer. It can provide a way to lower the students' level of anxiety. In addition, if students are genuinely interested in listening to our stories or jokes and can comprehend them, they can benefit.

What Problems Do Some EFL/ESL Teachers Face When Teaching English as Interaction among People?

Throughout this book, starting with this chapter, I devote a section to the kinds of problems EFL/ESL teachers report they have. In this chapter, I address the kinds of problems teachers have that block them from teaching English as interaction among people. I also provide suggestions on how teachers might resolve these problems.

A teacher telling a joke

Problems some EFL/ESL teachers face include the following.

The "bandwagon" problem. The teacher discovers a new exciting method and accepts this way of teaching with great enthusiasm as the best way to teach.

The "overly anxious" problem. Some students have such high levels of anxiety that they cannot take advantage of opportunities to learn English.

The "engagement" problem. The teacher is not fully committed to teaching English as interaction and will not fully engage in interacting with the students or arranging activities for them to use English as a means of communication in the classroom.

The "Bandwagon" Problem

A problem can occur in EFL/ESL classrooms when teachers jump on the latest methodological bandwagon. For the phrase *to jump on a bandwagon, Roget's Thesaurus* gives the alternatives "to float or swim with the stream; to join the parade, go with the crowd; to be in fashion, keep in step, keep up with the Joneses." With this in mind, as Mark Clarke points out, bandwagons are "the 'latest word,' the trendy, the fashionable, the most up-to-date in methods, materials, techniques."[8]

As Earl Stevick stated at the 1982 TESOL Conference, bandwagons provide confidence, the company of others who believe in the same thing, and useful techniques.[9] Those who are new to teaching often welcome a method of teaching that provides these things. So why is this problematic? It is only problematic if we teachers cannot see beyond the "in way" of teaching, cannot accept the bandwagon as simply other people's prescriptions about teaching, based on their personal set of beliefs about the relationship between teaching and learning. If we blindly follow a certain way of teaching because it is said to be the best way to teach, we become impervious to other possibilities. As I discuss in chapter 2, we teachers can be liberated, free to make our own informed teaching decisions, if we know how to become aware of teaching behaviors, analyze their consequences, and generate new teaching behaviors based on this awareness. Reflecting on our teaching through classroom observation, talking with other teachers, and writing about teaching are far more important to teachers than jumping on the latest bandwagon. While bandwagons provide us with confidence, company, and techniques, they do not liberate us to be able to make our own informed teaching decisions.

The "Overly Anxious" Problem

Tom Scovel defines anxiety as "a state of apprehension, a vague fear."[10] H. D. Brown adds that "it is associated with feelings of uneasiness, self-doubt, apprehension, or worry."[11] There are reasons for anxiety. Here are some of the factors that could raise the level of anxiety in language students.[12]

- Inability to pronounce strange sounds and words
- Not knowing the meaning of words or sentences
- Inability to understand and answer questions
- Reputation of the language class as a place for failure
- Peer criticism

- Not knowing or understanding course goals or requirements
- Testing, especially oral testing
- Previous unsuccessful language-learning attempts
- Encountering different cultural values and behaviors

In some EFL/ESL classroom settings, anxiety can create so much apprehension that the student cannot function normally. Most of us have experienced this type of anxiety. The teacher asks a question in the new language, and with heart slightly racing, all we can do is sit, mouths slightly open, staring at the book or at the teacher, nothing coming to mind. Facilitative anxiety, in contrast, can be motivating, creating just the right amount of tension to bring out the best in us. This is what happens to some actors and public speakers before they appear on stage. It can also happen to students before taking a test, and it can happen to EFL/ESL students in situations where they are given chances to use English.

If students in our classes have high degrees of anxiety that are debilitating them, there are things we can do to possibly reduce their anxious feelings. Students who have high levels of anxiety about being in an EFL or ESL classroom do not need criticism on their language performance. Rather than being critical, we can show understanding. To do this, when a student expresses an idea, we can use an "understanding response"[13] by really listening to the student and paraphrasing back to the student what he or she said. Such paraphrasing not only can provide a way for the student to reflect on his or her own language in a noncritical way but can also improve understanding. When we consistently and sincerely work at trying to understand the students' meaning without expressing verbal or nonverbal judgment of the language used by the student, a positive, trusting relationship between the student and teacher can develop, one that also reduces anxiety about being in a language classroom.

Tom Farrell, who teaches university students in Korea, suggests that students analyze their own propensity for anxiety through the use of personal diaries. If the student sees value in writing about his or her feelings in a journal addressed to the teacher, the topic of the student's anxiety could be pursued by the teacher or even initiated by the student. As pointed out by Farrell, "This use of a diary can show the students that they are not totally alone in times of emotional distress."[14]

The "Engagement" Problem

As I pointed out earlier in this chapter, promoting interaction in the classroom governs that the teacher step out of the limelight. It requires that the teacher yield to the students so that they feel free to interact with the teacher and each other. However, this is not necessarily easy for some teachers. As Wilga Rivers puts it, "Never having experienced an interactive classroom, [teachers] are afraid it will be chaotic and hesitate to try."[15] Adding to this problem are the students' attitudes. As I discussed earlier in this chapter, students quite often come to our classrooms with little experience in initiating and participating in interaction in English. As such, they will also hesitate to interact, afraid that things will become out of control, frenzied, and embarrassing.

To avoid this half-engagement problem, it is our responsibility, as leaders, to provide the kind of atmosphere that is conducive to interaction. As teachers, we need to show emotional maturity, sensitivity to the students' feelings, and a perceptiveness and commitment that interaction in English is not only appropriate but also expected and necessary for the students if they want to learn to communicate in English. As Rivers puts it, "when a teacher demonstrates such qualities, students lose their fear of embarrassment and are willing to try to express themselves."[16]

Teacher Self-development Tasks

Talk Tasks

1. The aim of this task is to consider ways to learn about the students in your classes (or future classes).
   a) Create a plan to get to know the students in your classes.
   b) Meet with other teachers. Share your plans. Together, create a master plan that combines your ideas.
2. The point of this task is to learn about the language-learning history of an EFL/ESL student.

a) Talk to an EFL/ESL student. Find out about his or her language-learning background. What kinds of language-learning experiences has he or she had? What kinds of classroom activities does he or she prefer? Why? Not prefer? Why?

b) Get together with other teachers who have talked with students. Explain what you have learned from the student you talked with. Listen to what other teachers have learned.

3. Imagine you are asked to teach a lesson on expressing ability through the use of the word *can,* as in "She can cook Mexican food."

a) Jot down ideas for a lesson for beginning-level students that takes them through a set of precommunicative and communicative activities.

b) Collaborate with other teachers on the design of this lesson.

4. Study the list of roles for EFL/ESL teachers given earlier in this chapter. Which roles do you believe you can easily adopt in the classroom? Which roles might be difficult for you? What additional roles can you add to this list? Compare your answers with the responses of others.

5. Earlier in this chapter I stated that I see value in the teacher taking on the role of entertainer. Do you agree with me? Why or why not? Find out what others think.

6. Study the list of problems teachers face given earlier in this chapter. Have you experienced any of these problems? How did you go about solving the problem or problems? Were you successful? Talk with other teachers. Find out about their problems and how they worked at solving them.

Observation and Talk Tasks

1. This task gives you a chance to reflect on your teaching. It involves four steps, each of which will take some of your time. You will need the cooperation of another teacher.

Step One: Tape-record or videotape a class you teach.

Step Two: Listen to or view the tape. As you do, take descriptive notes, draw sketches, and jot down samples of interactive dialogue. Avoid making judgments about your teaching as being good or bad. Simply describe the activities you and the students do.

Step Three: Get together with another EFL/ESL teacher. Take turns viewing or listening to sections of your tapes. Take turns describing what you did in your classes. Do not make judgments; just describe.

Step Four: Reflect on the experience. List three things you learned about yourself as a teacher and your teaching. List one or two new things you would like to try out in your teaching.

2. The point of this observation is to consider what happens in the classroom from the student's perspective.

Visit a class. Sit next to a student. Draw a line down the center of your notepad to make two columns. On one side write down everything the teacher does, including what the teacher asks that student to do. On the other side write down what the student does. For example:

What the Teacher Does	*What the Student Does*[17]
Tells class to open their books to page 103.	Opens book to page 33.
Calls on a student to answer question one.	Searches page 33 for question one. Looks at classmate's book. Sees she is on wrong page. Flips pages. Is silent. Looks at page. Looks at teacher.
Teacher calls on another student.	

At the end of the observation, consider the class from the student's point of view. Meet with other teachers who have done the same task. Talk about what some students experience in EFL classrooms.

Journal Writing Tasks

1. Write about the ways you can learn about the EFL students in your classes. Create a written plan to get to know your students.

2. Reflect on the kinds of roles you play in the classroom. Which roles do you like to play? Which roles are you not quite comfortable playing? What do you need to learn to play some roles more professionally? What additional roles could you play?

3. Consider the list of problems teachers face discussed earlier in this chapter. Write about some of your experiences related to these problems. Have you solved them yet? What could you do to work through yet unsolved problems? If you have had chances to talk with others about these same problems, write about what they feel and think about the problem and possible solutions.

Recommended Teacher Resources

Teaching Methodology Books

Celce-Murcia, M., ed. 1991. *Teaching English as a Second or Foreign Language.* Boston: Heinle and Heinle.

Fanselow, J. F. 1987. *Breaking Rules: Generating and Exploring Alternatives in the Language Classroom.* White Plains, N.Y.: Longman.

Long, M. H., and J. C. Richards, eds. 1987. *Methodology in TESOL: A Book of Readings.* Rowley, Mass.: Newbury House.

Nunan, D. 1991. *Language Teaching Methodology: A Textbook for Teachers.* Englewood Cliffs, N.J.: Prentice Hall.

Richard-Amato, P. A. 1988. *Making It Happen: Interaction in the Second Language Classroom.* White Plains, N.J.: Longman.

Rivers, W., ed. 1987. *Interactive Language Teaching.* New York: Cambridge University Press.

Scarcella, R. C., and R. L. Oxford. 1992. *The Tapestry of Language Learning: The Individual in the Communicative Classroom.* Boston: Heinle and Heinle.

Stevick, E. W. 1980. *Teaching Languages: A Way and Ways.* Rowley, Mass.: Newbury House.

Books on Teaching EFL/ESL to Children

Genesee, F. 1994. *Educating Second Language Children.* New York: Cambridge University Press.

Phillips, S. 1994. *Young Learners.* New York: Oxford University Press.

Samway, K. D., and D. McKeon, eds. 1993. *Common Threads of Practice: Teaching English to Children around the World.* Alexandria, Va.: TESOL.

Schinke-Llano, L., ed. 1996. *New Ways in Teaching Young Children.* Alexandria, Va.: TESOL.

Books on Theory and Classroom Practice

Crookes, G., and S. M. Gass, eds. 1993. *Tasks in a Pedagogical Context: Integrating Theory and Practice.* Bristol, Pa.: Multilingual Matters.

Ellis, R. 1994. *The Study of Second Language Acquisition.* New York: Oxford University Press.

Holliday, A. 1994. *Appropriate Methodology and Social Context.* New York: Cambridge University Press.

Johnson, K. E. 1995. *Understanding Communication in Second Language Classrooms.* New York: Cambridge University Press.

Oxford, R. 1990. *Language Learning Strategies: What Every Teacher Should Know.* Boston: Heinle and Heinle.

Reid, J. 1995. *Learning Styles in the ESL/EFL Classroom.* Boston: Heinle and Heinle.

Richards, J. C., and T. Rodgers. 1986. *Approaches and Methods in Language Teaching.* New York: Cambridge University Press.

Rubagumya, C. M. 1993. *Teaching and Researching Language in African Classrooms.* Bristol, Pa.: Multilingual Matters.

Notes

1. See Littlewood 1981.
2. Breen and Candlin (1980), Canale and Swain (1980), Nunan (1988), and Rivers (1987) agree that an interactive classroom requires a reduction in the centrality of the teacher.
3. Stevick (1978, 1980) discusses the concept of teacher control and student initiative.
4. I agree with Curran (1976) and Rardin, Tranel, Tirone, and Green (1988), who focus our attention on the "whole person" of the student.
5. Reid (1987, 1995) and Anderson (1988) discuss learning styles.

6. This list was generated from my own experience and from reading Altman 1981, Prodromou 1991, Richards and Rodgers 1986, Tudor 1993, and Wright 1987.

7. Anderson (1988) created a learning-style inventory, while Oxford (1990) asks students to evaluate their own language abilities in reading, writing, listening, and speaking. Brindley (1989) also created a needs analysis questionnaire.

8. The dictionary definition was discovered in Clarke 1982. The quote is also from Clarke (p. 439).

9. See Stevick 1982.

10. See Scovel 1978, 135.

11. See Brown 1987, 107.

12. This list was created from the work of McCoy (1979) and Alpert and Haber (1960).

13. See Curran 1978.

14. See Farrell 1993, 17.

15. See Rivers 1987, 9.

16. See Rivers 1987, 10.

17. This activity was originally designed by Robert Oprandy, Teachers College, Columbia University.

Chapter 4

Classroom Management

Success [in learning a language] depends less on materials, techniques, and linguistic analysis, and more on what goes on inside and between people in the classroom.

—Stevick 1980, 4

- What is classroom management?
- How can EFL/ESL teachers use knowledge of classroom management to create opportunities for students to interact in English in meaningful ways?
- What problems do some EFL/ESL teachers have in managing classroom interaction?

What Is Classroom Management?

Classroom management refers to the way teachers organize what goes on in the classroom. As the most powerful person in the classroom, the teacher has the authority to influence the kind of interaction that goes on in the class, and this interaction is created from a combination of many related factors. It includes such factors as how much the teacher talks and what the teacher says; the teacher's questioning behaviors; and how the teacher gives instructions, keeps students on task, and makes language comprehensible to the students. The goal of classroom management is to create a classroom atmosphere conducive to interacting in English in meaningful ways. It is through meaningful interaction that students can make progress in learning English.

How Can EFL/ESL Teachers Use Knowledge of Classroom Management to Create Opportunities for Students to Interact in English in Meaningful Ways?

My purpose in this section is to discuss how teachers manage classroom teaching so that students have opportunities to interact in

English in meaningful ways. Throughout my discussion, I emphasize that classroom management is a personal and creative endeavor in which a complex set of factors are combined and constantly tested through classroom use.

Teacher Talk

When asked to tape-record their teaching, listen to the tape, and add up the amount of time they talk, teachers are generally surprised to discover they spend much more time talking than they had imagined. Some teachers will react by saying that too much talk is bad and should be avoided. But this is not necessarily true. As David Nunan points out, "it can be argued that in many foreign language classrooms, teacher talk is important in providing learners with the only substantial live target language input they are likely to receive."[1] When it comes down to it, it is not how much time we spend talking but rather the way we use talk to promote meaningful interaction that is significant. Certain uses of teacher talk seem to lack this purpose and are not productive. Other uses seem purposeful and potentially productive.

Some EFL/ESL teachers think aloud in the classroom. Although some students might gain something positive from this authentic language experience, it can confuse students, and some might stop listening, even when the teacher has something important to say. Likewise, if the teacher gives long explanations about language or long-winded speeches on abstract ideas, some students will sit back and shift into a passive temperament, accepting English as a subject in which the teacher lectures, sometimes in abstract terms that are beyond comprehension. However, we can elect to use English selectively and purposefully to answer students' questions, give instructions, explain homework assignments, relate an amusing story that students can comprehend, participate in daily interpersonal communications with students in English, and use teacher talk as part of the students planned listening comprehension experience (e.g., in a dictation).

The Teacher's Questions

Teachers ask a lot of questions. For example, in a study of the frequency of questions asked by elementary school teachers in the

United States, Nash and Shiman discovered teachers ask between 45 and 150 questions every half hour.[2] My own observations show that EFL/ESL teachers also ask a lot of questions. For example, I recently observed six teachers who were all teaching in different contexts in Japan and found they averaged 52 questions every thirty minutes during teacher-initiated activities. It stands to reason that knowledge about questioning behaviors can benefit teachers who want to provide chances for students to interact in English in meaningful ways.

One way to focus on our questioning behaviors is to consider the purposes of questions (see Purposes of Teacher's Questions). For many teachers, one purpose is to ask students to "display" their knowledge. For example, when a teacher holds up a large paper

---

Purposes of Teachers' Questions[3]

Display Question	A question in which the teacher already knows the answer and wants the student to display knowledge ("What color is your shirt?")
Referential Question	A question in which the teacher does not know the answer ("What is your favorite color?")
Comprehension Check	A question to find out if a student understands ("Do you understand?")
Confirmation Question	A question to verify what was said ("You said you got up at 6:00?")
Clarification Check	A question to further define or clarify ("Did you say you got up at 6:00 or 7:00?")

clock and asks the students, "What time is it?", the teacher is asking students to show they know how to tell time in English. Likewise, when the teacher asks, "What is the past tense of 'to do'?", the teacher wants to see if they know this grammatical point.

For some teachers, another purpose for asking questions is to learn about the students, to discover things about them and their knowledge through referential questions. For example, if the teacher forgot his or her watch and wants to know what time it is, he or she would use a referential question: "What time is it?" The same is true if the teacher asks, "Who has been to a museum?" simply to know who has and who has not been to one.

Many of those who advocate an interactive approach to EFL/ESL teaching favor the use of referential questions over display questions. My own belief is that both have a place in the language classroom. Referential questions provide a means through which to bring "real questions" into the classroom. They can also be engaging for students because the questions are aimed at communicating with them, not testing their knowledge. However, display questions offer a way to practice language or drill students, something most students both like and need, and when students find display questions to be engaging, I see this as being meaningful to them.

Another purpose of teachers' questions is to check students' comprehension, and to do this, teachers often ask, "Do you understand?" Such "comprehension checks" are not as common outside classrooms as they are inside classrooms, and I wonder what real value they sometimes have. Much of the time, if asked, "Do you understand?", students will reply that they do, even when they do not. Perhaps such a question as "Who can tell me what I just said?" is more valuable as the question because it not only shows if the student has comprehended what was just said but also gives the student practice in paraphrasing.

Two other purposes of asking questions are to confirm and clarify understanding. For example, "We'll meet at 6:00. Right?" asks the listener to confirm something that the asker believes is true, while "Did you say you like strawberry or chocolate ice cream?" and "I'm a little confused. What time are we going to meet?" aim at clarification. Confirmation and clarification questions are used outside classrooms more often than inside, and because of this, I encourage teachers and students to confirm and clarify often, if for no other reason than to have more natural, and hopefully meaningful, conversations inside classrooms.

In addition to focusing on the purpose of questions, we can consider the content of our questions (see The Content of Teachers' Questions). Questions can include three possible content areas: study, procedure, and life. I have observed that many of the questions in EFL/ESL classrooms are about study, often on the study of language, such as on some aspect of grammar or vocabulary. Less often, teachers ask questions about content other than language, such as movies, trees, food, anything that is not about language itself. Questions can also have procedural content, such as questions used to take roll, give back papers, and ask about schedules.

Besides study and procedure, content of questions can be about life. As Fanselow points out, questions can be general to a group of people (life-general content), or specific to one person (life-personal content). Two examples of life-general questions are "How do people greet each other in Vietnam?" and "What is the most popular music among teenagers in France?" Examples of life-personal questions are "What is *your* favorite kind of music?" and "What did *you* do at the picnic?"

Some teachers believe that when we include study-other, life-general, and life-personal questions in our classroom interaction, we can provide greater opportunities for meaningful interaction than when our questions focus exclusively on the study of language and procedures. Study-other questions can involve students in using language to learn about a topic, rather than simply studying about the language itself. Likewise, life-general and life-personal questions can involve students in talking about their culture and themselves.

Finally, as teachers, we can consider "wait time" in relation to creating chances for students to engage in meaningful interaction. On average, teachers wait less than one second for a student to answer a question before calling on this student again or another student. In addition, teachers tend not to wait after a student gives a response, reacting very quickly with "Very good!" and the like. As a result, a usual pattern of classroom interaction emerges: the teacher ends up asking many questions, only students who can

The Content of Teachers' Questions[4]

Procedure	Questions that ask students about procedural matters ("Did you do your homework?")
Study of Language	Questions that ask students about aspects of language ("What is the past tense of 'eat'?" "What does the word *acculturation* mean?")
Study of Subjects	Questions that ask students about content other than the study of language ("How big is the Little Prince?" "How many countries are there in the world?")
Life-General	Questions about the lives of groups of people ("Do Japanese women like hot tea in the summer?" "How do Nigerians celebrate birthdays?")
Life-Personal	Questions about the lives of individuals ("Do you like to drink hot tea in the summer?" "How do you celebrate your birthday?")

respond quickly do so, and the teacher ends up reacting to the students' responses. However, if teachers wait a little longer (three to five seconds) and offer polite encouragement through nonverbal behaviors, this pattern can change. For some teachers, when they extend their wait time after asking a question, student participation increases in the following ways.[5]

• The average length of students' responses increases.
• Students ask more questions.
• Students react to each others' comments.

- The number of correct responses go up.
- More inferences are made by students.

I encourage you to increase your wait time. But I also caution that simply increasing wait time will not necessarily create changes in classroom interaction. The teacher needs to be sincere in waiting, genuinely wanting to hear the student's answer and what other students think about this answer.

Setting Up Classroom Activities

To manage and promote interactive classrooms, we also need to know how to arrange a variety of classroom activities. We can select to have students work (1) alone, (2) in dyads, (3) in small groups, or (4) as a whole class.

Look at the example of different seating arrangements, which shows that we have choices as to how we have students sit in the class. These arrangements also imply that we have a great many choices as to the activities we can have students do in class. They can sit in a traditional seating arrangement or in a semicircle during teacher-class discussions or lectures, or they can stand up and walk around as they study (e.g., to memorize lines in a poem). Students can also move their chairs or select a comfortable spot to sit alone or in groups while working on a task. Likewise, they can sit face-to-face—for example, as they interview each other. They can sit back-to-back as they simulate a telephone conversation, across from each other as they practice a dialogue, in circles as they solve a problem or discuss an issue, or next to each other as they study a reading selection, plan a party, or collaborate on a piece of writing. They can move around the class as they practice skits or role plays. The point here is that we teachers do not have to limit the students to traditional seating. If our goal is to provide lots of chances for students to use English to communicate meaning, we need to feel free to create seating combinations that make this possible.

Another aspect of setting up classroom activities is how we group students, and there are a variety of ways to do this (see Ways to Group Learners). One way is to select students in advance of the class based on personality characteristics or abilities and experi-

Seating arrangements: possibilities

ence. For example, shy students can be matched with other shy students or with talkative students, fluent students with other fluent students or with those who are not fluent.

Students can also make their own decisions about what group to join, or students can be grouped according to different physical characteristics, such as hair length, age, height, and so on. However, some students might be sensitive to being grouped in this way. For instance, in many countries, I do not recommend grouping adult women by age. We can also randomly group students, for example, by having students count off "One, two, three, four . . ." and having all one's form a group, two's another, and so on.

Ways to Group Learners

Selectively by the Teacher in Advance

The teacher can group students with the same characteristics or mix them. For example, shy students could be grouped together, or shy and outgoing students could be grouped.

By Ability and Experience:
Accurate/Not accurate
Fluent/Not fluent
Been abroad/Not been abroad
Use English at work/Do not
Use computer/Do not

By Personality Factors:
Shy/Outgoing
Front sitters/Back sitters
Stone faced/Smilers
Talkers/Nontalkers

Randomly in Class

By Characteristics:
Hair color, height, sex, age, favorite color, favorite rock group or singer, types of books read . . .

By Lottery:
Same flavor candy, same colored dot, same end of string, same number, same piece of picture, same line of sentence, same coin . . .

Students could also be given pieces of paper with colored dots. All the red dots form a group, blue dots another, yellow another. The same thing is possible with pieces of candy, feathers, coins, or anything that can be used to distinguish members of a group. Teachers can also cut pictures into pieces (like a puzzle) and hand the pieces out randomly. Students get up, walk around, and locate others who have the sections of the same picture.[6] This way of forming groups can also be an icebreaker, a possible way to reduce students' anxiety about speaking in English.

If the goal is to form pairs, we can simply have students sitting next to each other pair up or have students pair up on their own.

We could also have students randomly pair up through a pairing technique, such as having each student find the person with the other half of a picture. I find students are amused by a pairing technique in which the teacher holds up a set of strings numbering half the number of students in the class, letting the ends dangle. The students grab an end. Whoever ends up holding the ends of the same string is a pair.[7]

Giving Instructions

The way we give instructions is another aspect of managing a classroom, and it is worth taking time to consider how we can make our instructions clear to the students and at the same time provide opportunities through the instructions for students to interact in meaningful ways. One way is to write the instructions on the board or show them on an overhead projector screen. Sometimes I create a cloze activity from the instructions, leaving every fifth word blank. Students then complete the cloze and at the same time process what it is they are to do during the next activity. Another language activity is to give the instructions as a dictation. After giving the dictation, I have students correct each others' by comparing their dictation with a written version.

Some ways to give instructions include

- Writing down instructions and giving them verbally
- Giving instructions verbally and role-playing them; showing the students what they are to do
- Having a student read the instructions, then having a student or two paraphrase these instructions to the class
- Writing down the instructions, letting the students read them silently, then having them tell you what it is you expect from them
- Giving instructions as a dictation, then having the students check each others' dictations
- Miming the instructions as students guess and tell you what they are supposed to do
- Whispering the instructions as students lean forward in their

seats, having them repeat the instructions to the person next to them in a whisper

Keeping Students on Task

As teachers, we can group students, provide activities, and explore ways to give instructions, but this is not always enough. In addition, some teachers believe that keeping students on task is an important part of providing students with opportunities for meaningful interaction. However, this is not always easy, even when the students know what to do. For example, as a great number of experienced EFL/ESL teachers can point out, while working on tasks in small groups, students will sometimes have their own discussions on matters not related at all to the task. Personally, I have no problems with this, especially if their discussions are in English and they come back to the task and are able to complete it. (Perhaps they even benefit more from their own discussion than from working on the task.) However, students will sometimes use their native language during group or pair work, sometimes to work through the task and sometimes to talk about something else. And the students are very clever! Groups might use their native language while the teacher is on another side of the room and switch back to English as the teacher gets closer.

There are things we can do that aim at keeping students on task. The instructions themselves can be important. Some educators believe that students tend to begin working on a task sooner and work toward its completion when it is clear to them what the task involves.[8] Setting a reasonable time limit for the students to accomplish the task could also keep them on task. If students know they cannot possibly finish the task (e.g., if you ask them to answer a list of twenty questions on a long reading selection in thirty minutes), they might stop working on the task.

One thing that works for me is to require an oral or written report as a part of the task. For example, if a group task was to identify the traits of a good student, each group of students would be required to write down these traits on the board toward the end of the lesson. If the task was to write a dialogue, the students would be expected to act it out or read it to the class.

Finally, the teacher needs to stay out of the way, letting the students work on the task. This is not always easy to do! Some teachers have a tendency to talk to students while they work. I have seen some teachers, including myself, drawn to students in groups, circling, listening, and finally interrupting to make a comment or ask a question. Sometimes this keeps students even more intently on their task. But it can also do the opposite. By the time the teacher leaves, students can be totally off task.

In summary, here are some suggestions for keeping students on task.

- Give clear instructions. Make sure the students know what the goal of the task is.
- Let students know that you expect them to stay on task.
- Have students work on tasks that interest them.
- Have students work on tasks that they can accomplish in a set amount of time. Let students know how much time they have left to complete the task as they work on it.
- Give tasks that have a product. Let students know they are expected to report on their findings or conclusions—for example, to give their solution to a problem or their answers to reading comprehension questions.
- Appoint students to take on roles—for example, as recording secretary, timekeeper, discussion leader.
- Let the students work on the task. Do not interrupt without first considering your purpose. Let the students ask for your input.

Making Language Comprehensible to Students

As EFL teachers, we can also work at providing opportunities for meaningful interaction by making language comprehensible to the students. I believe that if the language used by the teacher or in materials is not comprehensible, students can lose interest, become anxious or frustrated, and sometimes go into a passive, nonattentive mood. As such, it makes sense to work at making language comprehensible, but how can this be done?[9] I suggest three ways to make language comprehensible to students.

- Simplify speech
- Add mediums
- Negotiate meaning

First, we can attempt to make language comprehensible by simplifying our speech. This includes using a kind of "foreigner talk," a simplified register or style of speech.[10] Foreigner talk, as it is sometimes used in the classroom, includes exaggerated pronunciation and facial expressions; decreased speech rate; frequent uses of pauses, gestures, and sentence expansion; and completing students' sentences for them. We can also simplify materials. This is what some writers of texts do. They present students with authentic materials (notes, newspaper articles, textbook excerpts, crossword puzzles, maps, letters, advertisements, etc.), but they also simplify the language to their estimate of the students' level of comprehension.

Second, we can add mediums, including those that are linguistic aural (speech), linguistic visual (print), nonlinguistic visual (pictures, objects, realia), nonlinguistic aural (bird chirps, the sound of water flowing, the sound of the wind in the trees, etc.), and paralinguistic (gestures, eye contact, touch, distance/use of space, etc.).[11] For example, if the students are to read an authentic restaurant menu and the text (linguistic visual/print) is too difficult for them, the teacher and students can bring in or draw pictures of the food on the menu (adding a nonlinguistic medium), bring in real food items for students to taste and smell (also nonlinguistic), write a short description of different foods (adding more linguistic visual), or act out how a particular food is eaten, such as how to eat a plate of spaghetti with a spoon and fork or Japanese ramen with chopsticks.

Third, we can work at making language comprehensible to students by negotiating meaning. As I discussed earlier in this chapter, the teacher can open up lines of communication by using questions that aim at clarification and confirmation. These same types of questions are useful to negotiate meaning for both the teacher and students, and when the students work at clarifying and confirming meaning, language can become more and more comprehensible to them.

Managing an Interactive Classroom: Questions Teachers Can Ask

As a way to conclude this section on creating opportunities for interaction, I offer the following questions for you to pose to yourself.

* How much do I talk in the classroom? What function does my talk serve? Does my talk seem to be productive? Unproductive? Are there times when I do not need to talk?
* What are the purposes of my questions? Do I mostly ask students to display their knowledge, or do I also ask questions to discover and learn about what the students know and do? Do I ask questions to clarify and confirm understanding of what students have said?
* How long do I wait after asking a question for the student to respond? If my wait time is short (about a second), can I expand the time I wait? What happens when I do this?
* What is the content of my questions? Are the majority of my questions about the study of language? Do I also ask life-personal and life-general questions? Questions about the study of things other than language itself? What consequences do questions with different content have on classroom interaction?
* What kinds of seating arrangements do I use? Have I explored a variety of arrangements? What happens when I try out different seating arrangements?
* Do the students stay on task during group work? If students go off task, what do they talk about? What language do they use? What are different ways to keep students on task? What happens when I use these ways?
* How do I make language comprehensible to students? Do I simplify my speech? If so, in what ways? Do I add mediums? How? Do I negotiate meaning? How? What happens when I try out different ways to make language comprehensible to students?
* How do I group students? What creative ways of grouping students would I like to try? What are the consequences of different ways of grouping students?
* How do I give instructions? Are my instructions clear to the stu-

dents? How can I give instructions differently? What happens when I give instructions differently?

What Problems Do Some EFL/ESL Teachers Have in Managing Classroom Interaction?

Problems some EFL/ESL teachers face include the following.

The "I never have enough time!" problem. The teacher wants to do a lot with and for the students but cannot find enough time to get everything done.

The "How do I get students to use English in class?" problem. The teacher wants to create a language-rich classroom where students listen to and use English. But the students limit their attempts to use English, not fully cooperating with the teacher's vision of the language classroom.

The "name remembering" problem. The teacher has trouble remembering students' names.

The "I Never Have Enough Time!" Problem

I have heard teachers say, "I never have enough time even to do half of what I planned!" Having faced this problem myself, I asked a number of EFL teachers how they save time. Here is what they suggest.

First, they suggest we build time constraints into our lesson plans. This includes estimating how much time it will take to do each step in an activity—for example, to give instructions to a group task, set up groups, and have students work on the task. Likewise, they suggest we keep track of time. Simply glancing at a watch and mentally noting how much time has gone by can be productive.

Teachers also suggest that when setting up group work activities, simply telling each group where to locate can save much time: "Group one, you are in the corner. Group two, please form up here, near the board . . ." In addition, during pair or group work, we can let students know how much time they are allotted to complete their task.

Finally, teachers suggest we reflect on how much time it took to do different activities and steps in these activities, as well as consider how we might use time differently the next time we do an activity. Keeping a record of our use of time (e.g., in a folder with the lesson plan and materials to do the activity) has proven useful to a number of teachers.

The "How Do I Get Students to Use English in Class?" Problem

I have met EFL/ESL teachers who strongly believe in an English-only policy. Some believe that to learn English, students need to interact only in English. When the goal is to get students to use English much of the time—a problematic goal—there are a number of things teachers have tried. Some put up signs that say, for example, "This is an English-only zone!" Others point at the student and say, "Speak English!" Others initiate a "chip" system in which students can cash in poker chips at times they want to use their native language. Still others make use of a "party fund" in which students give a coin toward a class party each time they speak in their native language.

Personally, I believe these techniques only work minimally for most teachers who face classroom English-use problems. If students are not motivated to use English in the classroom or are pressured by peers to follow a hidden set of classroom rules that includes interacting in the students' native language, then these more or less superficial techniques to compel students to use English can become novelties for the students, ones that will likely wane in their effect quickly.

If we truly believe that students need to use English to learn English and they are not doing so, I believe we need to negotiate with students why it is important for them to use English in class. It is important to gain their trust and commitment. They need to want to use English in class because they see value in doing so. We then are more likely to be successful in implementing techniques that focus their attention on using English to learn English.

The "Name Remembering" Problem

To my embarrassment, I never could remember my students' names. I decided names are important, as learning a student's name shows that I am interested, that I care enough to at least know his or her name. So I asked people who are good at remembering names what they do, and I read *The Memory Book*.[12] First, I discovered that people who remember names really listen to the name, and that they use it as soon as they hear it. They also study the person's face, and they match the name to the face, making mental notes: "This is Jacinta from India, with long black hair and a regal nose."

Surprisingly, simply paying attention to the name and face worked wonderfully for me when meeting individuals. But when faced with three or four classes of new students, I still had problems. So I decided to create ways to learn whole classes of students' names. I had students complete information sheets about themselves, and on these sheets, I asked them to draw pictures of themselves. (An alternative is to take Polaroid snapshots.) I could then take these sheets home, study them, and match the caricatures with their names.

My initial exploration into how I could better remember students' names inspired me to develop a number of first-day activities. Now, on the first day of each class, I do one of several activities that focus on learning the names of the students. One activity is to have students interview each other in small groups, and I join. We meet in groups (or pairs) to learn each others' names and at least three things about each other. We then form a new group to interview each other. After several switches, we form a large circle and list what we learned about each person in the class.

A second activity is a round-robin memory game. The students form a circle, and starting somewhere in this circle, a student will say, "My name is _____, and I like strawberry ice cream." The next student then says, "This is _____, and she likes strawberry ice cream. I'm _____, and I like to read murder mysteries." The next student introduces the first two and adds his or her own name and something he or she likes. This continues until the last person introduces every student. Of course, students can help out, and some students jot the names down as they hear them. The ultimate challenge for me is to be the last person to introduce the students in a class of thirty-five students.

A third activity is a "cocktail party."[13] I have each student write a variety of information on a name tag (for which I use a large self-stick note). The information might include, for example, the student's name in the center, a favorite food in the top right corner, a word recently learned in the bottom right corner, a hobby in the top left corner, and, in the remaining corner, the name of a person, dead or alive, whom the student would like to meet. We then walk around the classroom reading each others' name tags and striking up conversations. As I do this, I pay particular attention to the person's name and face.

Teacher Self-development Tasks

Talk Tasks

1. Study the list of questions in the section "Managing an Interactive Classroom: Questions Teachers Can Ask." Put a check next to those questions that interest you. Then study the ones you checked. Decide on three questions you would like to explore. Meet with other teachers. Who has similar interests to yours?
2. Study the seating arrangements given earlier in this chapter. Meet with other teachers. Design a lesson (on the content of your choice) that makes use of at least five different seating arrangements.
3. Study the list of ways I provide to give instructions. How many additional ways to give instructions can you think up?

Observation and Talk Tasks

1. Ask a friend or colleague who is also reading this book if you can visit his or her class to observe. Remind each other that your purpose is not to judge his or her teaching or the students but to collect descriptions of how he or she manages classroom interaction.

a) Before observing, consider what aspect of classroom management you will observe: for example, the teacher's questioning behaviors, the teacher's way of giving instructions, or the teacher's wait time and its consequences on students' behavior. Let the teacher to be observed pick the area of teaching on which he or she is interested in gaining descriptive feedback.

b) After deciding on an area of classroom management to focus on during the observation, consider how you will collect descriptions of teaching (see chapter 2). For example, will you take photos? Tally behaviors? Jot down sample dialogue?

c) Observe the class, collecting descriptions. Meet with the teacher (just after the class, if possible). Talk about the class, focusing attention on descriptions of teaching you collected. Avoid making judgments, the good teaching/bad teaching trap.

d) Reflect on what you have learned. Were you able to see your own teaching in this teacher's teaching? What does this teacher do that you would like to do? What do you think this teacher might do differently?

2. Work through steps a–d in question 1 again, this time with you as the observed teacher and your friend or colleague as the class observer.

Journal Writing Tasks

1. Answer the following question: What is the value of observing other teachers and of talking about the observation? If possible, base your discussion on your own experience in observing other teachers and then talking with the teacher about the class you observed.

2. Write up what you learned from doing the talk tasks in this chapter.

3. Write about your observation experiences from doing the first observation and talk task in this chapter. Include discussion on what you learned about your teaching, as well as on what you learned about how to go about studying your own teaching.

4. Select one or two aspects of classroom management you find

interesting. Using stream-of-consciousness writing, reflect on your way of managing classroom interaction.

5. Reflect on how language teachers you have had in the past (or present) manage classroom interaction. What do you like about the way they manage interaction? As a learner, what do you dislike?

Recommended Teacher Resources

Allwright, D., and K. M. Bailey. 1991. *Focus on the Language Classroom.* Cambridge: Cambridge University Press.

Fanselow, J. F. 1987. *Breaking Rules: Generating and Exploring Alternatives in Language Teaching.* White Plains, N.Y.: Longman.

Nunan, D. 1995. *The Self-directed Teacher: Managing the Learning Process.* New York: Cambridge University Press.

Notes

1. See Nunan 1991, 190.
2. See Nash and Shiman 1974.
3. The work of Barns (1975), Long and Sato (1983), Brock (1986), and Fanselow (1987) has had a direct impact on the way I understand the purpose of teachers' questions.
4. My ideas on the content of teachers' questions have been adapted from Fanselow 1987 and a personal communication with Fanselow.
5. See Rowe 1974, 1986.
6. This idea comes from Maley and Duff 1982.
7. This idea comes from Maley and Duff 1982.
8. See Brophy and Good 1986; Good and Brophy 1987.
9. Krashen (1982, 1985) discusses the concept of "I + 1." The "I" stands for the student's current stage of grammatical development, and the "1" stands for language just beyond the student's present comprehension. According to Krashen, when language input is at "I + 1," conditions are ideal for language acquisition to take place.
10. "Foreigner talk" was coined by Ferguson (1975).
11. The idea of adjusting mediums to make language more comprehensible comes from reading Fanselow 1980 and 1987.
12. See Lorayne and Lucas 1974.
13. I adapted this activity from Wright, Betteridge, and Buckby 1994.

Chapter 5

EFL/ESL Materials and Media

Reification of textbooks can result in teachers failing to look at textbooks critically and assuming that teaching decisions made in the textbook and teaching manual are superior and more valid than those they could make themselves.

—Richards 1993, 7

- Who creates the materials available to EFL/ESL teachers?
- How do materials reflect the beliefs of those who create them?
- What are the advantages and disadvantages of commercial materials?
- What are authentic materials? What types are available?
- What are the disadvantages and advantages of using authentic materials and media?
- How do EFL/ESL teachers use authentic materials and media?
- What problems do some EFL/ESL teachers have with materials and media?

Who Creates the Materials Available to EFL/ESL Teachers?

Basically, materials used in EFL/ESL classrooms are created by four groups of people. These include publishing companies, government agencies, curriculum development teams at the school level, and classroom teachers.

If you teach in a private language school or business, you probably use commercial materials. These include EFL/ESL texts, audiotapes with accompanying workbooks, videotapes with work sheets for students, and computer programs. In fact, there are now a large number of commercially made texts and other materials on the market for teaching reading, writing, listening, speaking, grammar, survival English, vocabulary building, cross-cultural communication, pronunciation, English for business, TOEFL preparation, vocational skills, literature, and more. In addition, publishing companies are producing a full series of texts, from beginner through advanced proficiency levels. (See list of publishing companies in app. B.)

If you teach in a public school in a country with a centralized educational system, you might find yourself teaching with materials produced (or selected) by a government education agency or committee. Some countries establish special committees that either produce their own texts or solicit proposals from teachers to produce texts. After being approved by this central committee, these texts are produced and used in the schools.

If you teach at certain universities, well-established private language schools, and corporations with language programs, you could find yourself teaching with locally designed materials. These "in-house" materials are usually produced by teachers who have some EFL/ESL teaching experience. Sometimes the writers of the materials are also members of a team who are responsible for designing the curriculum for the language program. As a result, classroom teachers are sometimes given a day-by-day lesson plan, which includes goals of the lesson, steps in implementing it, and the materials needed to teach it.

Finally, if you are among the teachers who are not satisfied with the text, you probably adapt the text or design entire lessons with materials you create yourself. Examples of such materials are illustrated later in this chapter and throughout this book.

How Do Materials Reflect the Beliefs of Those Who Create Them?

Materials differ according to the beliefs of those who create them. To make this point, in this section I provide a brief analysis of broad types of language teaching materials, including illustrations from commercial materials.[1]

Study of Structures

Those who create materials that emphasize grammatical rules believe students need to consider the linguistic makeup of English. Look at the example on page 91 from *English Structure Practices:*[2]

Lesson 17

Exercise 8 (B.1, pp. 188–89)
Write a complete answer to the question. Use *for* or *during* in your answer.

How long did you study? (two hours)

<u>I studied for two hours.</u>

When did you study? (the afternoon)

<u>I studied during the afternoon.</u>

1. When did you write letters? (my vacation)

_____

2. How long did you have the flu? (two weeks)

_____

3. How long did he talk to you? (twenty minutes)

_____

4. When did she study grammar? (the morning)

_____

5. How long did they stay with you? (a few days)

_____

Exercise 9 (B.2, pp. 189–91)
Write *while* or *when* on the line. Remember to use *when* for an action that is of short duration and *while* for an action that is of a longer duration.

She was studying __**when**__ the phone rang.

The phone rang __**while**__ she was studying.

1. We were watching television _____ our parents came home.

2. It began to rain _____ we were working in the yard.

3. She was cooking dinner _____ she dropped the plate.

4. The baby woke up _____ we were watching television.

5. I was writing a letter _____ I realized that I didn't have any stamps.

A lesson from *English Structure Practices*

Study of Language in Situations

Those who create materials that focus on the language used in particular situations believe that students can learn English by considering the language used within different social contexts—for example, in the doctor's office, shoe store, post office, department store, and restaurant. Look at the sample lesson on page 93 on using language in a restaurant from *Real Conversations: Beginning Listening and Speaking Activities.*[3]

Developing Communicative Skills

Those who create materials that focus on developing communication skills believe that the primary goal of materials is to teach communicative competence, that is, "the ability to communicate in English according to the situation, purpose, and roles of the participants."[4] Materials that emphasize the development of communicative competence combine topics, functions (making suggestions, asking for and giving advice, requesting, etc.), grammar, and development of skills (listening, speaking, reading, and writing). Look at the example on pages 94 and 95 of a lesson from *Interchange: English for International Communication.*[5]

Exploration of Personal Feelings and Attitudes

The writers of materials that explore personal feelings and attitudes believe that students gain much by expressing their feelings and attitudes in the target language. Their aim is to teach students self-expression, so that the students' use of the language might reflect their personality. Look at the typical example on pages 96 and 97 from a conversation book titled *Talk about Values.*[6]

Problem Posing

Writers who create problem-posing materials believe that students learn English by solving everyday problems in English. Look at the example on page 98 from *Springboards: Interacting in English.*[7]

★★

⭐5⭐ Try It Out

1. Go to two restaurants.

2. Look at the menus in the window.

3. Choose a breakfast (or lunch).

4. Fill in the chart.

	Restaurant 1	Restaurant 2
Name of restaurant	_____	_____
Breakfast	_____	_____
Price	$ _____	$ _____

⭐6⭐ Watch Out!

1. If the waitress offers something, the customer can
answer with: "I'd like...."

> **Example:** Waitress: "Would you like anything to drink?"
> Customer: "I'd like orange juice."

2. If the customer calls the waitress, the customer uses
a more polite form: "Can I have...." or "May I have...."

> **Example:** Customer: "Can I have some cream, please?"
> Waitress: "Sure."

Breakfast **25**

A lesson from Real Conversations

6 Do you play tennis?

1 SNAPSHOT

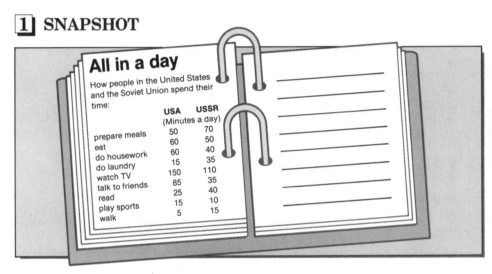

All in a day

How people in the United States and the Soviet Union spend their time:

	USA	USSR
	(Minutes a day)	
prepare meals	50	70
eat	60	50
do housework	60	40
do laundry	15	35
watch TV	150	110
talk to friends	85	35
read	25	40
play sports	15	10
walk	5	15

How much time do you spend each day on the activities above? Write down your information. Then compare with a partner.

2 CONVERSATION: Routines

Listen and practice.

Marie: What do you usually do on your day off, Chuck?

Chuck: Well, I always get up very early, around 5 o'clock. And I lift weights for an hour.

Marie: You're kidding!

Chuck: No, and then I usually run for about 2 hours.

Marie: Wow! You really like to stay in shape.

Chuck: And after that, I come home and eat a big breakfast. How about you?

Marie: Oh, on my day off, I just watch TV all day. I guess I'm a real couch potato!

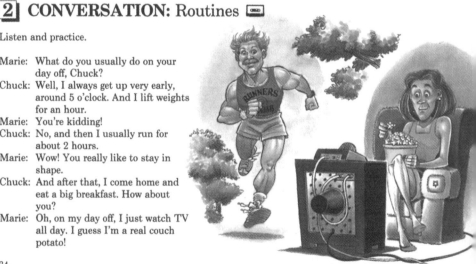

34

A lesson from *Interchange*

3 LISTENING 🔊

Listen to Mark, Sue, and Liz talk about what they do on their day off.
Who likes to exercise? Who doesn't?

4 GRAMMAR FOCUS: Adverbs of frequency (1) 🔊

What do you **usually** do on your day off?

I **always** get up early.
I **usually** run for about 2 hours.
I **often** eat a huge breakfast.
I **sometimes** go downtown in the afternoon.
Sometimes I just watch TV.
I **never** go to discos.
I don't **usually** eat out.

1 Put the adverbs in the correct place. Then practice the conversations.

A: What do you do on your day off?   (usually)
B: Nothing much. I sleep until noon.   (always)

A: Do you go out on Saturday night?   (usually)
B: Yes, I do.   (often)
I go roller-skating   (sometimes)
or I go to a movie.

A: Do you drive to school?   (usually)
B: No, I drive to school.   (never)
I take the bus.   (always)

A: What do you do after class?   (usually)
B: I meet friends for a drink   (often)
or I go straight home.   (sometimes)

A: Do you get much exercise?   (usually)
B: Yes, I play tennis after work.   (sometimes)
And on Sundays, I go to the gym.   (often)

2 *Pair work* Take turns. Ask the questions above,
but this time give your own answers.

3 *Class activity* Now write four questions like the ones above.
Then go around the class and ask your questions.

35

Borrowing and Lending

1 **Look at the pictures and answer the questions.**

1. How do the father, the co-workers and the friend seem to feel about lending something?
2. What are the advantages and disadvantages of lending or borrowing things?

For practice with vocabulary in Chapter 5, see page 80.

24

A lesson from *Talk about Values*

2 **Read the paragraph and answer the question.**

A Really Great Guy

All of Joe's friends say he's a wonderful guy. When a friend needs money, Joe is ready to lend it. When a friend needs a favor, Joe is there to do it. When a friend needs a ride, Joe offers to take him. When Joe and his friends go to a restaurant, Joe usually pays the bill. Everyone loves Joe. Everyone thinks Joe is great. Everyone, except Joe's wife. She thinks he's too generous.

Can a person be too generous? How?

3 **Think about your experiences and give your opinions. First answer the question by yourself. Then ask a classmate.**

Which statement is true about you?

	You	Your Classmate
1. I try never to borrow or lend money. I never like to ask friends or relatives for money. If I have to borrow money, I prefer going to a bank.		
2. I don't like to borrow or lend money. If I really need to, I reluctantly ask my family or close friends.		
3. I feel good about lending money to friends and relatives who need it. If I need some money, I feel good about asking my friends or relatives.		
4. I feel good about lending to friends or relatives. I hate to borrow money from anyone.		

continued

IT'S ONLY

LOGICAL

Each unit in this book includes a "logic puzzle." Using clues from a story, you fill in a diagram which helps you answer questions about the story. Here's the first of the logic puzzles.

1 HALLOWEEN PARTY

Halloween is the evening of October 31, when children play tricks while wearing strange clothes and false faces, or masks. Their costumes may look like the clothes of a sailor or cowboy, a queen or a clown. Or they may dress up to look like an animal such as a monkey or Bugs Bunny. Each child puts on a mask so that no one can know who he or she is.

Last year the three sons of Mr. and Mrs. Cooper attended a Halloween party. It was at the home of David, a friend of the Cooper boys. When Mr. Cooper went there to take his sons home, he was unable to recognize them. Everyone was dressed in costumes. Four children stood in front of him. One was dressed as Superman, one was a robot, one was Mickey Mouse, and the fourth was a ghost. Mr. Cooper was sure that the children were his three sons, Arthur, Billy, and Charles, and the host of the party, David. But he could not decide which was which.

Look at the clues below, and help Mr. Cooper decide the costume that each boy was wearing. Write + in the grid for *yes* and 0 for *no*. The first clue is done for you.

1. Mr. Cooper's wife had bought the costumes for their sons. He did not know exactly what costumes she had bought, but he knew she had not bought an animal costume.
2. Mr. Cooper was sure that Arthur, the oldest boy, was too tall to be dressed as the robot or the ghost.
3. He was sure that the robot was not Charles.

	SUPERMAN	ROBOT	MICKEY MOUSE	GHOST
ARTHUR				
BILLY				
CHARLES				
DAVID				

What costumes were the boys wearing?
Use the completed grid to find the answers.

Arthur: _____

Billy: _____

Charles: _____

David: _____

Be ready to explain the reasons for your answers.

A lesson from *Springboards*

Use of Language for Specific Purposes

Other writers of materials focus on the study of English for specific purposes. These writers believe that students in specific fields need to focus attention on the kind of language used within their particular field. These materials are geared specifically toward people working in different service industry occupations—such as hotel employees, restaurant chefs, factory workers, and secretaries—as well as toward students in academics. In classes teaching English for academic purposes, preuniversity students study listening and note taking or how to give an oral presentation. In classes for people already established in a profession, materials can be given specific content—for example, recommendations on how to pass a medical board certification exam.

What Are the Advantages and Disadvantages of Commercial Materials?

There are certain advantages and disadvantages associated with the use of commercially made EFL teaching materials. To begin, using commercial materials saves time. Another advantage, especially for teachers new to teaching, is that commercial teaching materials can act as a guide that will systematically take the teacher and students step-by-step through a series of lessons. Accompanying teaching manuals also provide lesson plans with some useful suggestions or techniques.

However, there are also disadvantages associated with using commercial materials. First, there is the possible problem of ideological conflict. Each text is usually based on the author's ideas about teaching. For example, some text writers believe students should memorize words and grammar rules before they practice speaking, writing, or reading; others think lots of practice in meaningful contexts is significantly more important. Given a prescribed text, the teacher has to accept the beliefs of the author. Conflict between the teacher's and author's beliefs about teaching and learning (even conflict at an intuitive level, from language-learning experience) can have negative consequences on what goes on in the classroom.

Second, when teachers blindly follow their assigned texts, they are trivializing the experience for the students, and if we teachers accept our role as simply taking students step-by-step through a book, "the teacher's role is marginalized to that of little more than a technician . . . and the level at which we are engaged in teaching is reduced to a very superficial one."[8]

Finally, commercially made textbooks are prepared for a wide audience, one that is culturally diverse and geographically dissimilar. As such, the "qualities which give teacher-made and audience-specific materials their authenticity and relevance are usually removed."[9]

What Are Authentic Materials? What Types Are Available?

To get beyond the limitations of a text, many EFL/ESL teachers adapt or create authentic materials and media. But what actually are authentic materials, and what types of authentic materials are available to us? Basically, authentic materials include anything that is used as a part of communication. To give you an idea of the scope of what I mean, here is a partial list of some authentic materials EFL/ESL teachers have used.

Authentic Listening/Viewing Materials
> silent films; TV commercials, quiz shows, cartoons, news, comedy shows, dramas, movies, and soap operas; radio news, dramas, and ads; professionally audiotaped short stories and novels; pop, rock, country, folk, and children's songs; home video; professionally videotaped travel logs, documentaries, and sales pitches.

Authentic Visual Materials
> slides; photographs; paintings; sketches; drawings by children; stick-figure drawings; wordless street signs; silhouettes; calendar pictures; pictures from travel, news, and popular magazines; ink blots; postcard pictures; wordless picture books; stamps; X rays.

Authentic Printed Materials

newspaper articles, cartoons, advertisements, movie advertisements, astrology columns, sports reports, obituary columns,
and advice columns; travel magazines; science, math, and history books; short stories; novels; books of photographs; lyrics
to popular, rock, folk, and childrens' songs; restaurant menus;
street signs; postcards; currency; cereal boxes; candy wrap-
pers; tourist information brochures and tourist guidebooks;
university catalogs; department store catalogs; telephone
books; world, city, and relief maps; calendars; TV guides; driv-
er's licenses; comic books; greeting cards; business cards; bank
checks and deposit forms; grocery coupons; hotel registration
forms; pins with messages; bus, plane, train, taxi, and jitney
schedules; teletext subtitles for the hearing impaired.

Realia Used in EFL/ESL Classrooms

dolls, puppets, currency, key rings, scissors, folded paper,
toothpaste, toothbrushes, combs, stuffed and toy animals, wall
clocks, balloons, walkie-talkies, candles, fly swatters, string,
thread, chewing gum, glue, rulers, tacks, paper clips, rubber
bands, trays, aprons, plastic forks and spoons, dishes, glasses,
bowls, umbrellas, wallets, purses, balls, phones, fishing reels,
furniture, people, cars, bug collections, play money, stones,
plants, sand, clay, ink, sticks, jars, coffee cans, chalk, credit
cards, hats, Halloween masks, rubber vomit, manikins.

What Are the Disadvantages and Advantages of Using Authentic Materials and Media?

As should be obvious, EFL/ESL teachers have access to a great number of authentic materials and media. However, as with commercially produced materials, using authentic materials and media has
disadvantages and advantages. One disadvantage is that it takes
time and effort to locate authentic materials. A second disadvantage
is that it is sometimes difficult to make authentic materials and
media comprehensible to the students. A third disadvantage is that

some students will not accept authentic materials and media as being a valuable learning source. For example, students will some-times reject TV comedy or games as a learning source, because they consider them as entertainment but view learning as a serious enterprise.

Although using authentic materials has disadvantages, there are very strong reasons to use them. Authentic materials and media "can reinforce for students the direct relation between the language classroom and the outside world."[10] In addition, authentic materials and media offer a way to contextualize language learning. When lessons are centered on comprehending a repair manual, a menu, a TV weather report, a documentary, or anything that is used in the real world, students tend to focus more on content and meaning than on language. This offers students a valuable source of language input, as students can be exposed to more than just the language presented by the teacher and the text.

How Do EFL/ESL Teachers Use Authentic Materials and Media?

Some teachers use authentic materials to get beyond the limitations of a text. To do this, they begin with an idea in a text and, based on their understanding of students' needs and interests, locate authentic materials, as well as create additional activities that make use of them. Here is an example of how one teacher did this. While engaged in a textbook activity, students in a functional English class expressed interest in learning how to order food in a restaurant. So the teacher pulled together pictures of food items from magazines, and he had students in groups study a photocopy of an authentic menu (which a restaurant manager graciously gave him) and match the pictures of the food items to some of those listed in the menu. He then had them create their own menus, including pictures of food items they cut out of magazines. The students next wrote their own dialogues about ordering food in a restaurant, and they practiced the dialogues and took turns presenting them in front of the class. The teacher also had students simulate being in a restaurant through the use of realia (e.g., plastic eating utensils and food order checks) and role-play cards similar to the following:

Waiter

You are a waiter. Your job is to greet customers and take their food orders. Make sure to write down each order.

Cashier

You are a cashier. Your job is to read the waiter's written orders, write in the price of each food item, add up the bill, and collect the money.

Customer No. 1

You are a customer. Go into the restaurant with a friend. Order from the menu. You want to treat your friend, but you only have $12.80.

Customer No. 2

You are a customer. Your friend will treat you to lunch.

As this teacher's set of activities illustrates, it is possible to adapt lessons to a text using authentic materials. However, some teachers also see the need to go beyond the text and to create their own lessons based solely on authentic materials and media, and there are many examples of how EFL/ESL teachers have done this. Garber and Holmes, for example, used authentic video as a means to have students in their French as a foreign language classes write and produce their own commentaries.[11] They prepared four, five-minute video segments on everyday themes, showed them to the students without a soundtrack, and asked them to write a commentary based on the video segment of their choice. The commentaries were corrected by the teachers and audiotaped by the students. After more teacher feedback, students rerecorded their soundtracks. They then watched the original video segments with sound and compared their versions with the original.

Another way to use authentic materials is to include them on reading boards.[12] A reading board looks similar to a bulletin board, but it is purposefully designed to promote interaction between the reader and the text. It can include quick quizzes, problems to solve, quotes from famous people, cartoons and jokes, and news items. Teachers who have created reading boards have used "Dear Abby" advice columns in which the problem is given without solutions.

An EFL teacher and her reading board

(Blank space is provided for readers to write in their own advice.) Some teachers have used advertisements that ask readers to compare prices and select the best buy on a product, as well as cartoons with blank bubbles, cultural quizzes, crossword puzzles, and funny pictures or photos of classmates under which readers can write in possible captions.

Melvin and Stout show how authentic mixed media can be used in a different way. They describe an activity called "Discover a City," in which students use authentic materials as a substitute for a trip to a particular place.[13] Some of the authentic materials include city street maps; tourist brochures; public transportation, shopping, hotel, and restaurant guides; menus from restaurants; cultural publications announcing museum, theater, and other shows; entertainment sections from newspapers; guides to sports and recreation events; samples of currency used; newspaper and magazine articles describing aspects of city life; and songs, films, television shows, and literature about the city.

The students begin by interacting with the materials and are given specific tasks. For example, they can be asked to pick a time of year for the visit and, based on the season, find recreational things to do; to select and figure lodging costs for four days; to select two places of interest they want to visit and find out the different transportation methods (e.g., subway, bus, or walking) and routes by which they can get to this place from their selected hotel; and create a budget based on a set amount of money, including hotel, meal, entertainment, and transportation costs. After searching through the materials to accomplish these tasks, students can be asked to create and present itineraries, justify each of their selections of places to visit, compare their itineraries with those of other students to determine whose plan is more expensive, carry out role plays related to things they would be doing in the city, and complete hotel registration forms.

What Problems Do Some EFL/ESL Teachers Have with Materials and Media?

Problems some EFL/ESL teachers face include the following.

The "I am forced to teach from the book" problem. Some teachers are required to follow a particular text and to use prescribed lesson plans.

The "let the textbook do the teaching" problem. Under the pressures of everyday teaching, it is easy to simply follow the textbook step-by-step, without giving much thought to the consequences this approach has on the students.

The "where can I find authentic EFL materials?" problem. EFL teachers new to teaching sometimes have problems locating authentic materials. Likewise, some teachers find themselves in remote places where even the simplest materials are not available.

The "I Am Forced to Teach from the Book" Problem

Some EFL/ESL teachers are required to follow a particular text, and they find that the administration's policy is stringent. Sometimes, actual lesson plans are handed to teachers, and supervisors make sure they are following the provided materials. When this happens, teachers can feel helpless in the face of being creative with materials and media. Unfortunately, some teachers give in under the pressure and simply follow the prescribed lessons.

However, some teachers find ways to incorporate additional materials, while adapting to the prescribed lesson. They might bring in photos or pictures that correspond to the story line in a required reading, to make the reading more vivid. They might have friends record a one-minute natural conversation based on language in a dialogue in the students' text. Or they might have students spend the last ten minutes of class using scrabble letters to spell out words found in their text and making up original sentences from these words. Some teachers also negotiate an "authentic English" day with the students, providing students with a lesson based on authentic materials and media each week.

Whether adapting a lesson or creating a special day every so often, the possibilities for making such small changes are endless, and the changes can be quite valuable. As I pointed out earlier, such small changes can ultimately have big consequences on the way students interact with each other and the teacher in English.

The "Let the Textbook Do the Teaching" Problem

Following a text has certain advantages. It saves time, and novice teachers can learn something about teaching from following a text and studying the accompanying teaching manual. However, following a text without considering the effects on the students—for example, whether or not they are negotiating meaning with each other and the teacher—can trivialize the experience for the students.

Of course, not all teachers accept the constraints imposed on them by the text. Some teachers want to be more than technicians, doing more than mindlessly following a text and its accompanying materials. They realize that texts are not meant to be blindly plodded through and that teaching guides are only other teachers' ways to teach lessons, which might not be appropriate for their own students. They also realize that much can be gained from exposing students to authentic language materials and media, and because they know these things, they want to make their own informed decisions about how to teach a particular, always unique, group of students.

The "Where Can I Find Authentic EFL Materials?" Problem

Teachers new to EFL teaching would like to use authentic materials as part of their teaching. However, they lack experience in locating such materials. Likewise, some teachers find themselves in remote parts of the world where authentic English language materials are difficult to find.

For the newcomer looking for authentic materials, it is simply a matter of searching. In many countries where English is a foreign language, for example, cable TV offers international news through British (BBC) and American (CNN) programs, as well as American, Australian, and British comedy, films, and talk shows. Most countries have English language newspapers, and in larger cities some bookstores have complete English language sections. English language videotapes and popular music are also easily accessible. Modern grocery and department stores carrying imported products offer other possible resources. The tourist industry offers additional sources. For instance, hotels have registration forms, lists of services with explanations, laundry forms, menus, tourist brochures and newsletters, fact sheets about the local culture, shopping guides, and more.

However, while authentic materials are readily available in many urban areas, it can be difficult to locate materials in remote areas of the world. Ed Black (in a personal communication) provides a vision of the worst possible scenario: "I was teaching English to Chinese immigrants in Jamaica. There was no chalk, no paper, no books. Me, no Chinese. They, no English."

I am very familiar with such settings. I have lived in them, and I visit them frequently. In these settings it is often difficult to obtain materials and media through which to teach. But as other teachers in difficult teaching settings have also expressed, I enjoy the challenge of creating materials out of everyday things. For example, we can teach students to write in the air and on the earth, make use of clouds (What do you see? I see a horse) and of folded leaves and sticks (e.g., to form a town to practice giving directions), and use our fingers to practice counting.

In fact, I believe that those who are fortunate enough to teach in such difficult settings have an advantage. They are challenged to reach deep within their creative selves and observe everyday things as possible teaching materials. This is an education within itself, one that provides an awareness that teaching first of all concerns what goes on between people, as well as an awareness that at our fingertips there is an infinite number of materials that are possible resources for teaching.

Teacher Self-development Tasks

Talk Tasks

1. Locate three different EFL/ESL textbooks. Study the introduction and a chapter or two in each. What are some of the obvious differences in the goals of each book? In other words, what does the author of each book intend for the students to learn through the use of the book? What kinds of activities does the author provide? After studying the books, get together with a friend who has also reviewed a few texts. Take turns showing the text materials and discussing the goals of each book.

2. Do you agree that following a text without using additional teaching materials places limitations on the teacher and students and trivializes the learning experience for the students? Explain what you think to a friend.

3. Study the list of authentic printed, visual, and listening materials given earlier in this chapter. Which do you personally find interesting? Select a combination of three or four items from the lists. Jot down ideas for a lesson that might use this combination of authentic materials and media. Then get together with another teacher to talk about your ideas for lessons using authentic materials.

4. Study this chapter's list of problems teachers have with materials and media. Which of the problems do you think you might be able to face and resolve most easily as an EFL/ESL teacher?

Which problem do you think would be (or has been) the most perplexing for you? Why? Ask other teachers if they have the same problems.

Observation and Talk Tasks

1. The point of this task is to consider how language-learning materials can provide or block opportunities for students to learn English. First, pair up with another teacher. Audiotape one of your classes. Then listen to the tape. As you do, make short transcripts of interaction going on in the class when students are focused on using materials. Study the transcribed interaction. Together, list several things you notice about the interaction and answer the following questions: How does the use of the material seem to provide opportunities for the students to learn English? How does the use of the material seem to block students? How could you use the same materials differently?

Journal Writing Tasks

1. Write up lesson ideas in which you use a variety of authentic materials and media.
2. Write up your reflections on your experiences as a language learner related to the materials you have used. What kinds of materials did you study as a language learner? How did these materials seem to help you to make progress in the language you were studying? How do they hinder progress?
3. Write up what you learned from doing the observation and talk task on materials use and classroom interaction.

Recommended Teacher Resources

Readings on Materials, Media, and Technology

Brinton, D. M. 1991. "The Use of Media in Language Teaching." In *Teaching English as a Second or Foreign Language,* ed. M. Celce-Murcia, 454–72. Boston: Heinle and Heinle.

Duncan, J. 1987. *Technology Assisted Teaching Techniques.* Brattleboro, Vt.: Pro Lingua Associates.

Fanselow, J. F. 1980. "'It's too damn tight'—Media in ESOL Classrooms: Structural Features in Technical/Subtechnical English." *TESOL Quarterly* 14:141–54.

Melvin, B. S., and D. F. Stout. 1987. "Motivating Language Learners through Authentic Materials." In *Interactive Language Teaching,* ed. W. Rivers, 44–56. New York: Cambridge University Press.

Moskowitz, G. 1978. *Caring and Sharing in the Foreign Language Classroom.* Rowley, Mass.: Newbury House.

Orem, R., and C. Holliday, guest eds. 1993. "Technology in TESOL." *TESOL Journal* 3 (1): entire issue.

Romo, R., and B. Brinson. 1982. *How to Make and Use Your Own Visual Delights.* Rowley, Mass.: Newbury House.

Stempleski, S., and P. Arcario, eds. 1991. *Video in Second Language Teaching.* Alexandria, Va.: TESOL.

Wright, A. 1989. *Pictures for Language Learning.* Cambridge: Cambridge University Press.

Wright, A., D. Betteridge, and M. Buckly. 1994. *Games for Language Learning.* Cambridge: Cambridge University Press.

EFL/ESL Textbook Series (Includes Texts, Workbooks, Audiotapes, Teaching Guides; Takes Students through Several Levels)

Brown, H. D. 1992. *Vistas: An Interactive Course in English.* Englewood Cliffs, N.J.: Prentice Hall.

Nunan, D. 1995. *Atlas: Learning-centered Communication.* Boston: Heinle and Heinle.

Richards, J. C. 1994. *Interchange: English for International Communication.* New York: Cambridge University Press.

Viney, P., B. Hartley, T. Falla, and I. Frankel. 1995. *New American Streamline.* New York: Oxford University Press.

Notes

1. In this section I make use of Wright's broad categories (1987) for identifying materials and beliefs that underlie them.
2. See Folse 1990, 242.

3. See Larimer and Vaughn 1993, 25.
4. See Richards, Hull, and Proctor 1990, ix.
5. See Richards, Hull, and Proctor 1990, 34–35.
6. See Schoenberg 1989, 24–25. One of the strongest advocates for exploration of personal feelings and attitudes is Gertrude Moskowitz, and in her 1978 book, *Caring and Sharing in the Foreign Language Class,* she includes 120 activities that provide opportunities for students to express their feelings and perspectives.
7. See Yorkey 1984, 7.
8. See Richards 1993, 8 and 9.
9. See Richards 1993, 6.
10. See Brinton 1991, 456.
11. See Garber and Holmes 1981.
12. Maurice, Vanikieti, and Keyuravong (1989) discuss how they created and used reading boards in an EFL setting.
13. See Melvin and Stout 1987.

Chapter 6

Culture and the Language Teacher

We speak of cultural adjustment, but in fact it is not to culture that we adjust but to behavior. Culture, a system of beliefs and values shared by a particular group of people, is an abstraction which can be appreciated intellectually, but it is behavior, the principal manifestation and most significant consequence of culture, that we actually experience.

—Storti 1989, 14

- What is a reasonable working definition of culture?
- What cultural adjustment process do most sojourners experience?
- What are the benefits of adapting to another culture?
- What cultural concepts can EFL/ESL teachers teach students?
- What problems do some EFL/ESL teachers have related to culture and language teaching and learning?

What Is a Reasonable Working Definition of Culture?

Although there are many ways to define culture, here it refers to the common values and beliefs of a people and the behaviors that reflect them. At the risk of overgeneralizing, it is possible to talk about common beliefs and values and about how they can differ from culture to culture, as well as about the behaviors associated with them.

To illustrate how values and beliefs can vary, let's look at the way people make use of time in two different cultures, mainstream North American and Saudi Arabian. Time, for the average American, is very important. Americans are constantly setting deadlines based on time, and they will stop conversations before they are finished, looking at their watches and saying, "Oh! Excuse me! I have to go or I'll be late." American English is filled with references to time. Time is something to be on, spent, gained, kept, filled, killed, saved, used, wasted, lost, and planned.

In contrast, Arabs see time as "flowing from the past to the present to the future, and they flow with it."[1] Social events and appointments do not always have fixed beginnings or endings. If a time for an appointment has been set, under many circumstances it is acceptable to be late, especially if the person is engaged in a conversation. It would be rude to leave in the middle of it, as maintaining friendships and engaging in human interaction is more highly valued than being on time.

The value assigned to equality among people is another way to illustrate different values and behaviors across cultures. For Americans, equality is a highly cherished value. Americans say that all people are created equal and that all people have an equal opportunity to succeed in life. Thus, an American ideal is to treat people as equals regardless of their status. For example, although a custodian and a professor at a university probably would not become close friends, they would engage in friendly chat in elevators and hallways, and neither would act in ways to make the other feel personally inferior or superior.[2]

Unlike Americans, the majority of the world sees equality quite differently. Rank, status, and authority are considered to be far more important. For example, in Thai society there exists the possibility of social mobility (a Thai peasant can end up being prime minister, for instance). However, while in a particular status or class, Thais, including those in the lowest status, tend to accept this condition as part of their fate.[3] Within this system, Thais value well-defined social behaviors that specify the status of each person. For example, if in the presence of a professor, a student would not engage in a friendly chat unless addressed, and he or she would be expected to behave in specific ways that show that the professor has a higher status. One way to reflect the other person's higher status is to show *kreeng jai,* defined as "a mingling of reverence, respect, deference, homage, and fear."[4] The Thai student would also keep his or her head slightly lower than the professor's while passing.

A final example of how values and behaviors across cultures can differ concerns the value associated with avoiding conflict and maintaining harmony among people. While some Americans value direct confrontation to solve conflicts, people from Asian countries generally value avoiding confrontations. They have developed subtle, indirect ways to resolve conflict. For example, if a person in Japanese society is upset with someone, he or she will likely not confront the other person directly but will behave in a particular way, such as being unusually silent or ignoring the person, providing the other person with clues that there is a problem.[5] Likewise, Laotians and Thais will avoid direct confrontation by being indirect. For example, if a Thai woman is angry at her friend, she will be indirect, perhaps by talking with another friend about the problem within earshot of the offending friend. Or she might invite everyone except the offending friend to eat lunch with her. For some Americans, especially males, being indirect would seem dishonest and insincere. Distrust can result. For many Asians, blatant, blunt, direct confrontation would disrupt the highly valued harmony among people.

Quite often, values and beliefs of a group of people have a deep philosophical foundation. For example, traditional Islamic Arab values can be traced in almost every respect to the Holy Koran. The belief that God alone, not humans, can control all events derives from the teachings in this holy book, as does the belief that each person's fate is in the hands of God. Likewise, Theravada Buddhism is at the heart of traditional Thai beliefs. For example, the belief that emotional extremes should be avoided stems from Buddhist teachings.[6]

What Cultural Adjustment Process Do Most Sojourners Experience?

Most of us have mixed emotions about moving to another country. This is true for those of us who have relocated to teach EFL or, in the case of nonnative speakers of English, to study and live in English-speaking countries. We are excited about the prospect of a new way of life. We are delighted about discovering obvious differences: the shape of buildings, the products in stores, and the way people dress. However, as we find places to live, begin our jobs, and use the transportation system, we begin to actually feel the impact of the culture on our lives. We discover that we have to think about, even prepare for, the most simplistic daily activities, such as paying bills, buying food, doing laundry, taking a bus, and using a telephone. These day-to-day activities soon weigh on us, resulting in culture shock. As Wallender, a Peace Corp volunteer puts it: "In a very real sense, all the convenient cultural cushions we have become accustomed to having around are in one moment totally dislodged. You're left flat on your back with only that within you for support."[7]

Some of us exhibit symptoms of culture shock. We may become depressed or nervous, and we may complain about the food, the weather, housing, and the host people's behavior. We might become physically ill, make irrational comments, have fits of anger over minor incidents, or become very homesick, spending endless hours writing to friends and family. At the workplace we may appear to be tired, disoriented, nervous, or confused. We give obviously wrong answers to students' questions, give unreasonable assignments, complain to the students about things that would ordinarily seem trivial, lecture obsessively, and complain about the administration and rules.

Some of us react to culture shock by withdrawing. We stay home, sleep, and generally avoid contact with people in the host culture. Some of us temporally withdraw to the expatriate community to ease the symptoms; we may seek refuge from everyday problems by avoiding participation with people in the host culture. Some end up staying in this safe harbor, as it is familiar and comfortable. However, by surrendering to the seemingly more pleasant world of people like ourselves, we sacrifice dreams; our visions of making friends, learning the language, and living among the people of the host culture becomes blurred. For some of us, what was a pleasant refuge becomes a void, one in which life can become vaguely unsatisfying.

Although some of us reach out to the refuge of the expatriate community to escape culture shock, others of us react differently to culture shock. We continue to endure, despite the discomfort. Instead of withdrawing, we reach out into the larger community, making friends and working out problems as they arise. We reflect on and learn from our experiences, and as we do this, we start to realize that we are adjusting. Everyday life becomes routine. We can get on a crowded bus like a native, give exact change for a purchase, have fun at a party, visit a friend in the hospital, or play games that were once foreign to us.

Such adjustments are typified by an understanding that cultural behaviors and values are simply different. We still have cultural stress and problems to contend with, but we become more empathetic, understanding that people in the host culture have been raised in a culture different from our own. Likewise, we "develop a greater ability to tolerate and cope with the external cultural patterns. . . . We acquire alternative ways of behaving, feeling, and responding to others."[8] As we adjust, self-confidence increases, and as we interact freely, a new self-image emerges, a new identity as a participant in the host culture. Quite often, when it is time to return home, some of us are sad to leave, and there are those in the host culture who are sad that we are leaving.

What Are the Benefits of Adapting to Another Culture?

Although adapting to another culture can be an arduous experience, there are benefits that make the effort worthwhile. The benefits of successful cultural adjustment include

- A fuller sense of security
- The possibility of more success in the workplace
- The possibility of establishing meaningful relationships with people from the culture
- The possibility of gaining fluency in the language of the host country
- A deeper understanding of one's own culture
- A deeper understanding of oneself

Storti points out that when living in another culture, "ignorance is the breeding ground for anxiety."[9] When we attempt to interact with people in the culture without knowing what is expected of us or what to expect, we become apprehensive. However, the more we learn about the culture through our experience,

An EFL teacher's successful adjustment to Thailand

the easier it is to make predictions, and this can reduce apprehension. Another benefit for some sojourning EFL teachers is that friendships with local people can develop over the course of living and working in the culture, and indeed, these friendships can become lifelong. Related to making friends is learning the language. Although some friendships are developed through the use of English, some can be built on the language of the host country. As we gain confidence through practice (and study) and control over the language, and as the local people get to know us, friendships develop. Although previously isolated, we are now invited to weddings and local religious events, to homes for dinner, and to participate in sports events.

Those of us who have successfully adjusted to the host culture also discover that we have a better understanding of our own culture. When in our own countries, most of us do not necessarily have chances to reflect deeply on our cultural selves as profoundly as we do during the cultural adjustment process. Having to face living in a place where values and behaviors are different from our own provides a way to reflect on our own values and behaviors. In short, "once we encounter another frame of reference, we begin to see what we never could before."[10]

Culture shock can be considered a deep learning experience that can lead to a high degree of self-awareness and personal growth. As a former Peace Corps volunteer from Ethiopia puts it: "It was the rebirth of me. I came away with a totally new concept of life and living, new values, stronger feelings, far richer experiences than I ever would have had in a lifetime in the states."[11]

What Cultural Concepts Can EFL/ESL Teachers Teach Students?

Teachers can teach concepts that not only can bring about appreciation for people and culture but also can be useful for students when the students are placed in cross-cultural communication situations. In this section I address four of these concepts, and I include activities that aim at teaching these concepts to EFL students. The four concepts are

• Cross-cultural communication includes adapting behavior.
• Cross-cultural communication involves problem solving.
• To understand a culture, get to know individuals.
• To understand another culture, study your own.

Cross-cultural Communication Includes Adapting Behavior

A part of learning to communicate with people from other cultures is knowing how to adapt one's behaviors, including one's nonverbal and discourse behaviors.

Nonverbal Behaviors across Cultures

Nonverbal behavior includes kinesics (facial expressions, gaze and eye management, gestures, touch, and posture and movement) and proxemics (the use of space, such as the distance people sit or stand from each other).[12] In this section I point out and illustrate some of these differences, ways in which they can be problematic during interaction, and activities teachers can use to teach students about these differences.

To introduce kinesic differences, I often begin by teaching students that people in different cultures walk differently. Wylie and Stafford, for example, observed that the French walk as if the space around them is extremely limited, while Anglo-Americans tend to walk with free-swinging arms and at a loose and easy gait.[13] To illustrate how people walk in different cultures, I ask volunteer students to let me follow them around the room, and I match their way of walking. Then we reverse roles: I walk; they imitate. After doing this, I ask students how important they think it is, while living in another country, to change their way of walking. Some students think I am being silly (or even crazy!). But as the discussion goes on, they hear stories about how foreigners bump into people in crowded streets, trip people, and even stop traffic because they are not walking like the people from the culture.

I also give lessons on how people shake hands differently in different cultures. For example, I show students that some Germans use a firm grip, pump the arm, maintain strong eye contact, and step closer during a handshake. Some Japanese use a weak grip, no arm pump, and no eye contact. I have students practice these different, culturally adapted handshakes, and we talk about why it is important to be able to change the way we shake hands. We talk about the international acceptance of the handshake as a form of greeting between people from different cultural backgrounds, and we discuss how adapting our way of shaking hands when visiting a country shows respect to those we meet. Further, we discuss how misinterpretations can result if we do not adapt our ways. For example, based on a handshake, Americans sometimes misinterpret Germans as too aggressive and the Japanese as shy or passive.[14]

Another area of kinesic behavior that varies from culture to culture is touch. For example, American males touch each other far more often and on more body parts than do Japanese males.[15] However, when compared to Arabs, Latin Americans, and Southern Europeans, these same Americans do not touch much at all.[16] As touch is a very personal behavior, it is well worth making students aware that differences in touching behavior exist.

Related to touch is the use of space and distance, and this can also vary greatly across cultures. According to Edward T. Hall, middle-class white Americans use space according to the following distance definitions.

Intimate distance. From body contact to a separation space of eighteen inches. An emotionally charged zone used for lovemaking, sharing, protecting, and comforting.

Personal distance. From one and one-half to four feet. Used for informal contact between friends. A "small protective sphere or bubble" that separates one person from another.

Social distance. From four to twelve feet. The casual interaction distance between acquaintances and strangers. Used in business meetings, classrooms, and impersonal social affairs.

Public distance. Between twelve and twenty-five feet. A cool interaction distance used for one-way communication from speaker to audience. Necessitates a louder voice, stylized gestures, and more distinct enunciation.[17]

People raised in other cultures adhere to different rules. For instance, "for Arabs the space which is comfortable for ordinary social conversation is approximately the same as that which North Americans reserve for intimate conversation."[18] Arabs tend to stand and sit very close, perceiving private space as "somewhere down inside the body."[19] Latin Americans, Greeks, and Turks are also from high-contact cultures and will also stand and sit much closer during everyday social interaction than will those from low-contact cultures, such as North Americans, Northern Europeans, and Asians. People from low-contact cultures, when interacting with people who like high contact, will back away, feeling very uncomfortable and perceiving the people who like high contact as invading their private space. Those from high-contact cultures might interpret this behavior as being distant and unfriendly.

As teachers, we can provide students with chances to gain awareness of the differences. Showing students clips from films and videotapes that record natural interaction among people from different cultures—using intimate, personal, and social space in different cultural contexts—can sometimes bring about awareness. We can also have students from the same cultural backgrounds measure the distance they sit from one another while doing pair work, then compare this with the distance between members of other cultures.[20] Choreographed role plays and dramas can offer another way for students to experience the distance they would encounter in a culture opposite from their own.

Discourse Behaviors across Cultures

In addition to nonverbal aspects of culture, EFL students can benefit from exposure to discourse behaviors that follow the rules of speaking. These include the appropriate ways people interact in social settings, such as how to greet, make promises, approve, disapprove, show regret, apologize, request, complain, give gifts, compliment, invite, refuse an invitation, offer, and thank. The ways people in different cultures do these things are often quite different, although there is some similarity across some cultures.

To illustrate how these discourse behaviors can be different across cultures, let's look at gift giving. In many countries, a person visiting a friend on a special occasion will take a gift. In America the hostess will open the gift and thank the person. However, in China and Thailand the receiver of a gift will often set it aside, not opening it in front of the guest. This is because the host does not want the guest to feel obliged to give a gift and does not want to hurt the guest's feelings if he or she does not like the gift and his or her true feelings are obvious.

The way people compliment each other can also differ from culture to culture. North Americans tend to compliment each other often. They compliment a person's new haircut, clothing, work, home, children, cooking, garden, choice of wine, grades in school—almost anything. In other cultures, people do not compliment each other as often, and the way the compliment is given is often different. In Japan, for example, a compliment will be slightly indirect, as was one I recently heard. "Your house is very big! It must be expensive!"

The way people react to compliments can also be different. Most North Americans will accept a compliment at face value, while Japanese and Chinese will often react with modesty. For example, an American hostess's typical reaction to the compliment

"This food is delicious!" would be "Thank you! I'm happy you like it." However, a Japanese hostess might react with something like "Sono koto nai desu" [That's really not so].

For further examples on discourse behaviors across cultures, see the readings I provide at the end of this chapter. As EFL teachers, we can teach students that knowledge about ways people interact with each other in culturally defined settings can be useful. We can provide readings and lectures on the topic, as well as have students do role plays and other activities. However, this is not enough. I believe we also need to teach them the value of problem solving.

Cross-cultural Communication Involves Problem Solving

Imagine the following scenario. Three people are going to meet in Paris to discuss a business idea. One is a Canadian who has lived in France for fifteen years and speaks fairly fluent French. A second is Indonesian and can speak fluent English, but only a little French. A third is French and can speak fluent English. Because all three share English as their common language, much of the interaction will be done in English. But there is still a problem. Which nonverbal behaviors—such as gestures, touch, and use of space—will they use? Which discourse behaviors—such as complimenting, apologizing, complaining, offering, and requesting—will they use? Whose cultural rules are followed? If all act in ways appropriate to their native cultures, how can they avoid misinterpretation of their behavior?

I pose these questions to introduce the idea that interacting with people from other cultures can be complex. Simply informing students that there are differences in culturally based nonverbal and discourse behaviors (and the values associated with them) is not enough. If our goal is to teach students how to interact in English in a variety of contexts with other nonnative speakers of English, as well as with native speakers, then, in addition to informing students about culturally defined behaviors, we can introduce them to the value of problem solving. It is through problem solving that our students can go beyond simply collecting interesting knowledge about cultures. They can have a way to assess a situation and identify or search out behaviors that they predict will be appropriate to use within the situation.

One way to teach this process is to have students introduce real cross-cultural problems they face. In ESL settings, this is easy to do. Students interact with people from the host culture and with ESL speakers from a variety of cultures. However, in EFL settings this approach is problematic. With the exception of some students who, for example, work in the tourist industry or do international business, most students do not have daily contact with people from other cultures. An alternative to using real cross-cultural problems is to use imagined or case history scenarios. For example, the following is an activity I wrote for America-bound Thai students in which the students read and talk about a situation involving an unhappy Thai, work at identifying the problem and the reasons it exists, and generate a list of suggestions that aim at solving the problem.

A Cross-cultural Problem: American University Dorm Life

Siriporn, a twenty-two-year-old woman from suburban Bangkok, had secretly dreamed of studying in the United States ever since she was a little girl. As an undergraduate at Thammasat University, she majored in English. Although Siriporn rarely spoke with her conservative merchant parents about going to the United States, they knew about her dream, and they had saved money through the years to send her to America. Siriporn applied to several universities in the United States, and together, she and her parents selected a university in Pennsylvania.

Siriporn arrived at her American university full of enthusiasm. She wanted to be an excellent student. Studying was the first thing on her mind. She attended all her classes and did her required readings before each lecture. However, Siriporn soon became more and more frustrated. She could not fully follow the lectures, and it took her a long time to comprehend the readings. She would study at the library until it closed and then would go to her dormitory room to study some more. She often studied until 2:00 A.M.

But she had a problem. Her American roommate had many

friends, and they all liked to meet in her room to talk and eat. They would simply walk into her room, sit down on her bed, and start to talk, eat potato chips, and play music. Sometimes they would stay up very late, and after they left, she had to clean potato chip crumbs and even dirt from their shoes off her bed.

Siriporn thought they were inconsiderate, and she attempted many times to get them to leave so she could study. Twice she walked out of the room without speaking. Another time she politely mentioned to her roommate that she likes to study in the room, but her roommate did not pay any attention to her comment. Another time, while walking with a friend from Japan, she said within earshot of her roommate, "I wish my roommate would not have parties every night." But nothing Siriporn said or did seemed to make a difference. Her roommate's friends kept coming into her room. She became more and more frustrated, sometimes feeling helpless and angry.

What is the problem? What conflict between Thai and American behaviors and values created this problem? Why do you think Siriporn's ways to solve the problem did not work? How could Siriporn solve this problem?

I suggest teachers write their own problem sets, as I did for my class of Thai students. Problems can be based on knowledge about the students and the types of culturally based situations they might someday face, or they can simply be based on the students' interests. One book that has given me ideas for developing problem sets is *Intercultural Interactions.*[21] It presents a host of situations and discourse-type problems to solve.

To Understand a Culture, Get to Know Individuals

It is possible, as I have done in this chapter, to generalize about the cultural values and behaviors of a large group of people. Such generalizations can be useful, for example, to gain a general idea of the differences (and similarities) among people from different cultural backgrounds. However, there is a danger in categorizing a group of people into one single set of values and behaviors. Not all British, for example, are reserved. Not all Japanese are indirect. Not all Americans are competitive.

As such, in addition to making generalizations, I teach students the importance of getting to know one person at a time, treating each as a distinct and unique individual. This includes how each individual behaves in different social situations, as well as the values each has. With this in mind, the question is, how can we teach students this concept? One way is to discuss it with them as a whole class, and for some students, especially those who already like to personalize their experiences, this can make a difference in the way they perceive learning about people from different cultural backgrounds.

Another way to focus on the individual is to draw the students' attention to the differences among individuals in their own culture and have them relate this knowledge to other cultures. For example, I sometimes do a values clarification activity I call "Who gets to test the drug?" In this activity students are asked to read statements about the lives of seven people, all quite different from each other. One is a homeless drug addict. Another is a bright college student, another a middle-aged scientist, another an elderly person who has worked all his life to solve societal problems, and so on. Each person has the same life-threatening disease, and the students are asked to select one of these people to participate in testing a new miracle drug that has the potential of reversing the disease. Students make their own individual choices and then meet in small groups to come to an agreement on their selection of one person to test the new drug.

One reason to do this activity is that it meets criteria, as discussed in chapter 3, for promoting interaction among students. It decreases the centrality of the teacher, provides students with chances to negotiate meaning, and allows them to decide for themselves what they want to say and how they want to say it. However, I also use this activity to show students how individuals in a culture can vary in their beliefs and values. After the students negotiate who should be given the chance to test the drug, I ask them what their individual choices are and why they selected a particular person. For example, one student might select the scientist because she is doing important medical research, another the student because he is young and has a bright future, another the elderly person because he has contributed so much to society and deserves to be rewarded. I also emphasize that some agree on what they value, while others differ in what they believe is important. I then make the point that it is important to get to know what it is that each person values, rather than making a generalization that all people in a culture believe in or value the same things.

To Understand Another Culture, Study Your Own

A fourth concept worth teaching is that much can be gained from studying one's own cultural behaviors and values. As acquiring the rules of one's own culture is a fairly unconscious process, students are most likely not aware of many aspects of their own culture. Even everyday behaviors—such as how change is given at a store or how people greet each other and bid farewell, complain, apologize, compliment each other, and enter and leave a classroom—are usually not apparent to most EFL students. By providing students with opportunities to consider how people interact in their own culture, as well as their own individual values and ways of behaving, they can gain the kind of insight useful to them when encountering people from other cultures. I base this assumption on the idea that by knowing one's own values and behaviors, it is easier to recognize those of others, as well as make necessary changes in behavior when needed. In short, contrasts help.

To teach students about their own cultures, the teacher can design questions for students to answer that provide them with chances to explain their own culture to the teacher and classmates. For example, a friend who is teaching EFL in Japan sometimes uses the text *Explain Yourself! An English Conversation Book for Japan.*[22] The entire book consists of different topics, sketches that illustrate the topic, and lists of questions. Topics include the Japanese New Year, sumo wrestling, baseball, funerals, weddings, public baths, university life, temples, different festivals, and so on. Here is a sample of the questions from the chapter on bathing:

How often do you use a public bath?
Why is bathing segregated? Has it always been so?

What are likely subjects of conversation in a public bath?

What is the most popular bathing time?

Why would it be inadvisable to have a hot bath if you had just eaten dinner?

Why has bathing always been such an important part of Japanese life?

My friend pointed out that students not only gain practice in talking about their own culture in English but also raise questions about his culture: "Do you have public baths in the United States? When is a popular time for Americans to take a bath?" I have also used this idea of explaining one's own culture in ESL settings by having small groups of students prepare oral presentations about their cultures. They collect objects and pictures, read about and consider behaviors and values, and create a presentation.

Another way to teach students about their own culture is to use photos and pictures. For example, by showing Thai students pictures that illustrate the ways Thais sit, it is possible to highlight that in their culture it is impolite to point one's foot at another person. By showing pictures of how people in other cultures sit, they can easily recognize the differences, especially noting that people in some cultures sit cross-legged, the foot pointing outward. The students could even practice sitting in foreign ways, providing a cross-cultural experience for them.

However, the teacher can go beyond simple behavior by also introducing readings or talking about the values associated with certain behaviors. For example, in the lesson on sitting in Thailand, the teacher could lead a discussion on reasons Thais sit the way they do. The teacher could make the point that Thais do not point their foot at others because it will disturb the other person's *khwan* or spirit essence. Many Thais believe that they have many parts to their *khwan* and that any part can escape the body if disturbed. As such, Thais do not point the foot (where the worst *khwan* are) at someone's head (where the best are), as this could be disturbing. Part of the *khwan* can escape, leaving the person less than whole.[23] Such knowledge can spark students' interest in values across cultures and deeper cultural knowledge.

What Problems Do Some EFL/ESL Teachers Have Related to Culture and Language Teaching and Learning?

Problems some EFL/ESL teachers face include the following.

The "I can't seem to adjust" problem. The sojourner finds that living in the host culture is more difficult than thought and is having problems adjusting. This is true for both sojourning ESL students and EFL teachers.

The "learning the language of the host country" problem. The EFL teacher finds learning the language of the host country to be a difficult challenge.

The "cheating" problem. Teachers and students sometimes have different attitudes and understanding as to what constitutes cheating.

The "I Can't Seem to Adjust" Problem

As I discussed earlier in this chapter, EFL teachers (and ESL students and nonnative EFL teachers studying abroad) go through a process of cultural adjustment that includes experiencing the loss of the familiar. Things taken for granted at home suddenly require close attention. Taking a bus, buying soap, doing laundry, paying bills, or looking up a telephone number can all require far more effort than expected. For some, these everyday problems create an emphatic emotional disruption, and it feels like cultural adjustment will never take place. But there are things we can do as an EFL teacher in a new culture to make the adjustment process easier. The following suggestions might help you adjust to another culture.

- Give yourself time.
- Recognize, accept, and treat symptoms of culture shock.
- Talk with others who have successfully adjusted.
- Learn as much as possible about the host culture.
- Get involved with people in the host culture.
- Study the language of the host culture.

First, we can recognize that cultural adjustment takes time. Adjustment is a gradual process. It will not happen over night.

Second, it is important to identify, accept, and treat the symptoms of culture shock. To identify the symptoms, it is necessary to step back and reflect on personal feelings and behavior. As I discussed earlier, symptoms include feeling emotionally distressed (homesick, easily angered, depressed, nervous, etc.), complaining about things that affect our lives (the students, housing, food, weather, etc.), and withdrawing (sleeping a lot, avoiding people from the host culture, spending free time with other sojourners). Recognizing the symptoms of culture shock can in itself be therapeutic. But it is also important to accept the symptoms. For example, if I am depressed, I recognize that I am depressed. I simply remind myself that it will not last long. I also do the opposite of what I have been doing as a result of culture shock. If I find I sleep a lot, I try not sleeping so much. If I find I complain too much, I try complimenting.

Third, talking with others who have successfully adapted to the culture can be useful. It lets others know that our uneasiness, lack of confidence, and everyday problems in getting around and doing simple things are temporary. It is also possible to learn about what others have done to adjust. People usually like talking about their experiences, and most sojourners are more than happy to act as mentors, especially if they have created a happy life for themselves in their second country.

Fourth, it helps to learn as much as possible about the host culture. While some want to know about geography, others are interested in history, art, education, politics, psychology, and religion. I personally like to read translated short stories and novels, as they give me a window, as reinvented as it is, into understanding much about the host culture.

Fifth, although not always easy, it is also possible to get involved with people from the host culture. In fact, this is very important. It is through daily contact with people in the host culture that we learn about what to expect and how to behave.

Sixth, when you learn the language of the host culture, it is possible to gain an even deeper understanding of the culture and its people, making adjustment not only possible but, at least to me, interesting and even fun.

The "Learning the Language of the Host Country" Problem

The problem of learning the language of the host country is specific to EFL teachers living abroad who want to learn the language of the host country. Most of us start out with great enthusiasm. However, many give up. It is not because we do not want to become fluent in the language. Most of us have a dream of gaining great proficiency. Rather, some give up because we get too busy to study the language or find we lack opportunities to actually use the language. We speak English to our students, office staff, and administrators. We make friends with other EFL teachers and with fluent English-speaking acquaintances from the host culture, and we end up speaking English with them outside the workplace. When we venture out into the country, we meet people who jump at the chance to use English with a native speaker, and we oblige. As it turns out, opportunities to use the language of the host culture become limited. However, some of us are determined, and based on our experience with learning second languages, we agree that learning the language requires a great amount of effort.

Suggestions for learning the language of the host country include

- Keep studying the language.
- Take on the responsibility for your own learning.
- Create and implement a learning plan.
- Build relationships with people in the community based on appropriate use of the language.

If we want to become fluent in the language of the host country, we have to devote considerable energy and time to studying the language. Some of us start out with wonderful intentions. We join a language class, do our homework, and attend classes regularly. But obligations get in the way, and gradually we attend classes less often and show up without completing our assignments. Eventually, we stop going, put the book on a shelf, and tell ourselves we will start up again when we have more time. However, studying a language is an ongoing process, and it requires consistent discipline and interest and a willingness to concentrate on studying. Basically, if our goal is to become very fluent and literate in the language, we have to be willing to devote years to this endeavor.

We have to take on the responsibility for our own learning, which includes creating a plan to learn the language. This plan might include attending classes and collecting and studying language texts. Perhaps more important is our need to have a plan designed to make use of all the resources available to us, including people in the community. For example, to gain spoken fluency, Terry Marshall[24] suggests we (1) decide on what to learn for the day (e.g., how to buy train tickets); (2) prepare an imagined conversation in the target language with the help of a native-speaking mentor/tutor; (3) practice the conversation with the mentor/tutor; (4) communicate the studied language to native speakers by going into the community, finding people, and speaking to them (e.g., at the train station); and (5) evaluate our progress.

Having a plan is a start. Implementing it is another matter. Going into the community to find people to use the language with is not always easy. However, it can be done. For example, when I moved to Japan, I purposefully lived in a place where no other foreigners lived, and when approaching the study of Japanese, I used the community. I talked with people at the public bath, the local stores, and the laundry. Being single at the time, I went on dates with women who I knew would be willing to speak Japanese with me. I also joined a yoga club where I could use Japanese, went on weekend hiking trips with a non-English-speaking Japanese, and drank a few beers each week at a place where few were interested in speaking English with me. During my lunch hour, I spent ten minutes chatting with a friend in Japanese on the phone, and I used Japanese with a group of American and Australian friends, all interested in mastering the language. I learned a lot from these friends, one reason I support teachers having students speak English with each other in class.

My efforts to find contexts to use Japanese did something unexpected for me. I established a network of people, becoming a member of several groups within the community—for example, the yoga club, a local restaurant, and the community center. I discovered that as my Japanese got better, my relationships with people in the community became more complex, and that as these relationships became more complex, I needed to learn more. For example, since I wanted to send New Year's greeting cards to my new friends, just before New Year's I learned how to use ink and a brush to write, as well as the formulaic language I needed. When the yoga club took a trip, I had to learn how to introduce myself to others in public fashion. When a friend's mother died, I had to learn what to say to him. The point is, as it relates to learning the language of the host country, it is important to build relationships with people in the community. It is through interaction with them that it becomes possible to make progress in the language, because language and culture are inexorably linked.

The "Cheating" Problem

Sometimes teachers and students have different beliefs about what constitutes cheating. The teacher is upset because the students are cheating; the students are baffled, thinking, "Why is the teacher angry at us?" In some cultures students have liberal attitudes toward copying homework and sharing answers on tests. In Thailand, for example, I have seen students very creatively design ways to help each other on exams. As I understand it, this is alright with some Thai students. It is more important for them to network, to create a strong working relationship with classmates, than to pass the test without help from classmates.

In other cultures—for example, in Latino culture—helping out others in this way also seems to be fairly valued. For example, based on a study of 151 students (44 North American, 21 Middle Eastern, 47 South American, and 39 Cuban), two researchers concluded that the students from Latino cultures believe that "cheating" is wrong but see no problem in occasional use of cribnotes, copying someone else's homework, and letting someone copy their work.[25]

As EFL/ESL teachers we need to recognize that "cheating" is a culturally based problem. We can learn about what cheating means to the students, what they believe is acceptable and not acceptable "cheating" behavior. Then we can teach them about our own values and, in ESL settings, the values of the people around them—for example, American professors and students. It is through mutual understanding that students can learn to change their perceptions and behaviors about cheating, if needed. In some EFL settings, it would even be a mistake to expect students to change the way they "help each other," as this is a deeply ingrained part of the students cultural identity.

Teacher Self-development Tasks

Talk Tasks

1. Culture can be defined in many ways. For example, I define culture as the shared values and beliefs of a group of people and the behaviors that reflect them.
   a) What merit do you think this definition has?
   b) What are other ways to define culture?
2. Review and discuss my points on teaching cultural concepts to students.
   a) What are the four concepts I discuss? Explain each.
   b) Why do I recommend that EFL/ESL teachers teach students cultural concepts? What are the benefits? Do you teach cultural concepts to students? If so, how?
   c) Select one of the cultural concepts. Design a lesson that aims at teaching this concept.
3. Here are three brief research tasks for you. Feel free to do one or more of them.
   a) The way names are listed in telephone books sometimes differs from culture to culture. Pick a culture different from your own. Locate a phone book from this culture. How are the names listed? Are they listed the same or differently from how they are listed in phone books in your native culture? What other differences, besides order of names, do you notice?
   b) Each culture has its own special holidays. Look into holidays in different cultures. See how many different types of holidays you can come up with.

c) Pick three different cultures. Find out how people in these cultures generally offer guests a drink (e.g., a cup of tea). Find out how people accept or refuse the offer.

4. Storti provides the following graphic model of the process of adjustment.[26]

Storti's Model of the Process of Cultural Adjustment

We expect others to be like us, but they aren't.

↓

Thus, a cultural incident occurs, causing a reaction (anger, fear, etc.).

↓   ↓

We withdraw.   We become aware of our reaction.

↓

We reflect on its cause.

↓

We observe the situation, which results in developing culturally appropriate expectations.

↓

And our reaction subsides.

Study this model. Notice that there are two possible ways for us to react to a cultural incident. We can withdraw (e.g., by moving into the expatriate community), or we can work at adjustment through reflection.

a) Explain what Storti's model means.

b) Talk about the benefits of taking the "reflective" path. You might want to refer to my discussion on the benefits of cultural adjustment.

c) Tell stories about your own and others' cultural adjustment.

Observation and Talk Tasks

1. Videotape one of your classes. Analyze the interaction by studying yourself and the students with regard to one or more of the following.

a) Use of eye contact while listening

b) Use of touch

c) Way of sitting

d) Distance kept while standing or sitting

How do your behaviors reflect your native culture? How are students' behaviors different or similar to yours? Meet with other teachers to talk about what you discovered.

2. Try out the following matching techniques. Then talk to someone who also has tried them. What did you learn from the experience? Consider how matching behaviors can be used as a way for you to learn a language, as well as the value it has for EFL/ESL students.

a) Sit next to someone who speaks a different language from you. Match this person's posture, gestures, facial expressions, and breathing. Do this for a few minutes.

b) Sit in the middle of a movie theater. Do whatever the audience does. Laugh when they laugh. Sigh when they sigh. Sit the way they sit.

c) Watch people doing things, such as paying for an item at a store, getting a waiter's attention, eating a dish of ice cream, and counting with their fingers. Imitate them. Try to match the behaviors they exhibited as they did these things.

Journal Writing Tasks

1. Write down your ideas about teaching students cultural concepts. If you try out any of the ideas, reflect on how you thought the lesson went.

2. If you now live in a foreign country or have lived in one, write about your own cultural adjustment process and problems. If you have never lived abroad, write about your imagined process and problems.

3. Write about what you have learned from matching people's behaviors. Make a list of possible behaviors you could match.

4. Review the problems of cultural adjustment, learning the host language, and understanding different perceptions of cheating as discussed in this chapter. Can you identify with any of these three problems? If so, select one problem and write about it.

Recommended Teacher Resources

Readings on Culture and Cultures

Bond, M. H., ed. 1986. *The Psychology of the Chinese People.* New York: Oxford University Press.

Damen, L. 1987. *Culture Learning: The Fifth Dimension in the Language Classroom.* Reading, Mass.: Addison-Wesley.

Fieg, J. P. 1989. *A Common Core: Thais and Americans.* Yarmouth, Maine: Intercultural Press.

Finkelstein, B., A. E. Imamura, and J. T. Tobin, eds. 1991. *Transcending Stereotypes: Discovering Japanese Culture and Education.* Yarmouth, Maine: Intercultural Press.

Hall, E. T. 1981. *Beyond Culture.* Garden City, N.Y.: Anchor Books.

———. 1990. *Understanding Cultural Differences: Germans, French, and Americans.* Yarmouth, Maine: Intercultural Press.

Luce, L. F., and E. C. Smith. 1987. *Toward Internationalism.* Rowley, Mass.: Newbury House.

Nydell, M. K. 1987. *Understanding Arabs: A Guide for Westerners.* Yarmouth, Maine: Intercultural Press.

Samovar, L. A., and R. E. Porter. 1993. *Intercultural Communication: A Reader.* New York: Wadsworth.

Stewart, E. C., and M. L. Bennett. 1991. *American Cultural Patterns: A Cross-cultural Perspective.* Yarmouth, Maine: Intercultural Press.

Readings on Teaching Culture

Brislin, R. W., K. Cushner, C. Cherrie, and M. Yong. 1986. *Intercultural Interactions: A Practical Guide.* Beverly Hills, Calif.: Sage Publications.

Gaston, J. 1984. *Cultural Awareness Teaching Techniques.* Brattleboro, Vt.: Pro Lingua Associates.

Heiman, J. D. 1994. "Western Culture in EFL Language Instruction." *TESOL Journal* 3 (3): 4–7.

Valdes, J. M., ed. 1986. *Culture Bound: Bridging the Cultural Gap in Language Teaching.* New York: Cambridge University Press.

Readings and Video on Cultural Adjustment

Adler, P. S. 1987. "Culture Shock and the Cross-cultural Learning Experience." In *Toward Internationalism*, ed. L. F. Luce and E. C. Smith, 24–35. Cambridge, Mass.: Newbury House.

Furnham, A., and S. Bochner. 1986. *Culture Shock: Psychological Reactions to Unfamiliar Environments*. New York: Methuen.

Lewis, T. J., and R. E. Jungman. 1986. *On Being Foreign: Culture Shock in Short Fiction*. Yarmouth, Maine: Intercultural Press.

Ogami, N., producer. 1988. *Cold Water: Intercultural Adjustment and Values of Foreign Students and Scholars at an American University*. Yarmouth, Maine: Intercultural Press. Videotape.

Storti, C. 1989. *The Art of Crossing Cultures*. Yarmouth, Maine: Intercultural Press.

Books for EFL Teachers Learning the Language of the Host Country

Brown, H. D. 1991. *Breaking the Language Barrier*. Yarmouth, Maine: Intercultural Press.

Marshall, T. 1989. *The Whole World Guide to Language Learning*. Yarmouth, Maine: Intercultural Press.

Rubin, J., and I. Thompson. 1994. *How to Be a More Successful Language Learner*. Boston: Heinle and Heinle.

Cross-cultural Texts (Mixed Skills)

Chan, D., J. Kaplan-Weinger, and D. Sandstrom. 1995. *Journeys to Cultural Understandings*. Boston: Heinle and Heinle. (High advanced)

Dresser, N. 1993. *Our Own Stories: Cross-cultural Communication Practice*. White Plains, N.Y.: Longman. (Intermediate)

Oxford, R. C. 1995. *Patterns of Cultural Identity*. Boston: Heinle and Heinle. (Advanced)

Wegmann, B. 1994. *Culture Connection*. Boston: Heinle and Heinle. (Low intermediate)

Zanger, V. V. 1993. *Face to Face: Communication, Culture, and Collaboration*. Boston: Heinle and Heinle. (High intermediate)

Notes

1. See Nydell 1987, 60.
2. It is worth noting that American cultural values represent a paradox. On the one hand, the majority of Americans will say they value equality. On the other hand, racism still exists in America. All one has to do is consider the Los Angeles riots of 1993 or talk to African-Americans. As one African-American stated on *CNN World News* (8 May 1994), "If you are young and black, it's like being a suspect. You can be arrested for simply walking down the wrong street."
3. This idea of fate in Thai culture comes from Fieg (1989), who has lived in and studied Thai culture for a number of years.
4. See Moore 1992, 83–84.
5. Doi (1973) discusses the psychological makeup of the Japanese.
6. As Fieg (1989) puts it: "Consistent with the Buddhist ideal that ultimate happiness (Nirvana) results from the total detachment of the self from feelings and desires, Thai emotional expression—whether it be positive or negative—is rarely extreme. Instead, Thais tend to neutralize all emotions" (41).
7. See Wallender 1977, 7.
8. See Lewis and Jungman 1986, xxi.
9. See Storti 1989, 94.
10. See Storti 1989, 94.
11. This quote was discovered in Adler 1987.
12. Morain (1987) offers a detailed discussion on nonverbal behavior.
13. See Wylie and Stafford 1977.
14. See Hoffer 1984 for more on handshakes.
15. See Barnlund 1975 for a discussion of touch in Japanese and American cultures.
16. Watson (1974) has studied touch in cultures around the world; Nydell (1987) writes about touch in Arab countries.
17. See Hall 1966, 15.
18. See Nydell 1987, 45.
19. See Hall 1966, 15.
20. This activity is discussed in Melamed and Barndt 1977.
21. See Brislin, Cushner, Cherrie, and Yong 1986.
22. See Nicholson and Sakuno 1982.
23. Heinze (1982) and Tambiah (1970) have done extensive research on the Thai *khwan*.
24. Marshall (1989) provides guidelines based on his Peace Corps experi-

ence. Brown (1991) and Rubin and Thompson (1994) have also written books with guidelines and advice for the language learner.

25. See Stanwyck and Abdellal 1984.
26. See Storti 1989.

Part 3

Teaching Language Skills

Chapter 7

Teaching Students to Comprehend Spoken English

There isn't any listening without someone speaking, and speaking without somebody listening is an empty gesture.
—Bowen, Madsen, and Hilferty 1985, 99

- What does the act of listening include?
- What kinds of listening activities do EFL/ESL teachers use?
- How do EFL/ESL teachers use the media to teach listening?
- What problems do some EFL/ESL teachers have in teaching students to comprehend spoken English?

What Does the Act of Listening Include?

I guide my discussion by focusing on four aspects of listening, including the nonpassive nature of listening, the way we normally process what we hear to make sense out of it, and two purposes for listening.

Active Listening

Listening is not a passive skill. Rather, listening places many demands on us. When we participate in face-to-face or telephone exchanges, we need to be receptive to others, which includes paying attention to explanations, questions, and opinions. Even when we listen during one-way exchanges—for example, while listening to lectures, radio dramas, films, television news, and musicals—we are active. Consider, for example, how many times you shouted at, laughed at, or agreed with (either out loud or inside your head) a person giving a television commentary on a hot topic. Active listening is even a part of our intrapersonal communication, in which

143

we pay attention to our own thoughts and ideas. For example, consider the last time you talked to yourself. "Where did I put my keys? Oh! There they are!"[1]

Processing What We Hear

Another aspect of listening is the way we process what we hear, and there are two distinct processes involved in comprehending spoken English, *bottom-up processing* and *top-down processing.* Bottom-up processing refers to a process of decoding a message that the listener hears through the analysis of sounds, words, and grammar, while top-down processing refers to using background knowledge to comprehend a message.[2] Here is an illustration of what I mean. Imagine that Joe is a tourist in a foreign country. He is staying at the Federal Hotel, and he wanders away to see some local sites, only to discover he is lost. Joe then decides to approach someone, whom he asks, "Excuse me, couldja tell me howta getto the Federal?" From a bottom-up point of view, the person listening to Joe arrives at meaning by identifying the specific words relevant to the message (such as recognizing that the "Federal" is a hotel), recognizing strings of sounds and being able to segment them (e.g., recognizing that "couldja" is two words, "could you," and that "howta getto" is "how to get to"), and identifying grammatical and functional clues pertinent to the message (e.g., recognizing that "could you" indicates that a request is about to be made and that "how to get to" indicates asking for directions).

While successful bottom-up processing relies on recognition of sounds, words, and grammar, successful top-down processing hinges on having the kind of background knowledge needed to comprehend the meaning of a message. This can be in the form of previous knowledge about the topic—for example, knowing the hotels in the tourist area. It can also be in the form of situational knowledge—for example, knowing there are lost tourists in the area who frequently ask for directions. Finally, background knowledge can be in the form of "schemata" or "plans about the overall structure of events and the relationship between them."[3] For example, when someone who looks lost approaches you in a tourist area and says, "Excuse me," you can predict this person is about to ask for directions, location, or something related to being a tourist.

This last kind of background knowledge or schemata relates especially to our real-world experiences and the expectations we have, based on our experiences, about how people behave. The schemata we draw from includes our experience in assigning specific kinds of interaction to an event—for example, knowing how to listen to jokes, stories, and requests. Likewise, it includes the way we categorize knowledge. For example, if we frequently walk through a tourist area, we will know the names of hotels, can group people as tourists and nontourists, and so on. Schemata also includes being able to predict a topic in discourse and infer a sequence of events—for example, expecting that a lost tourist will initiate and move through a conversational routine, including getting our attention, asking for directions, and possibly checking understanding by paraphrasing the directions.

The importance of background knowledge is especially obvious when we consider the language processing problems of foreign students who come to the United States. Many students are considered to be highly talented at bottom-up processing of English, and within their EFL settings they are considered to be very fluent speakers of English. Nonetheless, on arrival in the United States, some soon discover that they cannot communicate as easily as they had hoped. Here are two examples. The first is that of a student who came from Somalia.[4] This student went to McDonalds to get something to eat, and when he placed his order at the counter, the waitress asked him, "Would you like this forhereortogo?" He looked at her inquisitively and said nothing, as he could not understand her question. She repeated her question louder, "Forhereortogo?" The person behind him helped him with his bottom-up processing, telling him that the string of words consisted of "For here or to go", but he still had no idea what the waitress meant. Finally, the person behind him said, "Would you like to take this order out, or would you like to eat it here?" and the student finally understood, having gained the necessary background knowledge to process the culturally based question.

The second example is of an older woman from the People's

Republic of China.[5] She was a teacher for a number of years in China, and her dream was to go to the United States to study. She finally did, and during her first week, she was walking across campus when a classmate came toward her. He smiled and said, "Hi! What's up?" The confused newcomer looked at him for a brief moment, looked to the sky to see what was above her, looked down, scratched her head, and, with an unsure voice, said, "The sky?" Although this is an extreme example, it, along with the example of the student at McDonalds, does show the importance of background knowledge to comprehend spoken English.

The Purposes of Listening

In addition to bottom-up and top-down processing, we can consider interactional and transactional functions of language.[6] When language is used to fulfill an interactional communicative function, the focus is on creating harmonious interaction among individuals. As a social phenomenon, interactional use of language centers on such safe topics as the weather, food, and beautiful things. These topics are neutral, or noncontroversial, and shift quickly. Because these topics are noncontroversial, they promote agreement between speakers and listeners, which in turn creates a harmonious relationship.

Unlike interactional use of language, transactional use focuses attention on the content of the message. Emphasis is on transferring information, and unlike interactional uses of language, it is important for the listener to comprehend the content of the speaker's message. Topics vary from context to context and can include almost any content. Examples of interactional use of language include a doctor advising a patient how to take a prescription drug or a student listening to a lecture on marriage in the Philippines.

What Kinds of Listening Activities Do EFL/ESL Teachers Use?

An understanding of top-down and bottom-up processes of listening and of the transactional and interactional functions of language provides an awareness of what listeners do as they listen, and this knowledge is useful when we consider the kinds of listening activities we have students do in our classrooms. In this section I focus on activities we can use to provide EFL/ESL students with a variety of listening experiences.

Identifying Linguistic Features

The aim of activities that focus on identifying linguistic features is to make students more aware of the linguistic features of spoken English. As such, they center on bottom-up processing. As the aim is to provide chances for students to develop their perceptual abilities, little attention is given to transactional or interactional purposes. One activity is to give students practice in listening to the way sounds blend in spoken English. The teacher (or a tape-recorded voice) says a phrase, such as "didja," followed by a sentence, such as "Didja go to the store?" The student then identifies the written version from a list.[7]

The idea of the following activity is to show students what sentence stress is and how it influences the rhythm of spoken English. For example, after listening to and marking "He's a terrific actor," students can see that major words (nouns, main verbs, adverbs, adjectives) receive stress while minor words (pronouns, determiners, articles, prepositions) do not, and that when words have more than one syllable, only one syllable—for instance, "if" in "terrific"—receives primary stress.

A Stress and Rhythm Listening Activity

Instructions: Listen to the conversation. Put a mark over each stressed syllable.

    A: That was a really good movie!

    B: Yea. Robin Williams. He's a terrific actor. Very funny.

    A: What are your favorite Robin Williams movies?

To do the following activity, the teacher can use any minimal pair (two words that differ only in one sound), making the selection based on sounds that are new or problematic. Of course, the teacher can also select pairs that students can easily distinguish, so they feel successful. To do this activity, the teacher says the string of words, for example, "Liver. River. River." Each student puts up one finger each time he or she hears "Liver" and two fingers for "River." The teacher can challenge the students by increasing the number of words in the string and saying them faster.

A Minimal Pair Listening Activity

Directions: Listen to each word. Each time you hear "river," put up one finger. Each time you hear "liver," put up two fingers.

1. river
2. liver, river
3. liver, liver, liver

Responding to Requests and Commands

Listen and Respond activities highlight bottom-up processing because the listener listens to identify specific words and grammatical command structures. One activity is "Total Physical Response" (TPR).[8] Here is an example of a TPR lesson.

Teacher Command:	Stand up.
Student Response:	(Students stand up.)
Teacher Command:	Go to the blackboard.
Student Response:	(Students walk to the blackboard.)
Teacher Command:	Write your name on the board.
Student Response:	(Students write their names.)

While doing TPR with EFL/ESL students, I have found Berty Segal's advice quite useful.[9] Segal suggests that teachers begin by demonstrating the commands, doing them with the students. The teacher can also reduce anxiety by giving commands to the whole class, then to small groups of students, and finally, after the students have lots of practice, to individual volunteers.

There are many possible commands that students can practice. To create commands, we simply need to select "action" verbs, such as *stand up, sit down, walk, skip, hop, turn, stop, pick up, put down, sing, touch, point, smile, frown, laugh, throw, catch,* and so on. These verbs can be combined with nouns and other words to make up commands, each activity emphasizing listening for a purpose. For example, students can listen to the same verb said many times with different nouns, such as "Touch your nose. Touch your chin. Touch your mouth," or "Point at the clock. Point at the door." Or students can listen to different combinations of verbs, for instance, "Open your book to page 32. Close your book. Stand up. Point to the door. . . ." Some students appreciate humor, too. For example, the teacher might say, "Jose, put your nose in Maria's armpit."[10]

TPR is not just a listening activity for beginners. For example, EFL/ESL students could be asked to do different things with money: "Andre, please give $3.35 to Chang-wen." Teachers can also take students through each step in the process of doing something, such as brushing their teeth, getting dressed, meeting someone for the first time, and ordering food.

Another way to provide chances for students, especially children, to listen and respond is by playing "Simon Says." Like TPR, the teacher gives a command. But the listener is only supposed to follow the command if it is preceded by the phrase "Simon says." Most children love this game. Anxiety levels go down. Attention levels go up.

Another activity liked by both children and adults who are young at heart is the "Hokey Pokey." I usually do this activity along with a lesson on body parts. The students and teacher form a large circle, listen to the Hokey Pokey song, and follow the commands: "You put your right foot in, you take your right foot out. You put your right foot in and shake it all about. You do the Hokey Pokey and turn yourself around. That's what it's all about!"[11]

Interacting as a Listener

The goal of interactive listening activities is to focus students' attention on how they can maintain social interactive relations. Both bottom-up and top-down processes can be a part of these activities, depending on the design. One such activity is called "chat." Students view short videotaped segments of interaction in different settings—for example, at the dinner table, the fitness center, a grocery store checkout counter, and so on. The idea is for students not only to work at comprehending the interaction but also to consider what a "safe" topic is and how the interaction is maintained. To accomplish this, as students view the videotape, they can

- Check off those topics that were discussed from a list of possible topics
- Follow along with a written script, highlighting the things listeners do to keep the conversation going (e.g., listeners show they are listening by using head nods and encouraging remarks, such as "uh-huh," "What else?" and "No kidding!")
- Complete a set of multiple choice and true/false questions about the interaction (e.g., True or false? Josh likes to chuckle to show he is listening.)

Eavesdropping is another way to center students' attention onto the function of listening during conversations. The goal is to teach students the value of listening in on conversations and a few strategies for doing so. Here is one eavesdropping activity (from Porter and Roberts).[12] The students are told that they are guests at a party and they can eavesdrop on conversations. The students then listen to short segments of party conversation and complete a worksheet.

Eavesdropping
Directions: You are at a party given by the Director of Studies at your school. A lot of teachers and students are there. You can hear pieces of conversation. Try to guess what the people are talking about. You hear four different conversations. Would you like to join any of them?

Topic	Are you interested?
1. _____	_____
2. _____	_____
3. _____	_____
4. _____	_____

After students do such eavesdropping activities in class or in the listening lab, I ask them if they would like to try their eavesdropping skills outside the classroom. If they agree, I send them out in teams of two or three. Their task is to observe and capture pieces of conversation, including short dialogues, and to write up their eavesdropping experience and prepare to tell classmates something they learned. Of course, this is much easier in ESL settings, where there are plenty of English language conversations going on (e.g., in college dorms, grocery stores, and restaurants), but it is also possible for EFL students to listen in on English conversations, especially in big cities (e.g., at fast-food restaurants, tourist areas, and department stores). It is worth mentioning that not all students like to eavesdrop. Some consider it an invasion of privacy, and when students object, I respect their wishes not to practice this activity.

Another interactive listening activity is called "matching."[13] Although this activity is a little too outlandish for some, students can be asked to match others' nonverbal behaviors, including head nods, gestures, and facial expressions. The goal is to show the value of observing the behaviors others use as they listen, as well as to focus students' attention onto their own use of nonverbal behavior during a conversation. To introduce the concept of matching, I demonstrate by having one student talk on a familiar topic while another listens. At the end of their demonstration, I match a few selected aspects of the listener's behavior (e.g., quick Japanese head nods). I then have students practice matching other students' behaviors in the same way. Although students sometimes need lots of coaching and coaxing and have to work through fits of laughter, some students soon discover that to be a good listener in another language requires not only knowledge of "safe" topics and vocabulary and grammar but also adapting the nonverbal behaviors we exhibit as we listen.

Comprehending Extended Speech

Transactional in nature, comprehension activities center on comprehending stories, extended speech, and lectures. As with all the activity types in this chapter, there are many possible comprehension activities. One activity that can be used with beginners and more advanced students is a picture-ordering activity. This activity

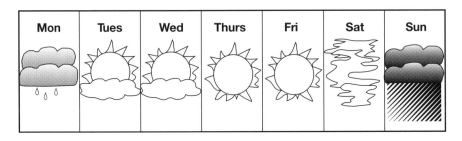

| Mon | Tues | Wed | Thurs | Fri | Sat | Sun |

A comprehension activity: students draw their own pictures

includes listening to a story and then putting pictures in the order of the events in the story. Students can also draw their own pictures. For example, students can view or listen to a weather forecast and, under the relevant days of the week, draw pictures that represent the forecast.[14]

Cloze listening tasks can also be used as comprehension activities. Here is an example.

Holidays

Instructions: Listen to the short lecture. As you listen, read the text. Listen a few times. Then complete each blank with one of the vocabulary words. Keep in mind, there are more words than blanks!

Vocabulary: restaurants, Hungarians, person's, includes, year, holidays, celebrate, name, birthday, treat.

Text: There are some very interesting _____ in different countries. _____, for example, have a Name Day. Each day of the _____ has a person's name. If it is a _____ Name Day, then he or she has to _____ friends. This _____ taking friends out to _____ for meals.

Taking notes can also engage students in listening to extended speech. Here is a sample activity.

The Joy of Traveling

Instructions: Listen to the travel story three times.

The First Time:
- What countries did the young woman visit?
- What types of transportation did she use?

The Second Time:
- Which country did she like the most?
- What are three things the woman says she likes about the country?

The Third Time:
- Listen to the woman's descriptions of the places she visited.
- Which place would you like to visit? Why?

Problem Solving

Problem-solving listening activities are transactional because they provide chances for students to comprehend content to solve problems through their use of both bottom-up and top-down processes. There are, of course, a variety of possible activities. In one of my favorite activities,[15] the students are detectives listening to a recorded report about a murder. As they listen, they complete a grid on the alibis of the suspects. Based on what they hear, their task is to narrow down the suspects to select the murderer. Here is my version of the report students listen to.

> Jerry Gebhard, an ESL teacher, was murdered between 8:00 P.M. and midnight yesterday at his home near campus. The suspects, his students, described their activities on the night of the murder. Yoko said she had dinner alone from 8:00 to 9:00, then practiced her flute. Several people heard her playing. She then watched TV for an hour with other students in the dormitory lounge. At 11:00 she was studying in her room. Several students saw her there. Andre said that he was watching TV from 8:00 to 9:00 and was studying alone in his room from 9:00 to 11:00, then went to bed. However, a classmate said he saw Andre and Lilia walking away from campus at 9:30. Bahlal said he was at the library from 8:00 until 10:00, then took a walk with his friend until around 11:00, when he went to his room to study.

Several people saw Bahlal at the library. Mohammad said he was talking with Lilia in the dorm hallway from 8:00 to about 9:15, was with another friend until 10:00, watched TV until 11:00, and then went to bed. Lilia claimed she talked with Mohammad from 8:00 to around 9:00 or so, then went to her room to study and sleep.

To add a touch of humor, teachers can use the names of students in their class. See the example of what the grid looks like when it is completed by the students.

Name	8:00-9:00	9:00-10:00	10:00-11:00	11:00-12:00
Yoko	Eating dinner alone	Playing flute	tv in lounge	Studying in room
Andre	tv in lounge	alone in room	alone in room	In bed sleeping
Bahlal	at library	at library	walking with friend	studying in room
Mohammad	with Lilia	with friend	tv in lounge	In bed sleeping
Lilia	with mohammad	studying in room	studying in room	In bed sleeping

A problem-solving activity grid

How Do EFL/ESL Teachers Use the Media to Teach Listening?

There are many ways in which we EFL/ESL teachers can make use of the media in our listening classes. Radio, for example, offers songs, advertisements, talk shows, and drama. Likewise, television offers an abundance of materials: quiz shows, situation comedies, soaps, cartoons, documentaries, educational programs, news, weather forecasts, movies, award shows, and commercials. Even when we consider a single item, we have plenty of choices. Take the news, for example. Though permission is needed, because of copyright laws, before some types of news programs can be shown in class, there remains available quite a variety, including the local news, world news, news shows with special topics (e.g., the American *60 Minutes* and *20/20*), and entertainment magazine shows, to name a few. As such, the difficulty is not in locating materials to teach listening from the media but in selecting and creating lessons from the materials available.[16]

Folk, rock, and popular songs offer students exposure to one form of authentic English through the media, and many students, young and old, enjoy listening to (and singing) songs. EFL/ESL teachers use a variety of different songs, including everything from "Puff the Magic Dragon" (by Peter, Paul, and Mary) to "The ABC Song" to "Yesterday" (by the Beatles). However, most agree that students benefit from the listening experience when the songs are taught so that the lyrics are comprehensible. One way to do this is to provide short lessons on vocabulary and grammar, followed up with different listening activities. For example, I observed a teacher have students listen to "Everything I Own" by Bread as a part of a lesson on the past tense. She had students listen to the song to get the gist, for example, that it is a song about lost love. She then played the song again, having students perform a fill-in-the-blank task with the past tense verbs they heard.

Singing lines in the song and participating in other ways can also help make the lyrics comprehensible. For example, as children listen to "Old MacDonald,"[17] they can point at pictures of animals, as well as sing animal sounds and the "E-i, e-i, ooh."

"Old MacDonald"

Old MacDonald had a farm

E-i, e-i ooh

And on this farm he had a cow

E-i, e-i ooh

With a *moo moo* here

And a *moo moo* there

Here a *moo,* there a *moo*

Everywhere a *moo moo.* . . .

As the following list of techniques shows, there are also creative things we can do in our classrooms with video clips from TV programs, films, commercials, and teacher-made videotapes of interactions.[18]

Techniques: Processing Authentic Video Materials

Silent Viewing: Students view video material without sound to let students consider what is going on and guess what speakers are doing and saying.

Soundtrack Only: Students hear the soundtrack without the picture. Based on what they hear, they speculate on what speakers look like, the setting, and the location.

Beginning Only: Students view the beginning of a sequence, then predict what will happen next.

Ending Only: Students view the ending and consider what happened earlier.

Split Viewing (One): Some students view the material without sound. Others listen without viewing. Groups come together to create a fuller understanding of context and content.

Split Viewing (Two): Half the class sits with back to screen. Half can see the screen. Both can hear. Pairs then build a fuller understanding of context and content.

To illustrate how teachers can process authentic video materials, here is an example from my own teaching of an episode of an American situation comedy, *The Wonder Years.* I began by writing a set of questions on the board: How many people are talking? How old do you think they are? What is their relationship? What are they talking about? We then listened to two minutes of the show without a picture and answered the questions written on the board, after which I gave them a new set of questions: What approximate year is it? What are the people doing? What do you think the story is going to be about? I then played the sound and picture of the first five minutes of the show, including the two minutes they had already listened to. After answering the questions, we viewed the show until just before the climax. I then had students meet in groups to write down and announce their predictions about how the show would end. We then viewed the ending to see if any of the predictions were correct and to compare the students' creative endings with the original.

What Problems Do Some EFL/ESL Teachers Have in Teaching Students to Comprehend Spoken English?

Problems some EFL/ESL teachers face include the following:

The "outdated listening lab" problem. Some EFL teachers find themselves teaching in a traditional-style listening lab where they believe it is difficult to be creative because of the lab design.

The "How can I judge the authenticity of commercial EFL/ESL listening materials?" problem. Some teachers question the authenticity of commercial listening materials, and they want to have criteria to judge the degree of the authenticity of the language used in them.

The "Outdated Listening Lab" Problem

Some EFL/ESL teachers find themselves in a traditional listening lab, where listening is considered to be a passive skill. Students sit at their carrels and listen to tapes, rarely speaking with classmates. When such a traditional, passive attitude permeates a language program, the role of the teacher in the listening lab is to broadcast a program to the whole class. The teacher acts as a monitor, listening in on students, correcting errors, and furnishing answers to listening exercises.

An EFL teacher showing a video he produced called *Interaction in a Bank*

There are problems with this traditional approach. Students complain that it is sometimes boring and that they do not necessarily gain from the experience. Teachers point out that there is little opportunity to interact with students on an individual level or to provide students with practice in listening to authentic English used as a means to communicate meaning between people.[19]

However, it is possible to transform a lab from a passive, traditional one into a place where students can work actively on developing their listening abilities while at the same time making use of the uniqueness of the lab system. In fact, many of the activities I discussed earlier in this chapter can be adapted for lab use. For example, using magazine pictures of crowded scenes, the teacher can create a verbal description of one person from the scene, audiotape this description, and have students listen, imagining they are supposed to meet the person in a crowded place. Students can then be given the picture to pick out the person from the crowd. Likewise, students can do jigsaw listening, in which they each have a piece of a puzzle, such as the alibis given by murder suspects in the activity discussed earlier in this chapter. Each student can listen to different alibies, then leave their carrels, meet in small groups, and share their knowledge about the alibies to determine who the murderer is. They can then return to their carrels to listen to an explanation on who the murderer is and to see if the explanation matches their group conclusion. Many such activities, created by the teacher or from the many new listening texts and tapes on the market, are possible.

In addition to breaking the traditional, passive idea of a lab through the use of interactive-style activities, some lab time can be devoted to allowing students to select their own listening materials. In such a lab, the teacher acts as a resource person by helping students select materials that are likely comprehensible and of possible interest. The advantage of this activity is that it teaches students to take on responsibility for their own listening development, as well as letting them work at their own pace and level. The disadvantage is that such an individualized system does not match all students' learning styles and expectations about what a lab is supposed to be. Some students become disconcerted because they believe that it is the teacher's job to select and teach specific listening materials. Considering advantages and disadvantages, some teachers use a fraction of the scheduled lab time as an open lab, while some programs include both regular and elective labs.

The "How Can I Judge the Authenticity of Commercial EFL/ESL Listening Materials?" Problem

Authentic listening experiences include pronunciation and intonation marked in a variety of ways.[20] For example, pronunciation includes simulation of sounds, such as blending two or more words into a single sound, as in "Didja" (Did you). Likewise, pitch and emphatic stress are used in ways to show nuance of meaning, and the rhythm of English is set through the use of sentence stress. Major words (e.g., nouns, verbs, adjectives, adverbs) receive sentence stress, while minor words (e.g., articles, prepositions, auxiliary verbs) do not, as in "You'll *find* the *book* on the *table.*" Authentic listening also includes hearing a variety of grammatical structures, not just one or two said over and over again—the use of fragments or sequences of loosely connected words and clauses, rather than well-formed sentences. It also includes interruptions and two or more people speaking at once (rather than each person taking a distinct turn), as well as one speaker dominating the interaction, lots of attention signals (such as "Mmmmm" and "Uh-huh" used by listeners), and different kinds of background "noise."

Unfortunately, in an effort to make language clear to students, some authors of listening tapes and texts eliminate authentic pronunciation, overuse emphatic stress, and give every word equal sentence stress, resulting in language that resembles the way "indulgent mothers talk to babies."[21] Likewise, when students listen to some audiotape materials, they hear conversations in which people speak in complete sentences, without interruptions, in a place void of background noise. Although there is likely some benefit from listening to such stilted use of spoken language, some EFL/ESL teachers believe that students gain more from practice in listening to authentic spoken English. If you are among those teachers who favor students listening to authentic speech, you can create some of your own listening materials or evaluate the authenticity of commercial listening materials (see the observation and talk task on recognizing authenticity in listening materials). You also need to make decisions about whether or not listening material is too authentic. Is the material so authentic that it is very difficult to make it comprehensible to the students? In such cases you might want to search for other material.

Teacher Self-development Tasks

Talk Tasks

1. Have you ever been in a conversation in English in which you lacked the appropriate background knowledge to completely comprehend what you were listening to? Describe your experience. What was the content? What background knowledge did you lack? Why did this lack of knowledge make it difficult for you fully to comprehend the content?
2. What kinds of listening activities have you experienced either as a teacher or as a student? Which activity types in this chapter

haven't you experienced? Which would you like to try out in your EFL/ESL classes?

3. Meet with another teacher. Together, select authentic listening material from the media (e.g., a song, film, TV situation comedy, cartoon, news show, or TV or radio advertisement). Based on the ideas in this chapter on using the media, and on your own ideas, create a step-by-step lesson plan that aims at making this authentic material comprehensible to a group of students with whom you are familiar.

Observation and Talk Tasks

1. Tape-record a conversation between friends. (Make sure you get their permission first.) Select three minutes from this conversation. With other teachers/friends, analyze what goes on in the conversation. What gives the conversation its authenticity?

2. Visit a listening lab. Observe what is going on in the lab? What are students listening to? Are the students all doing the same listening activity? How interested do the students appear to be in the listening activity? Also talk with the teacher in the listening lab. What activities go on in the lab? How does the teacher interact with the students in the lab? Think of your own questions, too.

3. Locate commercial listening materials that focus on person-to-person interaction in social contexts (rather than, for example, on teaching students to listen to the news). Using the criteria for authenticity and the worksheet I provide at the end of this self-development tasks section, evaluate the authenticity of these materials. How authentic is the language in the materials? If they are authentic, what value do they have for students? If they do not use authentic language, can students still benefit from listening to them? What are the benefits?

Journal Writing Tasks

1. Write up what you learned from doing the observation tasks.
2. Consider your own experience in learning to listen in a foreign/second language. Based on your reflections, what listening

experiences do you believe helped you to gain in your abilities to comprehend the language? What experiences do you believe did not help you? Do you believe this is the same for other language learners?

3. Write freely on your ideas for teaching students to comprehend spoken English.

Evaluating the Authenticity of Listening Materials

The following criteria provide a way to judge the authenticity of language used in commercial listening materials, by people as they interact in social contexts. Please refer to this criteria while completing the accompanying worksheet.

Intonation: Criteria
Intonation is not authentic when marked by exaggerated and frequent pitch movement. Likewise, it is not authentic when each word receives equal stress.

Intonation: Questions
- Is the intonation marked by exaggerated pitch or is it natural?
- Does the intonation amuse you? Remind you of an indulgent mother talking to a baby?

Pronunciation: Criteria
Pronunciation is not authentic when each word is clearly enunciated. Rather, assimilation (or blending of sounds) is normal.

Pronunciation: Questions
- Does the pronunciation seem artificial? Too correct?
- Do speakers enunciate all the words? Or do they blend sounds?

Structures: Criteria
Normal speech makes use of multiple structures. Nonauthentic English includes repetition of the same structure with obtrusive frequency.

Structures: Questions
- Do particular structures recur over and over again?
- Are grammatical structures varied?

Complete Sentences: Criteria
Informal speech is characterized by fragmentation. In short, people talk in clauses and single word utterances.

Complete Sentences: Questions
- Do speakers use all complete sentences? Or do they use short loosely connected clauses and words?

Distinct Turns: Criteria
In authentic situations, people do not wait for others to stop talking. They interrupt.

Distinct Turns: Questions
- Do speakers wait for others to finish? Or do they sometimes speak at the same time?

Speaker Domination: Criteria
In normal conversation, speakers do not usually take equal amounts of talk time. One person usually dominates.

Speaker Domination: Questions
- Are all speakers saying an equal amount? Or does one person say more than the others? Do some speakers play subsidiary roles?

Pace: Criteria
Authentic speech is characterized by relative rapidity and variability of pace. Uniform pace is not authentic, especially an unusually slow pace.

Pace: Questions
- Are all the speakers speaking at the same pace? Are they talking too slowly?

Background Noise: Criteria
Normal listening situations include background noise: passing cars, radios, barking dogs, wind in trees.

Background Noise: Questions
- Is there normal background noise?

Evaluating the Authenticity of Listening Materials: Worksheet

Title:

Author:

Publisher:

Level:

Overall Evaluation of Authenticity:

1 ————— 2 ————— 3 ————- 4 ————— 5

Not authentic   Very authentic

Evaluation of Authenticity of Particular Components:

Intonation   1 ---- 2 ---- 3 ---- 4 ---- 5

Pronunciation   1 ---- 2 ---- 3 ---- 4 ---- 5

Structures   1 ---- 2 ---- 3 ---- 4 ---- 5

Complete Sentences   1 ---- 2 ---- 3 ---- 4 ---- 5

Distinct Turns   1 ---- 2 ---- 3 ---- 4 ---- 5

Speaker Domination   1 ---- 2 ---- 3 ---- 4 ---- 5

Pace   1 ---- 2 ---- 3 ---- 4 ---- 5

Background Noise   1 ---- 2 ---- 3 ---- 4 ---- 5

Recommended Teacher Resources

Readings on Teaching Listening: Concepts and Activities

Anderson, A., and T. Lynch. 1988. *Listening.* Oxford: Oxford University Press.

Lonergan, J. 1984. *Video in Language Teaching.* Cambridge: Cambridge University Press.

Long, D. R. 1989. "Second Language Listening Comprehension: A Schema-theoretic Perspective." *Modern Language Journal* 73: 32–49.

Morely, J. 1991. "Listening Comprehension in Second/Foreign Language Instruction." In *Teaching English as a Second or Foreign Language,* ed. M. Celce-Murcia, 81–106. Boston: Heinle and Heinle.

Nunan, D., and L. Miller, eds. 1995. *New Ways in Teaching Listening.* Alexandria, Va.: TESOL.

Peterson, P. W. 1991. "A Synthesis of Methods for Interactive Listening." In *Teaching English as a Second or Foreign Language,* ed. M. Celce-Murcia, 106–22. Boston: Heinle and Heinle.

Rathet, I. 1994. "English by Drawing: Making the Language Lab a Center of Active Learning." *TESOL Journal* 3 (3): 22–25.

Stempleski, S. 1992. "Teaching Communication Skills with Authentic Video." In *Video in Second Language Teaching,* ed. S. Stempleski and P. Arcario, 7–24. Alexandria, Va.: TESOL.

Ur, P. 1984. *Teaching Listening Comprehension.* New York: Cambridge University Press.

Listening Texts: Authentic Listening

Helgesen, M., and S. Brown. 1994. *Active Listening: Building Skills for Understanding.* New York: Cambridge University Press.

Jones, L., and V. Kimbrell. 1987. *Great Ideas: Listening and Speaking Activities for Students of American English.* New York: Cambridge University Press.

Lim, P. L., and W. Smalzer. 1990. *Noteworthy: Listening and Note-taking Skills.* Rowley, Mass.: Newbury House.

Numrich, C. 1995. *Consider the Issues: Advanced Listening and Critical Thinking Skills.* White Plains, N.Y.: Longman.

Listening Materials from *English Teaching Forum*

English Teaching Forum, a United States Information Agency
(USIA) publication given free to American EFL teachers
through the American Embassy, periodically includes listening
materials in their journal. Here are references to some of this
material:

"Stories to Listen To." 1990. *English Teaching Forum* 27 (1):
19–28.

"Music on the Mississippi." 1991. *English Teaching Forum* 29 (1):
22–29.

"The American Cowboy." 1992. *English Teaching Forum* 30 (1):
28–37.

"A Weekend in Boston." 1993. *English Teaching Forum* 31 (1):
20–31.

"Atlanta: City for the Future." 1994. *English Teaching Forum* 32
(1): 28–37.

"African American Women in Literature." 1995. *English Teaching
Forum* 33 (3): 25–38.

Notes

1. See Anderson and Lynch 1988 and Morley 1991a for more on active
   listening.
2. Listening processes are also discussed in Anderson and Lynch 1988,
   Chaudron and Richards 1986, Helgesen 1993, Morley 1991a, and
   Richards 1990.
3. See Richards 1990, 51.
4. See *Cold Water,* a videotape produced by Ogami (1988), to view the
   Somalia student tell this story.
5. This example comes from my own observations.
6. Brown and Yule (1983) and Richards (1990) discuss the functions of
   language as they relate to listening.
7. Bowen, Madsen, and Hilferty (1985) offer additional activities to focus
   attention onto linguistic features of spoken English.
8. "Total Physical Response" (TPR) was developed by James Asher. His
   1982 book, *Learning Another Language through Actions,* outlines
   his beliefs and teaching practices. Larsen-Freeman (1986) and
   Richards and Rodgers (1986) also discuss TPR theory and practice.

9. See Segal 1983.

10. This is a line from Segal and Sloane's 1983 videotape, *TPR and the Natural Approach.*

11. The "Hokey Pokey" can be found on *It's Toddler Time,* produced by Bueffel and Hammett (1982).

12. This listening activity is from Porter and Roberts 1987.

13. I learned about matching behaviors to gain rapport by studying the work of Bandler and Grinder (1979), Lankton (1980), and Rosen (1982).

14. This idea is from Rathet 1994.

15. The idea for this activity comes from Ur 1984.

16. It is important to note that some programs are copyrighted. As Lonergan (1984) points out, "The legal situation concerning the use of video for educational purposes (such as language teaching) can be confusing. It varies not only from country to country, but can also vary from programme to programme. . . . The safest way to avoid infringing copyright is to contact the broadcasting company concerned" (80).

17. The "Old MacDonald" song can be found in *Action Songs for Indoor Days,* produced by David White (1978).

18. The techniques discussed here on how to have students process authentic video materials come from Allen 1985, Kajornboon 1989, Kitao 1986, Lonergan 1984, and Stempleski 1992.

19. Tanka (1993) points out problems with a traditional notion of a language lab and offers some useful ideas that help create an interactive lab.

20. Celce-Murcia and Goodwin (1991), Morley (1991b), Pennington (1989), and Pennington and Richards (1986) discuss normal uses of intonation and pronunciation.

21. See Porter and Roberts 1987, 177. My ideas on judging the authenticity of listening materials are directly influenced by the work of Porter and Roberts.

Chapter 8

Teaching the Conversation Class

It is through talk that people construe their cultural worlds, display and
recreate their social orders, plan and critique their activities, and praise
and condemn their fellows.

—Frake 1980, 334

- What does it mean to converse in a second language?
- How do EFL/ESL teachers teach conversation to beginners?
- What kinds of activities do EFL/ESL conversation teachers use
  with postbeginners?
- How do EFL/ESL teachers teach pronunciation?
- What problems do some EFL/ESL teachers have in teaching stu-
  dents to converse in English?

What Does it Mean to Converse in a Second Language?

Conversing in a second language means knowing how to maintain
interaction and focus on meaning, use conversational grammar,
introduce, develop, and change topics, take turns, apply conversational routines, and adapt style.[1]

Maintaining Interaction and Meaning

As I discussed in chapter seven on listening comprehension, conversations include both transactional and interactional purposes. In
relation to speaking, when the purpose is transactional, the focus is
primarily on the meaning of the message. For example, imagine
explaining how to find your residence to a new friend or describing your aches and pains to a doctor. When the purpose is interactional, the focus is on maintaining social relations, for example,
greeting, complimenting, and chatting with friends. Many conversations include both interactional and transactional purposes.

Using Conversational Grammar

In addition to transactional and interactional purposes, conversing means using conversational grammar, different from standard grammar because it is based on how people actually talk. It includes small chunks, mostly clauses and single words, rather than complete sentences. This is true for both interactional and transactional turns. Here is an example.

Jack: Hi. What's up?
Jane: Not much.
Jack: Headed to the bookstore?
Jane: Yeah. Have to buy my Art course supplies.
Jack: Oh! Good! Glad I ran into you! What do we have to buy?
Jane: Colored chalk, ah, sketch pad. Hmmm, charcoal sticks.

Introducing, Developing, and Changing Topics

Carrying on a conversation also requires speakers to introduce, develop, and change topics. This aspect of conversational management can be complex, the selection and development of a topic done through a process of negotiation. This includes opening a conversation with a formula such as the "What's up?" routine given above. Getting past this initial greeting, before going into a topic, other steps might be needed, for example, asking the person (or guessing from the context) if he or she is busy or free to talk, how much time is available, and what topic should be talked about.

Although in our mother tongue it is natural for us to select topics to talk about, it is not necessarily easy to do this in another language. Take for example, Japanese students who go to the United States to study English. When talking with strangers and untrusted acquaintances, including new classmates and the teacher, some of these students will be hesitant to talk about a variety of different topics used in conversations between American strangers, including sex standards, social standards, the physically and mentally challenged, personal income and financial needs, and family illnesses. This is because these topics are not generally discussed with strangers or acquaintances in Japan.[2]

Taking Turns

Carrying out a conversation also means taking turns, and there are both short and long turns. A short turn includes just one or two utterances, such as in the following.

Kamel: Want to go for a walk?
Yoshi: Sure.
Kamel: Where to?
Yoshi: Around the park.
Kamel: Sounds good. Let's go.

A long turn takes place when it is necessary for a speaker to elaborate on, explain, or justify something, provide an anecdote, or tell a story. Many EFL/ESL students have a much harder time taking long turns in a conversation because they take on responsibility for generating a sequence of utterances which must give the listener a coherent mental understanding of what is said, something not necessarily easy to do in a first language, much less a second.[3] Some students have trouble taking both long and short turns, perhaps because of their past language-learning experiences, but possibly also because they lack strategies in English for taking a turn, such as using interjections like "Mm-hmm" to signal a request to speak, using facial expressions to indicate a need to speak, and quickly adding something to what a speaker just said.[4]

Carrying Out Conversational Routines

Conversing also means carrying out conversational routines, many which require a sequence of short turns. These include routines used in many of our daily interactions, for example, paying for a newspaper, greeting a friend in the street, leaving a party, apologizing to a teacher, complimenting a friend, and offering something to a guest. Although there is some creative license, carrying out a routine within a specific context is fairly consistent in its pattern and rules. For example, consider the following interaction at an American dinner party.

> *Mrs. Jones:*   Ann, would you like some more chicken?
> *Ann:*   Oh, no thanks! Delicious! I can't eat another bite.
> *Mrs. Jones:*   Well, there's plenty. Help yourself!

Here is the same interaction at a dinner party in Beijing.

> *Mrs. Liu:*   Ann, some more? (Mrs. Liu reaches for the plate)
> *Ann:*   No thank you!
> *Mrs. Liu:*   No. I insist. Have some more.
> *Ann:*   No thank you.
> *Mrs. Liu:*   Have some more.
> *Ann:*   (Silent)
> *Mrs. Liu:*   (Puts the chicken on Ann's plate)

While an American routine is to offer something to a guest one or two times, often indicating the guest help herself, the pattern in China is often for the guest to refuse the offer several times, waiting for the host to insist. As there are a huge number of such routines to carry out daily functions, and because they can vary from culture to culture, problems quite often arise for EFL/ESL students, especially when they try to directly transfer a routine from their native cultural experience into their English.

Adapting Style

Conversing also includes the selection of conversational style to match the formality of the situation. Jack Richards provides an example of how native speakers of English adapt style when asking someone the time.[5] From informal to formal, language is adapted in social settings the following ways: "Got the time?" "What's the time?" "Do you have the time?" "Would you know what time it is?" "Could I trouble you for the time?"

EFL/ESL students have trouble adapting style, sometimes being too formal in an informal setting, in part as a result of applying the style rules from their first language. For example, in the United States some Asian students will use last names in situations which call for first name use, such as Mr. Brown, rather than John. German students are similar in this regard. Further, ESL students who are not used to calling elder or higher status people by their first names will often avoid addressing people by any name.

Some students in an effort to be more informal in their use of English, miss the mark. This is what happened to the rural Thai adult I was tutoring some years ago. I was invited to a reception at a hotel in a northeast Thai town, mostly for Americans. I thought this would be a perfect time to expose this young man to conversations beyond ours. So, I invited him to go along. At the reception, he was doing fine, when suddenly, while in the middle of a conversation about Thai food, he smiled, looked at the elderly husband and wife, and said in an eloquent manner, "Please excuse me. I have to take a piss." Of course, no one took offense and even found it amusing, knowing he was learning English. But, it does show the need for us to teach students how to adapt style to different contexts.

How Do EFL/ESL Teachers Teach Conversation to Beginners?

With beginners, teachers usually limit the scope of the conversations so that these conversations are manageable and the students are successful. One way teachers do this is to control the kinds of questions they ask, using yes-no, either-or, and identity questions. As these question-types only require students to give short answers, they can focus attention on comprehending the meaning in the questions.

As the students' vocabulary grows and they learn to recognize more and more spoken words, conversations can become quite elaborate through the simple use of these three types of questions. As discussed in chapter four on classroom management, the teacher can ask display questions, perhaps to test students' knowledge, or ask referential questions, ones which the teacher does not know the answer before asking. For example, if the teacher, the asker, already knows the student can speak French, then "Can you speak French?" is a display question. If the teacher does not know, it is a referential question. Likewise, the teacher can ask about different content, including questions about the study of language ("Is Piroska's sweater blue or green?"), about the study of things other

---

Conversations with Beginners: Using Short-Answer Questions

Question-Type	*Example Questions*
Yes-No Questions	Is Piroska's sweater blue?
	Do Nigerians like to play soccer?
	Did you get up early?
	Can you speak French?
Either-Or Questions	Is Piroska's sweater blue or green?
	Do Nigerians like to play or watch soccer?
	Did you get up early or late?
	Which can you speak better, French or English?
Identity Questions	What color is Piroska's sweater?
	Which sport do Nigerians like to play most?
	What time did you get up?
	What languages can you speak?

---

than language ("Do many Nigerians like to play soccer?"), about the lives of people ("Did you get up early?").[6]

A second way teachers limit the scope of a conversation is through the use of what Littlewood calls "quasi-communication" activities.[7] As I discussed in chapter three, the objective of these activities is for students to practice using English with reasonable fluency, but without having to be overly concerned with communicating meaning effectively. To create such an activity, some teachers use charts which simply require students to identify words and give short responses to questions:[8]

New York	Pittsburgh	Flight
lv 10:15 am	ar 11:05 am	121
lv 12:45 pm	ar 1:35 pm	232
lv 4:40 pm	ar 5:30 pm	330

Using this schedule, it is possible to ask a variety of different questions: What time does flight 121 arrive from New York? (11:05 A.M.). Does the flight leaving New York at 4:40 P.M. arrive in Pittsburgh at 5:35 P.M.? (No). How long does it take to fly from New York to Pittsburgh? (Fifty minutes). This same type of questioning activity is also possible with simple class schedules, advertisements, and other simple charts using numbers, prices, and time.

Another quasi-communicative activity is dialogue practice. Most EFL/ESL texts include dialogues, and some teachers write their own short dialogues. By writing their own, they can control the content. At a beginning level, such dialogues can include useful conversational routines. Here is a short example.

> *Person A:* Could I borrow your pen?
> *Person B:* Sure. No problem.
> *Person A:* Thanks.

Some teachers have students practice through the use of a technique called "Read and Look Up," in which students look down at their line, look up and at the other person, and say the line, rather than just reading it.[9] After practice students gain confidence. As beginners gain vocabulary and routines, the task can be more complex. In the following dialogue, students select from the available choices based on levels of formality needed in a situation. Notice that Person B can either accept (+) or turn down (-) the request; person A then reacts appropriately.

Person A:	*Person B:*
Could I borrow your pen?	Sure. No problem. (+)
May I use your book?	Yea. Here you go. (+)
Got a pencil?	I'm sorry! I need it right now. (-)

As students become more proficient, teachers also create open-ended dialogues such as this one, allowing students to draw from their memory:

> *Person A:* Could I borrow five dollars?
> *Person B:* _____.
> *Person A:* _____.

What Kinds of Activities Do EFL/ESL Conversation Teachers Use with Postbeginners?

Some teachers continue to use quasi-communicative activities with postbeginners as a way to warm up, review, or teach a new concept. However, with postbeginners, most teachers go beyond these quasi-communication exercises in order to give students chances to interact freely in English. The sample activities in this section, aim at providing students with the kind of language practice that will enable them to express themselves in spoken English, although they also include some reading and writing.

Dialogue Writing, Skits, Role Plays, and Improvisations

Some teachers have students write their own dialogues, and students generally like this because they can consider their own interactive needs. When students act out their dialogues, they become skits, the idea being for students to practice and then give a performance in front of the class. Role play activities are similar to skits in that students are expected to act. However, unlike skits, students are not provided with lines but are given a situation and roles to play. In chapter five I give an example of a role play in a restaurant.

Video drama is similar to role play. However, each role play is video taped, providing a way for students to reflect on their use of language. Tracy Forest, for example, uses video to have students do improvisation, which she points out is, "organized around a general framework of imagined facts, based on a particular scene, within which students interact and communicate spontaneously."[10]

To prepare students for doing their improvisation, Forest has students work in groups to specify the framework (Examples my own). She includes specifying when and where the scene takes place (In a cafeteria at noon on a Friday), who is participating in the scene (Two close friends), and a recent event shared by the participants (Student B had borrowed $10.00 from student A and promised to pay it back last week). She also has students describe how they feel about the other person and what is taking place (Student A sees that student B has money and feels student B should pay him back. Student B only has $12.00 and wants to go to a movie with friends that evening). She also has students define what they are doing when the scene begins (Standing outside the cafeteria) and decide on an opening line (Student A: "Do you have the $10.00 you borrowed from me?").

Foster points out that the goal of preparation is for the students to create a basic set of facts which will build a conversation, using a wide range of linguistic options. She also points out that although the actual improvisation takes only about five minutes, its success depends on the longer thirty minutes or so of preparation time. Also, the video tape of the performance can provide rich materials for follow-up lessons.

A similar use of video is to have students produce their own news broadcast. Sainz,[11] for example, draws students' attention to the five key questions which take place at the beginning of a news story (Who or what is the story about? What happened? When did the event occur? Where did the event take place? Why did the event take place?). She also introduces students to different types of news, including world news, local news, sports, cinema, weather, and fashion. Students also watch and do comprehension exercises from video clips of the news, followed by making decisions on how they will go about creating their own news broadcast. They write their own news stories (including, as I adapt this activity, news about classmates and their teachers), as well as decide who will deliver the news and play other roles, such as sound technicians and set designers. Students then use their created news reports to practice giving the news, and after several practice rounds with feedback, the students are video taped. They can then view the tape, an option being for the teacher to design lessons which provide constructive feedback for students on their language use.

Buzz Groups

Buzz groups got its name because students sound like a group of busy bees while working on a task. To create a Buzz group, the teacher needs to select a topic which will likely interest students and have some purpose. Some teachers use real tasks for groups to work on, such as planning an actual trip to a museum or planning a party or picnic. Other topics are based on questions, such as "How can the police protect the public against crime?" and "What is a good education?" Here is an example of a Buzz group I have used with a variety of EFL/ESL students.

Who's a Good Language Learner?

In your group, make a list of the kinds of things a good language learner does. You will be asked to list these things on the board. To stimulate your thinking, before you make your list, answer these questions.

- What do good language learners do in class? At home?
- What do you do that helps you to learn English?
- What do you do that could be hindering your language learning?

Although some Buzz group activities can be done with almost any group of students, some can be contextually designed for a specific group. To illustrate what I mean, here is a Buzz group activity,

Students at Korea University engaged in discussion

"Who will be the next student director of the ALI?" I designed for ESL students studying at the American Language Institute (ALI), an intensive English program at Indiana University of Pennsylvania. After dividing students into small groups, I gave them the following handout.

Who will be the next student director of ALI?

We are going to elect a student director of the ALI! This person will attend some meetings with the director and staff and will be your representative in the director's office.

So, here's your chance to change the ALI. In your group, talk about what you want at the ALI. What do you want to keep? What do you want to change? Do you want . . .

a student lounge?	smaller classes?	more chances to
more electives?	more trips?	write?
more homework?	less homework?	more time on
a pop machine?	guest speakers?	computers?
a more active ALI club?	an ALI baseball team?	

Consider other ideas, too! What kind of language program would you really like to have at ALI?

After discussing what you want at the ALI, select a member of your group to run for student director. As a group, write a speech for this person to deliver. Help this person to practice the speech. After each of the group's candidates gives his or her speech in front of the student body, we will vote, by secret ballot, for the next ALI student director.

Games and Related Activities

EFL/ESL teachers also use games in the conversation class, and there are a huge number of possible games. There are games to teach grammar, vocabulary, spelling and pronunciation. There are picture, psychology, memory, guessing, card and board games.[12]

One game most teachers are familiar with is "Twenty Questions." This game gives students chances to use English to narrow down possibilities through the use of yes-no questions. To play this game, two students pick something in the room, for instance, the teacher's pen, the fan, or the calendar. Classmates have twenty chances to narrow down and guess what that object is.

Another game is "Paraphrasing Races."[13] In this game, the teacher divides students into groups, gives a sentence, and allows three minutes for the students to come up with as many rephrasings as they can. Each group then gives their rephrases, receiving one point for each acceptable one. The team with the most points wins.

Another game is "The Strip Story."[14] Students are put into small groups and given one or two lines of a short story. They are told not to show their lines to other students and to put the story together. They have to negotiate who has the first line, second line, and so on. An alternative way to do this is to take the strips away, having them put the story together from memory. There is also a cartoon version of a strip story in which students put a cartoon sequence together, each describing his or her strip to others without showing it to them.

Teachers sometimes make up their own strip stories while some others discover stories used by other teachers, passed down through the years. Here is an example of a strip story I discovered while teaching at a Thai University.[15]

Who's the Laziest Boy?
   An old man was walking along the road.
   Suddenly he saw three boys lying on the grass under a tree.
   He said, "I'll give a gold coin to the laziest boy. Who's the laziest boy?"
   The first boy jumped up, ran over to the old man and said, "I'm the laziest boy. Give me the coin."
   The old man shook his head and said, "No, you aren't. Go lie down again."
   The second boy held out his hand. "I'm the laziest boy. Give me the coin."
   The old man shook his head again. "No, you aren't. Lie down again."
   The third boy said, "Please come over and put the coin in my pocket."
   "Yes," said the old man, "You're the laziest boy!"
   And he put the coin into the boy's pocket.

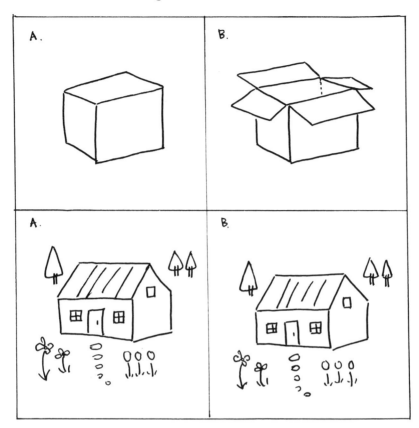

A "Same or Different" activity

Another activity is a matching game called "Same or Different?"[16] Students are divided into pairs, and they are given a set of pictures, Sets A and B. Some of the pictures in the set are the same. Some are different. Without showing the pictures, and within a limited amount of time, the two students must decide which pictures are the same and which are different.

How Do EFL/ESL Teachers Teach Pronunciation?

Some teachers prefer to have students systematically work through a pronunciation text.[17] Such texts provide explanations, drawings which illustrate how sounds are made, and lots of practice activities for students in pronunciation of consonant and vowel sounds, intonation patterns, sentence stress placement, emphatic stress placement and more. Most teachers find these texts to be quite useful. However, some teachers also prefer to go beyond the text or to develop their own approach to teaching pronunciation and activities for students. In the rest of this section, three ways teachers approach the teaching of pronunciation are discussed, including the use of creative activities, teaching pronunciation as communication, and teaching students strategies for self-improvement.

Teaching Pronunciation: Creative Activities

There are many creative activities to teach pronunciation, far more than I can possibly discuss here.[18] However, I can describe some of the activities teachers have reported on and I have used in my own teaching. One activity makes use of minimal pairs (two words pronounced exactly the same except for one difference—e.g., lice and rice, lap and lab). The teacher selects pairs which are problematic for students and lists them on the board. For example, students from Spain might benefit from grappling with these minimal pairs.

| List A: | seat | eat | each | sheep |
| List B: | sit | it | itch | ship |

The teacher can begin by calling out a word, having the students tell the teacher whether it is from list A or B. Once the students understand the rules, they take turns selecting and pronouncing words, while classmates and the teacher tell the speaker the column letter.[19]

Another activity makes use of a kazoo to focus on patterns of intonation.[20] By using a kazoo, the teacher can take away words and grammar, leaving only intonation patterns. And, there are a number of intonation patterns that can be taught, for instance, patterns for declarative sentences, yes-no questions, and tag questions. It is possible for the teacher to demonstrate the pattern by humming into the kazoo, as well as to have students practice the patterns without the words. In addition to intonation patterns, a kazoo can be used to show students correct accent placement on words (e.g., Interesting rather than interesTING), as well as how sentence stress works (major words, including nouns, main verbs, adjectives, and adverbs receiving stress, while minor words, such as prepositions, pronouns and articles not receiving stress).

Games are another way to provide students with intonation practice. For example, here is a game which gives students practice with surprise questions and short assertions.[21] Before class, the teacher gives a few students different objects, for instance, a watch, a pen, a pin, and a rubber duck. The teacher tells these students to keep this a secret. At the start of class, the students form a tight circle, and after explaining the rules, the teacher begins by saying, "I lost my watch and number six has found it." The students listen for the number, and the sixth person from the teacher will reply. This continues until the person who was given the watch before class is called on. Then the teacher starts the search again, this time for another item planted with a student. The figure on page 184 shows an example.

Another activity is "The Pronunciation Computer."[22] To prepare to do this activity, the teacher needs to collect samples of students' English during classroom activities. The teacher then writes these samples (words, phrases, sentences) on the board, numbering each item. The students, who are sitting in a semicircle facing the board, are then told to study the list of language items and to raise their hands if they would like to practice an item. They are also told that the teacher is now a computer and the students have to turn the computer on and off by saying "start" and "stop." The students are also told that they have to pick an item from the board and say it before the computer will model the English pronunciation. The job of the pronunciation computer is to stand behind the students and to continue to give the pronunciation by whispering the line given by the student, each time the student says it, into the student's ear until the student tells the computer to stop.

Teaching Pronunciation as Communication

Teachers who approach teaching pronunciation as communication use activities that focus on meaning. However, they also build into the activity an aspect of pronunciation. One example activity, created by Marianne Celce-Murcia, focuses students' attention on words using a voiceless "th" sound, such as in *Th*ursday and *th*ird.[23]

Number 6:   Who? me, mr. Smith?

Teacher: Yes, You, No. 6.

Number 6:   Not me, mr. Smith.

Teacher: Then who, No. 6.

Number 6:   Number Nine mr. Smith.

Number 9:   Who? me, No. 6?

Number 6:   Yes, You, No. 9.

Number 9:   Not me, No. 6.

Number 6:   Then who, No. 9?

Number 9:   Number three, No 6.

Practice of surprise questions and short assertions

As I adapt this activity, students are paired, one student receiving a calendar with notes written on it, especially on dates which begin with "th," for example, the thirteenth. The other student is given written cues for questions he or she should ask the other student: (1) Date of Mary's birthday? (2) Date of the first Thursday? (3) 13th on a Friday? (4) Date of American Thanksgiving? Day of the week? (5) Catherine's brother's third birthday?

Another communicative activity with an added pronunciation component is a version of bingo. Students are given bingo boards, and the squares include pictures and words based on a minimal pair. For example, if the teacher wants students to practice words with /r/ and /l/, the squares would include words (and possibly pictures) such as "red," "led," "ray," "lay," "crowd," "cloud," "free," "flee," "crime," "climb," and so on. Of course, each bingo card has different word combinations. Students take turns pulling words from a bowl, calling out each word while paying attention to pronunciation. They can also use the word in a sentence.[24]

Teaching Students Strategies for Self-Improvement

We can also teach students how to take on responsibility for improvement of their own pronunciation. The following list, created by Joan Morley, provides self-improvement strategies teachers can teach students to use.[25]

Strategies to Improve Pronunciation

Strong, Vigorous Practice
Use vigorous practice with strong muscular movements. Use slightly exaggerated mouth movements, overly articulating words. Don't hurry. Take time to articulate as clearly as possible.

Self-Monitored Practice
Listen closely to and monitor yourself on both the sounds and the rate, rhythm, and vocal qualities. Pay attention to stress points, pitch rises and falls, and rhythmic patterns.

Slow-Motion Practice: Half-Speed Practice
Try slow-motion, or half-speed, practice for a strong sense of kinesthetic touch-and-movement feedback and for the feeling of articulation.

Loop Practice ("Broken Record" Practice)
Use an endless-loop practice of twenty or more strong and vigorous repetitions of a phrase or word with focus on kinesthetic feedback.

Whisper Practice (Silent Practice)
Use whispered or silent practice to focus on articulation and the feeling of articulation.

Mirror Practice, Video Practice
Use mirrors to view the articulation of specific sounds. If possible, zoom in on a close-up of your face as you articulate words.

Practicing exaggerated mouth movements

What Problems Do Some EFL/ESL Teachers Have in Teaching Students to Speak in English?

Problems some EFL/ESL teachers face include the following.

The "students won't talk" problem. EFL/ESL teachers point out that some students, including advanced students, are so shy or have such high levels of anxiety over speaking that they will not speak in class.

The "error treatment" problem. Some teachers are concerned that students do not change their language, even after receiving feedback on their language errors.

The "any native speaker can teach conversation" problem. There is a false assumption among some administrators and teachers that any native speaker of English can teach the conversation class.

The "Students Won't Talk" Problem

Some students will not talk in class because they are too shy or anxious. This is not only true for beginners, but also for some students who are fairly advanced in their listening, reading and writing abilities. Perhaps they are anxious because they have not had many chances to speak or because teachers in the past have been critical of their English. Whatever the reason, when faced with quiet anxious students, the problem for the conversation teacher is how to get them to open up, to talk.

So, how can teachers get such students to talk? Before anything else, as teachers, we need to gain the trust of the students.[26] To gain trust, the students need to know that we are on their side. They need to know that we do not expect them to speak perfect English, and that we realize it takes time and effort for them to learn to converse in English.

As teachers, we also need to provide opportunities for students to feel at ease in the classroom. One way to do this is through warm-up activities. In fact, the objective of using warm-up activities is to relax students, to help get them over their classroom apprehensions. There are, of course, a great number of possible ways to warm students up for a conversation class. One way is through the use of techniques used by drama teachers.[27] Here are a few examples.

A Breathing Warm-Up Exercise: The students and the teacher close their eyes, breathe slowly in through their noses for three seconds, hold that breath for nine seconds, then slowly release it through their mouths for six seconds. This is repeated several times.

Walking Warm-Up Exercise: The teacher and students clear away furniture from the center of the room. While standing, they form a circle. They then begin to walk in a circle in their usual way. After a turn or two around the circle, the teacher then calls out commands, such as "Walk like you are chest high in water," "Walk on clouds," "Walk like you were a marionette," and "Walk like you are on hot sand."

A Voice Warm-Up Exercise: While sitting or standing in a circle, the
teacher begins by whispering a word or phrase, for example,
"Hello!" The next person says the word a little louder, but still
in a whisper, the next a little louder, and so on, until the word
comes back to the teacher, perhaps even as a shout. A variation
is to slow down or speed up the way the word or phrase is
said.[28]

The use of quasi-communication activities, such as dialogue
practice, can also engage "quiet" students in speaking. As students
can rely on context and print, they are sometimes more willing to
speak. As students become more and more comfortable with these
precommunicative activities, we can coax them to participate in
the fluency-type activities, such as problem solving, skits, and buzz
groups. And, success builds success. From my experience, as students feel the success they have at negotiating meaning, the more
risks they will be willing to take in expressing their ideas in English.

The "Error Treatment" Problem

Most EFL/ESL teachers now believe that students need to be given
an acquisition rich experience in the classroom, providing them
with opportunities to listen to, read, write and speak lots of
English. Some of these teachers also believe that students will
naturally acquire the language through an unconscious process of
second language acquisition.[29] As long as language input is comprehensible to the students, they will acquire the grammar of the language on their own. Many of those who believe in acquisition point
to the research on the acquisition of grammar by second language
learners. This research shows that some grammatical features are
acquired early and others later for learners. For example, the ING
(progressive), as in "He's going to work" is acquired early while
possessive (-s), as in "That's Ann's book," is acquired later. Likewise, the ability to use irregular past tense of verbs, such as ate,
slept, drank, and swam, is acquired before regular past tense. Some
acquisition believers point out that error treatment will do little to
change this natural process.

However, others believe that feedback on language errors can be used as a type of input by students to promote the acquisition process.[30] In short, some educators suggest that error treatment can provide the kind of feedback that will help the student to work through the different stages of acquisition, especially in EFL settings where students do not have access to lots of authentic language outside classrooms.

Taking this controversy into consideration, as EFL/ESL teachers, we have choices. We can decide not to treat language errors. Or, we can decide to treat them. If we decide to treat them, then there are other decisions that need to be made. When should errors be treated? Which errors should be treated? Who should treat them? How can they be treated?[31] As for when to treat errors, they can be treated at the moment the error is made or treatment can be delayed. A problem with instant treatment is that it can disrupt communication. A problem with delaying treatment is the possibility that students who made the errors will not recognize the errors as being theirs.

Making decisions about which errors to treat is not an easy task for the teacher. Some teachers base their decision on their estimate of the stage of acquisition of the student, for example, treating irregular past tense verb errors such as "He eated it" (an early stage error) while ignoring regular past tense verb errors (a later stage error). As Allwright and Bailey put this, "the dilemma . . . to English teachers is the question of whether or not treatment of learners' errors . . . will help speed the acquisition of the correct form, or simply be futile until the learners reach a stage of development where they can make use of such feedback."[32] Faced with such a dilemma, some teachers take a different approach. Instead of considering the acquisition stage of the student, they base their treatment on whether or not the error interferes with meaning during communication. For example, if there is some confusion over the meaning of "I am very enjoy," the teacher might treat the error: "Do you mean, 'I enjoyed the movie'?"

As for who treats the errors, the teacher also has choices. The teacher can treat the error, have the student who made the error treat it, or have the whole class treat the error. However, a problem with asking students to treat each others' errors is the very real possibility that they will not cooperate.

Even more problematic is how to treat the errors. Some teachers will treat the error in ways that are not obvious to the student, as the following example shows.[33]

Anna: I have no brother.
Teacher: Two sisters? (using rising intonation).
Anna: Because my mother she dead when I was three years old.
Teacher: She *died* when you were three?
Anna: Yes. She dead when I was three years old.

However, it is possible to make it clear to the student that errors are being treated, as well as offer an activity which draws the students attention to the error and the correction.[34] One way is to involve the student in a discrimination exercise.

Maria: I have thirty years.
Teacher: Which is correct: "I have thirty years" or "I am thirty years old"?
Maria: I am thirty years old.

Another error treatment activity involves classification. For example, when a student makes an error such as, "I sleep late" (meaning "I slept late"), the teacher can write the error and the correction on the blackboard for the student to see.

Correct	*Incorrect*
I slept late.	I sleep late.
I am thirty years old.	I have thirty years old.
I'm going to study.	I going to study.

The teacher can also do a mini-lesson or conversation to let the student practice the correct form.

Teacher: Jose, did you get up early this morning?
Jose: No, I slept late.
Teacher: Do you sleep late everyday?
Jose: No, I usually get up early. Today I slept late.

The "Any Native Speaker Can Teach Conversation" Problem

Native speakers of English are frequently asked to teach conversation simply because they are native speakers. This idea is based on two assumptions. First, the native speaker is most qualified to expose learners to authentic use of English. Second, those who teach the speaking course do not need special qualifications as teachers (unlike teachers of reading and writing). The idea is that if you are a native speaker of a language, you can teach others to speak it simply by using the language with them.

The first assumption is partially true. Native speakers of English likely expose students to the teacher's culture and fine nuances of English simply by interacting with them. Of course, this depends on how they interact with students. For example, I have observed native speakers who have lived in a country for several years interact with students by using behaviors of the students' culture. Likewise, teachers do not necessarily speak in the same way inside the classroom with students as they do outside the classroom with natives from their own English speaking culture.

The second assumption is false. As I have tried to show throughout this chapter, teaching students to converse in another language is quite challenging. It requires those who teach it to develop an understanding of what learning to converse in a second or foreign language entails, as well as be able to make use of activities which provide opportunities for students to speak. In addition, teachers need a great variety of skills in classroom management, as well as in interpersonal and cross-cultural communication.

Teacher Self-development Tasks

Talk Tasks

1. Have you learned to converse in a foreign or second language? What was the experience like? What problems did you have? Can you relate your experience to the learning experiences of EFL/ESL students?
2. Using the pictures of the four seasons, create a lesson for beginners. Imagine that you will show the pictures on an overhead,

The four seasons

and that you, the teacher, will have a conversation with the class about the seasons. To prepare for your conversation, write down a series of yes-no questions, either-or questions, and identify questions. See how many possible questions you can list. Consider both display and referential questions, as well as the content you include in your questions. After listing your questions, meet with another teacher who has also made a list. Compare your lists. Combine your list of questions.

3. Review the activity types in this chapter. Then, meet with other teachers to answer these questions: Which activities do you like the most? Why? Which have you used as a teacher or experienced as a learner?

Observation and Talk Tasks

1. Listen to a conversation between two EFL/ESL learners. Quickly jot down examples of the errors the students make. Do you believe that these students will someday speak without making these same errors if given lots of opportunities to speak English?
2. Tape-record a class you teach. As you listen to the tape, jot down examples of your error treatment behaviors. Do you treat their errors? If so, how? When? What types of errors? Look for a pattern you use to treat errors. Then, talk with other teachers who have also analyzed how they treat language errors. Do you treat errors in similar ways? Together, generate an alternative plan for treating students errors. Implement it to see what happens.
3. Observe a friend's conversation class. What kinds of speaking activities does the teacher use? What do you see this teacher doing in the class that you would like to use in your teaching?

Journal Writing Tasks

1. Write down your ideas to teach beginners through the use of yes-no, either-or, and fact-type questions and quasi-communication activities. Feel free to draw sketches and list procedures you would use in your teaching.
2. Write about your own experiences in learning to converse in a foreign or second language.
3. What do you think makes students anxious about speaking a foreign or second language? What ideas do you have about reducing students' anxieties?

Recommended Teacher Resources

Readings on Teaching Speaking: Concepts and Activities

Bailey, K. M., and L. Savage, eds. 1994. *New Ways in Teaching Speaking*. Alexandria, Va.: TESOL.

Brown, G., and G. Yule. 1983. *Teaching the Spoken Language: An Approach Based on the Analysis of Conversational English*. Cambridge: Cambridge University Press.

Bygate, M. 1987. *Speaking.* Oxford: Oxford University Press.

Klippel, F. 1984. *Keep Talking: Communicative Fluency Activities for Language Teaching.* Cambridge: Cambridge University Press.

Morley, J., ed. 1994. *Pronunciation Pedagogy and Theory: New View, New Directions.* Alexandria, Va.: TESOL.

Olshtain, E., and A. Cohen. 1991. "Teaching Speech Act Behavior to Nonnative Speakers." In *Teaching English as a Second or Foreign Language,* ed. M. Celce-Murcia, 154–65. Boston: Heinle and Heinle.

Ur, P. 1981. *Discussions That Work: Task-centered Fluency Practice.* New York: Cambridge University Press.

Wofson, N. 1983. "Rules of Speaking." In *Language and Communication,* ed. J. C. Richards and R. W. Schmidt, 61–87. White Plains, N.Y.: Longman.

Some Textbooks Used in Conversation Classes

Folse, K. S. 1993. *Talk a Lot: Communication Activities for Speaking Fluency.* Ann Arbor, Mich.: University of Michigan Press. (Intermediate)

Jones, L., and V. Kimbrough. 1987. *Great Ideas: Listening and Speaking Activities for Students of American English.* New York: Cambridge University Press. (High intermediate)

Larimer, R., and S. Vaughn. 1993. *Real Conversations: Beginning Listening and Speaking Activities.* Boston: Heinle and Heinle. (Beginner)

Porter, P. A., and M. Grant. 1992. *Communicating Effectively in English: Oral Communication for Non-native Speakers.* Belmont, Calif.: Wadsworth. (High intermediate/Advanced)

Wall, A. P. 1987. *Say It Naturally: Verbal Strategies for Authentic Communication.* Orlando, Fla.: Harcourt Brace. (High intermediate/Advanced)

Watkins, D. 1995. *The Idiom Advantage: Fluency in Speaking and Listening.* Reading, Mass.: Addison-Wesley. (High intermediate)

Notes

1. My ideas here are influenced by the work of Brown and Yule (1983), Bygate (1987), McCarthy and Carter (1995), and Richards (1990).
2. Barnlund 1975 discusses conversation topics in Japan.
3. The complexity of turn taking is evident through reading the collection of articles in Atkinson and Heritage 1984 and Schenkein 1978.
4. See Wardhaugh 1985.
5. See Richards 1990, 73.
6. Fanselow 1987 discusses the content of teacher's questions.
7. See Littlewood 1981.
8. This activity is adapted from Krashen and Terrell 1983, 83.
9. West (1960) and Fanselow (1987) elaborate on the value of using the technique "Read and Look Up," as well as ways students can use it.
10. See Forest 1992, 81.
11. See Sainz 1993.
12. Several sources describe and illustrate games used in conversational classrooms, including Wright, Betteridge, and Buckby's *Games for Language Learning* (1994), Rinvolucri's *Grammar Games* (1984), and the "Games and Speaking" section in Bailey and Savage's *New Ways in Teaching Speaking* (1994).
13. This game is described in Harsch 1994.
14. "The Strip Story" was created by Robert Gibson (1975).
15. To the best of my knowledge, this strip story was created by a materials writer at The Language Center, Chulalongorn University, Bangkok, in the mid-1970s.
16. This problem-solving game or versions of it have been described in different publications, including Klippel 1984; Wright 1989; and Wright, Betteridge, and Buckby 1994.
17. There are numerous pronunciation texts on the market, including books by Morley (1979), Orion (1988), and Dale and Poms (1995).
18. Pronunciation activity ideas can be found in the pronunciation section (199–262) of Bailey and Savage 1994, in Carruthers 1987, and in Gilbert 1987 and 1994. Views and knowledge about pronunciation can be found in Morley 1987, 1991b, and 1994; Pennington 1989; and Pennington and Richards 1986.
19. Folse (1994) has published a version of this activity.
20. Gilbert (n.d.) discusses the use of the kazoo to teach intonation.
21. I adapted this activity from Lee 1979, 81.

22. "The Pronunciation Computer" was originally designed by Charles Curran (1976) as a part of his counseling-learning approach to second language teaching and learning.
23. See Celce-Murcia 1987, 7.
24. Greenfield (1994) does a similar bingo activity using street names.
25. See Morley 1987, 86.
26. Trust is important to Curran (1976, 1978) and Stevick (1980). Their work has made it obvious to me that trust is an extremely important aspect of the teaching process.
27. The warm-up activities I give are from Via 1987 and my own experience.
28. Chan (1994) gives a number of pronunciation warm-up activities—for example, having students stretch mouth muscles by making funny faces and waggling the tongue in and out, hitting the teeth, to loosen the tongue.
29. See Krashen 1982, 1985; Krashen and Terrell 1983.
30. Allwright and Bailey (1991) offer views on error treatment and acquisition.
31. See Allwright and Bailey 1991 for a review of literature on the when, what, and how of error treatment. Long (1977) offers a discussion on the decision-making process teachers sometimes go through in relation to error treatment.
32. See Allwright and Bailey 1991, 102.
33. This example is from Gebhard, Gaitan, and Oprandy 1987, 228.
34. The error-treatment techniques discussed here are adapted from Fanselow 1977b.

Chapter 9

Teaching Students to Read for Meaning

> Comprehension may be regarded as relating what we attend to in the world around us—the visual information of print in the case of reading—to what we already have in our heads. And learning can be considered as modifying what we already have in our heads as a consequence of attending to the world around us.
>
> —Smith 1994, 53

- What does reading include?
- How do EFL/ESL teachers teach beginners to read?
- What kinds of reading activities do EFL/ESL teachers use with postbeginners?
- What problems do some EFL/ESL teachers have as reading teachers?

What Does Reading Include?

Reading includes discovering meaning in print and script, within a social context, through bottom-up and top-down processing and the use of strategies and skills.

The Social Context of Reading

As the following list of things we read shows, we read a great variety of things. We read some of these alone—for example, a newspaper over morning coffee or tea. We also read things and talk about them with others. For example, we might read the movie listings in the newspaper to a friend to choose a film to see, or we might read a menu item at a restaurant to the waiter to ask if he or she recommends it. We read some things while sitting, others while walking, others while driving. The point is, reading is not done in a vacuum. It is done within a social context.

Things We Read

Calendars; addresses on envelopes; numbers and addresses in telephone books; name cards; bank statements; credit cards; maps; diplomas; product warning labels; washing instruction labels; shoe size labels; shopping ads; coupons; money; food product nutrition labels; cereal boxes; messages on coffee cups; graffiti on walls; children's scribbling; letters from friends; business letters; electronic mail; junk mail; postcards; greeting cards; comic books; newspaper columns; magazine articles; advertisements; posters; travel guides; cookbooks; repair manuals; product instruction manuals; notes from mothers; memos; train, bus, and air schedules; place mats in fast-food restaurants; street signs; textbooks; overhead projector notes; syllabi; journal articles; short stories; novels; plays; poems; theater, gallery, and museum programs; store catalogs; song lyrics; film subtitles; subway ads; ads in taxi cabs; job application forms; name tags; names of banks, restaurants, shops, and stores on buildings; pins; T-shirt messages; and messages written by airplanes in the sky.

Processing What We Read

In chapter 7 I discussed auditory bottom-up and top-down processes involved in listening comprehension, and these same processes are active in a visual sense when we read.[1] To comprehend written language, we rely on our ability to recognize words, phrases, and sentences (bottom-up or text-driven processing), as well as on our background knowledge related to the content of what we are reading (top-down or conceptually-driven processing). These two processes interact as we read, resulting in some degree of comprehension.

Quite often, comprehension is difficult for EFL/ESL readers because of cultural factors. For example, a study by Kate Parry[2] shows that failure of Nigerian students to achieve high scores on the English language section of the West African School Certificate (WASC) exam is due in large part to two cultural factors. First, the West African physical and social environment of the children is very different from that reflected in European-influenced passages in the English reading section of the exam. Second, the act of reading itself is cultural, as the Nigerian students live in an oral culture where complex thoughts and ideas are remembered and expressed orally.

Another study that also shows how the lack of cultural knowledge can affect comprehension was done by Steffensen, Joag-Dev, and Anderson.[3] They had subjects from India and the United States read two texts describing an Indian and American wedding, later asking them to recall the passages. They discovered that when readers have the background knowledge assumed by the writer, comprehension is high; correct inferences are made. If they do not have the background knowledge, they distort meaning as they attempt to adjust the writer's intent to their own knowledge of the world. For example, while the American reader could make sense out of references to the engagement ring and stag party, the Indian reader could only guess, sometimes making wrong inferences.

Strategies Used by Readers to Comprehend Text

Here is what fluent readers say they do to be successful at comprehending reading materials.[4]

- Skip words they do not know
- Predict meaning
- Guess the meaning of unfamiliar words from the context
- Do not constantly translate
- Look for cognates
- Ask someone what a word means
- Have knowledge about the topic
- Draw inferences from the title
- Make use of all information in the paragraph to comprehend unfamiliar words
- Try to figure out the meaning of a word by the syntax of the sentence.
- Read things of interest
- Study pictures and illustrations
- Purposefully reread to check comprehension

In addition to what readers say about their own strategies for comprehending reading materials, research on the eye movements of fluent readers shows another reason for success: they read most words on a page, including 80 percent of the content words and 40 percent of the function words. They do not simply sample a small piece of text and try to guess what the rest of the text is about. Instead, they read in a very precise way. Even when reading fast, they identify the majority of the words.[5] Also, readers who consistently read with success do not read once in a while but spend much time reading.

Skills Used to Read

In addition to the strategies readers use to make sense out of print, successful readers also learn basic reading skills.[6] They can skim a text to get the general idea of a passage. For example, most readers are able to read a newspaper headline and the first paragraph or two to determine what it is about and whether or not they want to read the article. Successful readers can scan things they read to locate facts or specific information, for example, to locate a number in the phone book or a file from a list on a computer screen.

Successful readers can also read for thorough comprehension. This means they read to understand the total meaning of a passage. This kind of reading is often done in academic and other settings where complete comprehension is necessary. In addition, successful readers can read critically. Critical reading requires that readers evaluate what they read, considering whether or not they share the author's point of view or are convinced by the author's argument or position. Finally, successful readers read extensively. This means they read broadly in areas of interest, such as mystery novels, or in a field of study, such as history or cooking.

How Do EFL/ESL Teachers Teach Beginners to Read?

Before being able to skim, scan, read for thorough comprehension, read critically, and do extensive reading in English, students need chances to build their bottom-up processing abilities in the language.[7] In other words, they need time and practice building knowledge of sentence structure and vocabulary, as well as experiencing reading within meaningful contexts.

There are a number of ways to have students build their knowledge of sentence structure and vocabulary. One way, of course, is to use texts, and there are a number of beginning-level grammar and vocabulary texts on the market. Most of these books include lots of exercises, charts, graphs, illustrations, and photos.[8] Reading texts written for beginners also offer students tightly controlled grammatical structures and vocabulary while providing stories relevant to a particular reading audience (e.g., young adults).

As discussed in chapter 5 on EFL/ESL materials and media, teachers often go beyond the text by creating their own materials and activities. As beginning readers, EFL/ESL students can greatly benefit from teacher-created vocabulary-building activities, especially if these activities are based on the students immediate, or at least felt, needs. Examples of such activities are offered later in the problem-solving section of this chapter.

Some teachers also create activities that provide contextualized reading experiences. One way to do this is through pen pals. Students in one class can write to students in another, or the teacher can link students across schools, even countries. These letters can be handwritten, or, if available, electronic mail offers speed and often an exciting way for students to write to each other. The letters from students become the reading text, and when students truly connect, the letters offer students a valuable reading and learning experience. If students' oral skills are more developed than their reading skills, they can generate their own reading texts by tape-recording their life stories, which the teacher (or advanced students) can transcribe and edit. These stories then become reading material for the students.

What Kinds of Reading Activities Do EFL/ESL Teachers Use with Postbeginners?

As students gain in their processing abilities, teachers can have them do activities to develop their skills to skim, scan, read for thorough comprehension, read critically, read extensively, and read dramatically.

Skimming Activities

Readers skim to gain a general impression of a book, story, essay, or article and to determine whether or not to read it more carefully. The following activities[9] illustrate ways that students can practice doing this. The first example of a skimming activity asks the reader to skim a passage and then identify the best title.[10]

The Best Title

Instructions: Read the passage quickly. Then select the best title.

Mary Ashworth couldn't believe it! She had purchased a lottery ticket six months ago, put it in her wallet, and forgot about it. One day while at the store, she found the ticket and decided to see if she had won. To her amazement, she had won top prize of two million dollars! She remarked enthusiastically, "I really couldn't believe it! I almost threw the ticket away without checking to see if I won anything!"

Which title is best?
(a) "The Good Shopper"   (b) "The Lucky Lottery Winner"
(c) "Six Months Ago"   (d) "The Lost Wallet"

A second example of a skimming activity is more extended in that students are given a topic and expected to select relevant books, newspaper articles, magazine articles, and other reading materials from a library collection. To prepare, the teacher collects reading materials on a variety of narrowed topics, such as sports of Chinese origin, Italian fashion, computer games, and travel in eastern Europe. The teacher also adds readings (comprising about half the total readings) on closely related topics, such as sports in Latin America, New York fashion, computer programs used in business, and travel in western Europe. The teacher sets up the class library, has each student select a specific topic from a list, and has them locate and skim readings from the class library, searching for readings specifically on their topic. The idea is to see how many of the topic-specific readings the student can discover.

Students skim a passage

Scanning Activities

While skimming is quick reading to find the general idea, scanning is quick reading to locate specific information.[11] For example, we scan telephone books, catalogs, dictionaries, event calendars, book indexes, menus—basically any source in which we need to locate specific information. Here is an example of a scanning activity that makes use of the classified ads.

Scanning the Classified Ads

Instructions: Scan the newspaper classified ads on page 204 to find answers to the following questions:

1. What number would you call if you were interested in buying a car?
2. If you wanted to house sit, which number would you call? Do you have to like cats?
3. If you know someone who wants a student to do lawn work, who would you tell him to call?

4. Imagine you would like to live in a house rather than an apartment. How many houses are for rent?

5. How many apartment rentals include utilities? How many do not?

6. Who would you call if you were interested in finding a new apartment?

7. Could you buy a computer for less than $1,000? What would this computer include?

8. Which employment listing seems like the best opportunity for a student? Do any of the jobs interest you?

9. What is the phone number for the dormitory office at Moore Hall?

FOR SALE

1993 IBM PS 1 486 sx 33mhz cpu - 14" svga color monitor 2MB RAM, 270MB hard drive, 3.5" and 5.25" 1,44MB disk drive, modem and 101 keyboard. Microsoft mouse, Windows and lots more software! $800-357-2272, Dave

For sale '92 Honda Accord. Auto, 4-door, A/C, P/W, Cruise, Power-lock. 55,000 mi. Must see and drive. $3800. 463-1978

WANTED

Wanted: Apartment needed for fall semester. Call 463-9897

Student needs part time work. Will do lawn work. Experienced at home repair. Reasonable rate. Call Matt, 357-5466.

APARTMENTS

1 bedroom apartment for two students, no smokers, unfurnished, 1662 Philadelphia St, $750, 349-2786.

1 female needed to fill 4 person apartment close to campus. Fall and spring, $900/semester. All utilities included. Call 676-5793. Ask for Beth.

2 bedroom duplex for 3 females. Fall and spring. 349-9333.

Apt. for three. One half mile from campus, fully furnished with carpeting, large back yard, off street parking. $900/semester, includes utilities. (412) 668-7765.

Large, furnished, four girls $675 each + utilities. Fall & Spring, 463-1990.

Need one female for five person house. Close to campus. Available now.

Looking for a summer apartment? 2 person, 2 bedroom, 1 block from campus. Only $300/both summer sessions. Non-smoking females only. Call 357-4425 after 6 pm

Summer apartment, own room, $250 for ten weeks. Utilities included. Call 463-0220, between 6-9 pm.

Moore Hall. Single dorm rooms available. Fall and Spring. 463-6665.

New! New! New! Murphy Apartments. Available now. Call 357-2402.

House sitting. Free rent to the right person. Walking distance to campus. Must like cats and lawn care. Non-smoker. 463-1969 after 6pm.

EMPLOYMENT

Need extra cash? Clinical Psychologist needs 50 students. Call 357-1339.

Needed. Mature older student to manage apartment. Call Steve, 357-0183.

B&B Cruise ships now hiring. Earn big $ and travel the world. No experience necessary. 800-377-5577.

Employment Clearing-house will help you find a good job. 800-667-0909.

A scanning exercise: using the classified ads

Another way to give students practice with scanning is to have a contest. Students form teams, and each student receives a handout that includes lots of facts. I sometimes use fact sheets on different countries—for example, on China's fourteen coastal port cities.[12] Equipped with a long list of questions and answers, the teacher throws a question out to the class. The first team to answer the question correctly, gets two points. If a team gets the answer wrong, they lose a point. The team with the most points wins.

Reading for Thorough Comprehension: Activities

Unlike skimming and scanning, activities that aim at having students read for thorough comprehension require students to read meticulously. The goal is for the students to understand the total meaning of a reading selection, and there are a number of techniques teachers can use to get students to interact with the reading material. Here are some of these techniques.[13]

- Students study the title and skim to capture the main idea.
- Students read two paragraphs and predict what will follow.
- Students do several different scanning tasks, such as underlining past tense verbs in red and adverbs indicating sequence (e.g., *first, second, next,* etc.) in blue, circling words they do not recognize, and putting stars next to words that seem important. After each task, they briefly discuss what they underlined, circled, or starred.
- After students have a sense of what the reading material is about, they read silently while answering true-false or multiple-choice questions.
- Students meet in groups, consider the text, write down questions, and give them to another group to answer.
- Students draw pictures of the main characters in a story or draw pictures that illustrate the story line.
- Students, working in groups, reconstruct material previously cut into pieces (also called a jigsaw task).
- Students read a story with the conclusion missing, then write their own endings.

- Students give the reading material a new title.
- Students put a set of pictures or photos in order to show the story line or content.
- Students meet in groups to summarize an article and to separate main ideas from supporting ideas and examples.
- Students listen to the teacher discuss how the piece of writing is organized.

This list illustrates some of the activities teachers use in reading classes, and there are, of course, other ways to teach reading, as well as ways to creatively combine a number of reading activities into a single lesson. And it is through such combination of activities that students have chances to read thoroughly. With this in mind, and as a way to conclude this section, I provide here a reading lesson I designed for a lower intermediate ESL class, including a story I wrote and a combination of activities. Through this example, I encourage you to write your own stories and activities for students in your classes. Here is the story.

My wife, Yoko, and I got up very early on Saturday. We had a busy day ahead of us. Before leaving the house, we shut the windows. Then we noticed our cat, Kiku, sitting comfortably on a chair. "This won't do," Yoko said. "We better put Kiku outside for the day."

Yoko said goodbye to Kiku just before she got into the car. The cat didn't look happy. He wanted to go back into the house to rest comfortably on the chair! But this was impossible. At least, this is what we thought!

We then drove to my mother's place, a retirement home. But my mother wasn't home. So we walked in the garden. Yoko spent some time at the small white fountain in the middle of the garden.

After we walked in the garden, we drove to the countryside to join relatives at a family reunion. Yoko talked with Aunt Nita and my cousin Ann for a long time. She also talked with Uncle Gene, who always seems to be wearing white slacks and shoes.

We left the reunion early to go to a wedding party. Our friend Agnes is from Poland, and she married her childhood sweetheart, Wojtek. They had a wonderful time, although they missed their families in Poland on such an important day.

Finally, late at night, we went home. And guess what! We found Kiku in the hall of the house! How did that cat do that!?

Here are the activities students did.

- Students answered questions before they read (e.g., How many of you have ever had a pet cat? How many cats? What do cats like to do?).
- Students studied a blown-up photo of Kiku the cat next to a drawing of a chrysanthemum while listening to an explanation about the meaning of Kiku's Japanese name, meaning chrysanthemum.
- Students looked at the reading while tracing some of the script with their finger, spelling out words. As a class, they wrote the same words in the air using their index fingers.
- Students looked for words they had studied the week before, such as "fountain," "garden," and "countryside."
- Students underlined verbs in the past tense, then counted the number of past tense verbs.
- Students read the story silently and responded true or false to such statements as (1) Kiku is a dog, (2) Yoko and her husband visited three places, (3) Yoko and her husband visited his mother after going to a picnic.
- While in groups, students read each paragraph together, then had one person in each group summarize it.
- After students finished reading and summarizing, they arranged seven drawings into the same order as the story.
- As a group, students answered the following question: How did Kiku get back in the house? Then each group gave their answer to the whole class.
- As a class, students gave the story possible titles while the teacher wrote them on the board.

Critical Reading

There are at least three things to remember when asking students to do critical reading. First, when students are asked to read critically, they still need to do the kinds of activities that lead to full comprehension, as discussed earlier in this chapter. Second, students are asked to make judgments about what they read: Do I agree with the author's point of view? How is my view different? Does the author persuade me to change my view? Is the author's evidence strong? Third, we need to be careful about what we ask students to make judgments on. In other words, we need to select content that is not only interesting to the students as readers but also something they can relate to. For example, young adults from Japan, Mexico, and California will likely be more interested in reading and giving opinions about earthquake survival than will people in places not affected by earthquakes. Likewise, young students are apt to have more-informed opinions about popular rock stars and youth fashion than is the average adult.

Extensive Reading

The goal of extensive reading is to improve reading skills by processing a quantity of materials that can be comprehended and pleasurable. Teachers who implement extensive reading set up an open library (in the classroom or school library) where students can select from an assortment of reading materials.[14] The teacher's job is to guide the reader to materials that are comprehensible, letting the students make their own choices.

As a part of the extensive reading experience, teachers often ask students to report on what they have read. One way to do this is to have students interview each other through the use of question prompts. For example, if a student reads a short story, the question prompts might include[15]

- What the story title is
- What kind of short story it is
- Whether the student liked the story
- Why the student liked it, or why not

Students thinking critically

- Whether the student would recommend the story
- Who the story's author is
- What main message is in the story

What Problems Do Some EFL/ESL Teachers Have as Reading Teachers?

Problems some EFL/ESL teachers face include the following.

The "I want to read faster" problem. Students want to read faster, but they do not know how to increase their reading speed.

The "vocabulary building" problem. It is not just beginners who need lots of vocabulary. All students need to work constantly on building vocabulary, and teachers can show students how to do this on their own.

The "background knowledge" problem. Most teachers recognize that before students read, it is important to build students' background knowledge. And they can do this in interesting and creative ways.

The "getting students to read" problem. It is sometimes difficult to get young students to read outside class. Meeting students real-life interests could be the catalyst needed to spark an interest in reading.

The "I Want to Read Faster" Problem

Some students, including some at an advanced level, complain that they read too slowly. One reason is because the material is too difficult. There are too many new words, the grammar is too complex, the reader does not have the background knowledge to process the intended meaning, or, more likely, the reader is faced with a combination of these problems. Another reason students read slowly involves the way they read. Some students read a word at a time and look up many words in a dictionary, even words they know.

Realizing these two reasons, how can we provide chances for students to increase their reading speed? First, we can select materials that are comprehensible to students. Second, we can teach students strategies they can use to read faster. For example, as I discussed earlier in this chapter, we can teach them to make predictions from the title and headings, as well as to begin by skimming the material to locate main ideas. We can also teach them to guess the meaning of a word from the context. Here is an example of an activity that addresses this last point.[16]

Guessing Words from Context
Instructions: Work through each step.
1. Read through the text once. Circle the words you do not know, but do not stop to look them up in a dictionary.
2. Read through the text again, checking the underlined words that you can now understand.
3. Locate words you do not yet understand and believe are important. Ask a classmate or the teacher what they mean or look them up in a dictionary.

Third, we can do activities that directly aim at increasing students' reading speed. One such activity gives students chances to read fluently by reading and rereading the same material.[17] The teacher hands out reading material he or she predicts students will easily comprehend. The teacher then tells the students to read as much as they can for one minute, timing the reading. The students mark where they stopped with the number one. Then the teacher tells the students to return to the beginning of the passage and to read again for one minute, and students then mark where they stopped with the number two. This procedure goes on for a third and fourth time, the idea being for students to read further each time, as well as gain a sense of how a fluent reader reads.

The "Vocabulary Building" Problem

Students quite often ask the teacher how they can increase their vocabulary knowledge, and there are a number of things teachers can have students do.[18] First, as teachers, we can have students read extensively, as this is one way for students to acquire a larger reading vocabulary, especially if what they read is comprehensible to them and if they are good at guessing the meaning of words from the context.

As teachers, we can also teach students how to use a dictionary, with an emphasis on word study. If the teacher emphasizes the dictionary as a source of knowledge about words, and not necessarily as a productive way to increase reading comprehension and speed, dictionary study can be a productive way for students to increase their word power. There are a number of English-English dictionaries on the market. One is the *Longman Dictionary of American English.* It is easy to understand and easy to use; provides cross-references to other words, such as synonyms (words with similar meaning) and antonyms (words with opposite meanings); separates noun, verb, and adverb forms of words into separate entries; includes a clearly written guide to using the dictionary; and includes a workbook through which students can learn about how to use the dictionary.[19]

Another way to have students work on their vocabulary development is to have them create their own dictionaries. As I have done this, students generate ideas for the layout and content of the dictionary, and these dictionaries can range from being simple to very elaborate. Students have included phonetic break-

Two EFL teachers talking about activities to teach idioms

down of words; the student's own definitions; quick sketches; pictures cut out of magazines and newspapers; noun, verb, adjective, and adverb forms of words; translations; and sample sentences. They have kept their dictionary in three-ring binders, on index cards, or in a computer file. Students have reported that they learn much from keeping their own dictionary, including the knowledge that they are indeed increasing their lexicon, and a deeper discernment about the uses of words.[20]

The "Background Knowledge" Problem

As I pointed out earlier in this chapter, students' ability to comprehend the content of reading material depends in part on their knowledge about the topic of the reading selection. To increase students' potential comprehension, the teacher can do a variety of prereading activities that build background knowledge.[21]

One activity is to have a short discussion about the topic. For example, the teacher might lead off discussion with the following set of questions before having students read an article on the lifestyles of sumo wrestlers: How many of you have ever watched sumo on TV? What happens during a match? What are some of the rules in sumo? What do you know about the lifestyles of sumo wrestlers? If time is limited, written reading previews could be used. Similar to a movie preview, a reading preview introduces the student to the main idea of the reading. Pictures, sketches, or photographs can also be used to introduce the topic of a reading.

Another prereading activity is to take a field trip to a historical or cultural place or event or to watch a film or video clip about the topic of the future reading. For example, students could watch part of a videotaped sumo match and view a short documentary on the lives of famous contemporary sumo wrestlers.

The "Getting Students to Read" Problem

In some EFL/ESL teaching settings students do not necessarily value reading. It is a constant struggle for teachers to get students to attend to reading material in and out of class. In short, students, young and old, are not always motivated to read. And when faced with such an attitudinal or motivational problem, teachers are often at a loss about what to do.

Although there is no single or simple way to change students' attitudes toward reading, there are things teachers can try.[22] First, we can begin with the following assumption: "People learn better when what they are studying has considerable meaning for them . . . when it really comes out of their own lives . . . when it is something that they can in some way commit themselves to or invest themselves in."[23] Second, we can work at discovering what brings meaning to the life of each student in our classes. We can do this by observing students: What do they talk about? Show interest in? Carry around with them? Some nonreaders will read if the reading matches their interest, such as learning how to develop photos or learning to cook. When given the right conditions, problem readers will spend time reading because they have an invested interest in learning something they consider to be important or useful.

Third, we can do our best to introduce students to readings that match their interests, mostly through extensive reading activities. By putting together a library collection that includes the kinds of readings and content in which students express interest, we can most easily guide students toward materials that interest them and new attitudes about reading. Such a collection includes mysteries, how-to books, old letters, grammar books, catalogs, sports magazines, newspaper clippings, poems, application forms, menus, academic books, and more.

Teacher Self-development Tasks

Talk Tasks

1. Meet with others who are interested in teaching reading. Ask each other questions about learning to read. Here are a few questions to get you started: How did you learn to read your native language? Have you learned to read a second language? How did your teacher manage the reading lessons? Do you think there were differences in learning to read your first and second languages? If so, what are some of these differences?
2. Meet with a friend. Work through the following steps:
    a) Make a list of materials that students can use to practice scanning.
    b) Locate one of these materials.
    c) Create a scanning activity.
3. Meet with a friend. Work through these steps:
    a) Locate a reading passage. If you are now teaching a reading class, you might want to select material you plan to teach or are required to teach.
    b) Study the list (given earlier in this chapter) of techniques teachers can use to have students interact with reading materials.
    c) Based on the list of techniques to have students interact with reading materials, and on your own creative ideas, generate a detailed reading lesson that contains at least five different reading activities, all which help students process the passage you selected.
    d) Find others who have done this same activity. Give each other copies of your lesson plans.

Observation and Talk Tasks

1. Try out one of the reading lessons you created in talk task number 2 or number 3. Tape-record the lesson. Then select three two-minute sections from the tape to listen to. As you listen, jot down alternative ways you could teach the same aspect of the lesson.
2. Study the following partial checklist. Add behaviors of your own. Then observe a reading lesson. Use the checklist. Add behaviors you observe that are not on the list.

Teaching Reading: A Partial Checklist

	Yes	No
1. Teacher introduced material to be read		
a. related it to students' lives	___	___
b. discussed topic of the reading	___	___
c. used visual aids to introduce reading	___	___
d. selected words from reading to discuss/define	___	___
e. selected structures from reading to practice	___	___
f. other: _____	___	___
2. Teacher set goal(s) for reading		
a. to read for literal meaning: words, ideas	___	___
b. to read for inference	___	___
c. to read critically	___	___
d. to read for enjoyment	___	___
e. other: _____	___	___
3. Students read in class		
a. silently	___	___
b. orally	___	___
c. chorally	___	___
d. as a dramatic reading (like a play)	___	___
e. other: _____	___	___

(Checklist adapted from Fanselow n.d.)

Journal Writing Tasks

1. Study the activity types discussed in this chapter. Which do you like the most? Why? Which types have you used as a teacher or experienced as a learner?
2. Write about your experiences in learning to read a second language.
3. Select one of the problems from the section "What Problems Do Some EFL/ESL Teachers Have as Reading Teachers?" Write about why this is a problem for some teachers, and perhaps for yourself as a teacher.

Recommended Teacher Resources

Readings on Teaching Reading: Concepts and Activities

Carrell, P. L., and J. Eisterhold. 1983. "Schema Theory and ESL Reading." *TESOL Quarterly* 17:553–73.

Day, R. R., ed. 1993. *New Ways in Teaching Reading.* Alexandria, Va.: TESOL.

Grabe, W. 1991. "Current Developments in Second Language Reading Research." *TESOL Quarterly* 25:375–406.

Grellet, F. 1981. *Developing Reading Skills: A Practical Guide to Reading Comprehension Exercises.* New York: Cambridge University Press.

Nation, P., ed. 1994. *New Ways in Teaching Vocabulary.* Alexandria, Va.: TESOL.

Silberstein, S. 1987. "Let's Take Another Look at Reading: Twenty-five Years of Reading Instruction." *English Teaching Forum* 25 (4): 28–35.

Smith, F. 1994. *Understanding Reading.* New York: Holt, Rinehart, and Winston.

Textbooks: Teaching Reading

Baudoin, E. M., E. S. Bober, M. A. Clarke, B. K. Dobson, and S. Silberstein. 1988. *Reader's Choice: Second Edition,* Ann Arbor, Mich.: University of Michigan Press. (Intermediate/Advanced)

Davies, E., N. Whitney, M. Pike-Baky, and L. Blass. 1990. *Task Reading*. New York: Cambridge University Press. (High beginner)

Dubin, F., and E. Olshtain. 1990. *Reading by All Means: Reading Improvement Strategies for English Language Learners*. Reading, Mass.: Addison-Wesley. (Intermediate/Advanced)

Heyer, S. 1992. *Even More True Stories: An Intermediate Reader*. White Plains, N.Y.: Longman. (Intermediate)

Ligon, F., and E. Tannenbaum. 1990. *Picture Stories: Language and Literacy Activities for Beginners*. White Plains, N.Y.: Longman. (Beginner)

Low, M. 1995. *Thresholds in Reading*. Boston: Heinle and Heinle. (High intermediate)

McConochie, J. A. 1995. *Twentieth-century American Short Stories: An Anthology*. Boston: Heinle and Heinle. (Advanced)

Miller, J. N., and R. C. Clark. 1993. *The World: The 1990s from the Pages of a Real Small-town Daily Newspaper*. Brattelboro, Vt.: Prolingua Associates. (Multilevel)

Pickett, W. P. 1995. *The Pizza Tastes Great: Dialogues and Stories*. Englewood Cliffs, N.J.: Prentice Hall. (Beginner)

Shulman, M. 1991. *Selected Readings in Business*. Ann Arbor, Mich: University of Michigan Press. (Advanced)

Notes

1. Many sources address second language reading processes. Some include Bernhardt 1991; Carrell 1987; Carrell and Eisterhold 1983; Carrell, Devine, and Eskey 1988; Grabe 1991; and Wallace 1992.
2. See Parry 1987.
3. See Steffensen, Joag-Dev, and Anderson 1979.
4. Most of this list is from Papalia 1987, 72.
5. See Adams 1990; Rayner and Pollastek 1989.
6. The way I categorize reading skills has been influenced by Day (1993), Grellet (1981), and Baudoin, Bober, Clarke, Dobson, and Silberstein (1988).
7. Eskey (1988) and McLaughlin (1990) have stressed the importance of automatic lower-level processing. This means that students are encouraged to make guesses about the meaning of words, to test their own hypothesis. However, beginning readers do not necessarily do these things. Rather, they focus on one word at a time, because, as

Grabe (1991) points out, "they are not yet efficient in bottom-up processing. . . . Students do not simply recognize the words rapidly and accurately but are consciously attending to the graphic form" (391). In addition, as Eskey (1986) and Swaffar (1988) make clear, syntactic and vocabulary knowledge are critical to reading comprehension, because they provide the fundamentals to process the language so that readers can more automatically process meaning.

8. Three very different beginning-level grammar books include *Beginning Interactive Grammar* by McKay (1993), *Grammar One* by Zukowski-Faust and O'Brien (1991), and *Grammar Work* by Breyer (1995). Grammar activities can also be found in *New Ways in Teaching Grammar,* edited by Pennington (1995).

9. In a book of this scope, I can only give a few example activities. Other activities can be found in Baudoin et al. 1988, in Grellet 1981, and in published EFL/ESL reading texts.

10. The idea for this activity came from Grellet 1981, 69–70. The passage and titles are my own.

11. Baudoin, Bober, Clarke, Dobson, and Silberstein (1988), Day (1993), and Grellet (1981) provide an abundance of ideas on how to teach scanning skills.

12. EFL teachers can obtain from the tourist information center fact sheets about the country they are visiting or living in. Some tourist hotels also have useful information sheets.

13. Ideas from Papalia 1987 and Fanselow 1987 are included in this list of teaching techniques.

14. Shanefield (1993) offers advice for teachers who want to set up their own open library, including ways to catalog, gain support from school administrators, and locate and order appropriate books. Major publishing companies (see app. B) market graded readers (beginner through intermediate) for children and adults, which can be a part of the extensive library materials.

15. These prompts were designed by Kluge 1993 who also offers procedures for setting up and carrying out interviews.

16. Pearson-Hamatami (1993) does a similar activity called "Without a Dictionary."

17. This activity was created by Anderson (1993).

18. Nation (1994) and Allen (1983) provide other ideas on how students can study vocabulary.

19. The *Longman Dictionary of American English: A Dictionary for Learners of English* (Stenton 1983) is for advanced learners. The workbook was written by Fuchs (1992).

20. Schmitt and Schmitt (1995) have students keep "vocabulary note-books." They base the content on knowledge we have of memory and vocabulary acquisition. For example, they discuss eleven factors, two of which are "The best way to remember new words is to incorporate them into language that is already known" and "Word pairs can be used to learn a great number of words in a short time."
21. I also discuss ways to build students' background knowledge in Geb-hard 1987.
22. The three ways are also discussed in the article "Teaching Reading through Assumptions about Learning" (Gebhard 1985).
23. See Stevick 1978, 40.

Chapter 10

Teaching Students How to Process Writing

> We cannot teach students to write by looking only at what they have
> written. We must also understand how that came into being, and why it
> assumed the form it did. . . . We have to do the hard thing, examine the
> intangible process, rather than the easy thing, evaluate the tangible prod-
> uct.
>
> —Hairston 1982, 84

- What does writing include?
- How do EFL/ESL teachers teach beginners to write?
- What kind of writing activities do EFL/ESL teachers use with postbeginners?
- What problems do some EFL/ESL teachers have as writing teachers?

What Does Writing Include?

The usual things associated with writing are word choice, use of appropriate grammar (such as subject-verb agreement, tense, and article use), syntax (word order), mechanics (e.g., punctuation, spelling, and handwriting), and organization of ideas into a coherent and cohesive form. However, writing also includes a focus on audience and purpose, as well as a recursive process of discovering meaning. In this section I consider these last two aspects of writing.

Audience and Purpose

When we write, we usually have someone in mind who will read what we wrote. On a personal level, we write notes and letters to friends, relatives, and lovers. We also write diary entries to ourselves. As teachers, we write memos to colleagues, notes to students, and reports to parents and administrators. We might also write articles and newsletter items about teaching and learning for other teachers, conference papers to deliver at professional meetings, reading materials for students, and grant proposals to government agencies, cooperations, or a private funding source. In short, when we put pen to paper or fingers to keyboard, we usually have a specific audience in mind.

We also have a purpose, a reason to write. We want to thank a friend or colleague for doing a favor, wish a relative a happy birthday, or tell a lover how we feel. We want to convince administrators to change policy, colleagues to change attitudes, or agencies to give us money. Even when we write to ourselves, through a diary, we have a purpose, perhaps to know ourselves or the world around us differently.

A Recursive Process of Creating Meaning

When we write, especially something that is fairly complex, we do not ordinarily write a perfect letter or memo or essay or proposal in a single draft. Rather, we go through a process of creating and re-creating this piece of writing until we discover and clarify within ourselves what it is that we want to say and until we are able to express this meaning in a clear way.[1]

To prepare to write, some of us make lists, sketch, cluster our related ideas, or outline our thoughts. Some of us prefer to think about our topic, create mental notes and images, then begin to write. As we write, we put ideas into draft form, and as we do this, we create meaning.

As we write, we also take breaks to read the draft, and as we read, we reflect on whether or not our writing reveals our intended meaning. We might also consider our purpose and audience, and as we read over what we wrote, we cross out paragraphs, sentences, and words; reorder the way we present ideas; and jot down notes about how to revise our writing. We continue to write and read and draft changes until we are satisfied with the piece of writing. If the piece of writing is important enough, we ask a trusted friend to read it and give us feedback. We then use this feedback as a way to further revise our writing.

Students writing

How Do EFL/ESL Teachers Teach Beginners to Write?

Teachers generally agree that beginning-level EFL/ESL writers need to learn the basic conventions of writing. This includes being able to identify and write down letters, words, and simple sentences, as well as learning spelling and punctuation conventions. Teachers use a number of different types of activities to teach these conventions.[2]

One basic activity is tracing letters, words, and sentences. Although such a task may seem trivial, it can teach students letter recognition and discrimination, word recognition, and basic spelling, punctuation, and capitalization rules. One way teachers have students trace letters and words is to utilize tablet-style sheets used to teach American children. Students use pencils to trace letters and words written in an appropriate size and shape. In addition, students can use their index finger to trace letters and words cut from felt. This can be especially useful for students whose learning modality is more kinesthetic than visual. Some students also benefit from saying the letters and words aloud as they trace them.

Another widespread activity is called "Copy and Change." Students are given a passage and asked to copy it. But they are also required to change one aspect of the passage—for example, to change the subject from "he" to "she" and make accompanying changes (for instance, all references to "him" would need to be changed to "her"). This activity can be done with other grammatical features, such as changing verb tense from present to past time and changing the subject from singular to plural form.

A similar activity involves teaching students a grammatical pattern and functional rules. For example, we can teach students that we use simple present tense to describe everyday routines, and we can provide a model sentence pattern, such as this one:

Subject + Adverb + Pres. Tense Verb + Object + at + Time
I   usually   eat   lunch   at   noon.

Based on this pattern, students make up new sentences by exploring different grammatical conventions, such as investigating the use of other adverbs of frequency (*never, rarely, seldom, sometimes, often, frequently, always*), as well as changing the verb (*have, go out for, make*), object (breakfast, dinner, a snack), or time (3:00 A.M., 8:30).

Another beginning-level activity is to have students unscramble muddled sentence parts. For example, students are given a list of words—such as *school, goes, friend, everyday, My, to*—and they are asked to form a sentence.

After students gain some of the grammatical, mechanical, spelling, punctuation, and other conventions of written English, they can take on more demanding tasks. One idea is to have students plan a party by making two lists, "Things to do" and "Things to buy." Students work in groups or pairs to create their two lists, as well as practice related tasks, such as writing invitation notes and addressing envelopes.[3]

Another activity for advanced beginners is to read and write public notices, such as the ones on supermarket or dormitory bulletin boards. I have had ESL students in my beginning-level classes practice reading notices I bring to class, as well as copy down notices they see on bulletin boards and bring them to class. We also prepare for and do role-play telephone conversations to practice asking questions related to a notice. Based on their reading, copying, and conversation experience, students write their own notices. It is interesting that some students have been able to make connections with the larger community outside the classroom through actual use of their notices, thus expanding their language-learning opportunities. For example, one student started a haircutting business, another found a job doing lawn care, and another found a free ride to a distant city.

What Kind of Writing Activities Do EFL/ESL Teachers Use with Postbeginners?

After students have gained some control over the convention of writing, they can focus more easily on communicating their ideas through writing. And there are a variety of writing activities students can do.

Composition Writing

As writing teachers, we have students write short stories; descriptions of people, places, or objects; comparisons; elaborate definitions; arguments; and more. Quite often we find ourselves giving a composition assignment, such as to write about the character of a person we know, and we immediately focus on vocabulary and grammar that can be used to complete this assignment. When the composition is completed, we read each student's work and mark the errors with red ink. We might also write comments in the margins, such as "Very interesting" or "Good use of the present tense." But is it enough to give an assignment, to let the students write, and then to evaluate the product of their work? It is not. In fact, as writing teachers, we are advised to take students through a nonlinear process whereby, as writers, they can discover and rediscover their ideas as they attempt to put meaning into prose.

Our role is to provide chances for students to develop workable strategies for getting started (finding topics, generating writing ideas, focusing, planning content and organization), for drafting (working through multiple drafts), for revising (deleting, adding, reorganizing, modifying), and for editing (working out problems with word choice, grammar and mechanics, and sentence structure). To accomplish this, we are encouraged to have students work through a process of prewriting, drafting, revising, and editing.[4] Although each of these activities does not take place in a linear fashion, let's look at each separately.

Prewriting Experiences

One popular activity is called "Brainstorming," in which a topic is introduced by the teacher or students, after which students call out ideas associated with the topic while the teacher (or a student or two) write the ideas on the board. Although there is no right or wrong association in this activity, some EFL/ESL students will shy away from calling out their ideas. As such, some teachers have students brainstorm first in small groups, then as a whole class.

Similar to brainstorming is an activity called "Clustering" (or word mapping), in which students' associations are clustered together and stem off of the central word.

There are other prewriting activities. "Strategic questioning"[5] lets students consider their topic through a series of questions. By answering such questions as "What do you know about your topic?" and "What do you still need to learn?" students are given chances to consider what they know and need to learn about their writing topic. "Sketching" offers a more visual idea-generating strategy, useful, for example, when visualizing descriptions or showing the plot of a story. "Freewriting" provides students with chances to put ideas into writing.[6] Students are asked to write continuously for a set amount of time (e.g., eight minutes). They are told not to stop writing, continuing to write even if the only words that come to mind are "The teacher is crazy!" The students then read and consider what they wrote, after which they freewrite again. Freed from worrying about grammar and word choice, students generate lots of raw material for their essays.

Prewriting: Ways to Get Started[7]

Brainstorming. Based on a topic of interest, students call out as many associations as possible while the teacher (or students) jots them down.

Clustering. Using a key word placed in the center of a page (or board), a student (or teacher) jots down all the free associations students give related to the word, clustering similar words.

Strategic Questioning. Students answer a set of questions designed to guide their writing, such as "What do you want to write about?" "What is your goal?" "What do you know about this topic?" "What do you need to find out?" "What interests you or surprises you about this topic?" "Who might want to read what you are about to write?"

Sketching. Students draw a series of sketches that represent ideas for an essay—for example, the plot of a short story.

Freewriting. Students write nonstop on a topic for a set time (e.g., eight minutes). They stop to read and consider what they wrote and then write nonstop again for another set amount of time.

Exploring the Senses. Suitable for generating ideas for descriptive essays, the teacher guides students through their senses by asking them to visualize, hear, smell, and feel a person or place.

Interviewing. Students interview each other or go outside the classroom to interview people on a particular topic.

Information Gathering. Students collect information about a topic through library research.

I developed a prewriting activity, "Exploring the Senses," to facilitate idea gathering for descriptive essays on a place or person.[8] I begin by having students relax (sometimes doing deep-breathing exercises). I then take them through a series of "daydreaming" experiences by guiding them to see, hear, smell, touch, and feel a place or to see, listen to, smell, and have feelings about a particular person. As I do this, I do not get too specific but rather act as a guide and create an opportunity for the students to capture their own descriptions: "See the person. Zoom in on this person's face. Study the face. (Silence.) Now back away from the person. Look at this person from different positions, as if you are walking around the person. (Silence.)" After several minutes as a visual guide, I switch the students' experience to another sense: "Now, sense what it is like to be with this person. What feelings do you have when you are with this person?" I also guide students through smelling, touching, and listening experiences.

Teachers can have students experience a combination of prewriting activities. After taking students through the activity exploring the senses, I have students list their visual, auditory, kinesthetic, tactical, and other sensual experiences. If students are willing, I then have them meet in groups, each taking turns describing their person or place, after which I take them through a freewriting experience.

Drafting

After students have generated ideas, they need to write them down, and teachers have students draft their ideas in a number of ways. One way is to have students do component writing, in which they write different components of their texts within a certain period of time. Another way is to have students do one-sitting writing, in which they are encouraged to write a draft of their entire essay, from beginning to end, in one sitting. Another way is through leisurely writing, in which students begin a draft in class and are asked to finish it at their leisure at home.[9]

Revising

Once students have generated a draft, they can consider revision of the content and organization of their ideas. However, this is not necessarily easy for students to do. Some students have a limited understanding about what revision includes, and some lack the patience needed to go through a time-consuming and sometimes

A teacher working with a student on his writing

frustrating revision process. However, there are things teachers can do to teach students the concept of revision.

In the university ESL writing courses I teach, I make revision a required part of the students essay-writing experience, but I also teach them how they can explore the revision process. Here are the instructions I use when I teach narration:

1. Write and hand in three versions of your essay. Mark the essay you like the most with an asterisk (*) next to the title. Add a note explaining why you like it the most.
2. Here are some ways you can revise. Consider changing one or a combination of the following: (a) the beginning, (b) the climax, (c) the events in the steps that build up to the climax, (d) the sex of the main character, (e) the person in which the story is told (e.g., from first person, "I," to second person, "he" or "she"), (f) the setting in which the story takes place (for instance, from an inner-city high school to a summer camp), (g) any major content or organization change you would like to make.

Editing

Editing is another aspect of writing and requires recognizing problems in grammar (e.g., subject-verb disagreement, improper pronoun use, incorrect verb tense), syntax (e.g., fragments and run-on sentences), and mechanics (e.g., spelling and punctuation errors). Editing is not problematic in the way that revision is, because most students are willing to work hard at editing their work. However, it does take much time, knowledge, experience, and commitment to become a good editor, and some students (and teachers) can become preoccupied with editing, so much so that they equate good writing with correct grammar, syntax, word choice, and mechanics rather than with the expression of meaning, of which editing is simply a part.

Nonetheless, teaching students how to edit their work is important, and teachers approach this task in a variety of ways. Some teachers proceed by going through each student's paper and, with the use of a red pen, circling errors and writing notes, such as "wrong tense" or "awkward sentence." Although we teachers have good intentions and spend hours marking papers, students do not always appreciate our efforts and can even be confused by many corrections and comments. Realizing this, some teachers select one or two aspects of the student's work, such as a particular grammatical error and punctuation problem, and mark only these errors. There are, of course, other ways to respond to students' work, and these are discussed in the problem section at the end of this chapter.

Language-Play Writing

Some EFL/ESL teachers use language-play activities in writing classes. Such activities can be fun and engage students in writing. There are, of course, a great number of language-play writing activities, and here I only provide a few examples. One activity is called "Name Poems."[10] Students, either alone or in groups, are asked to create a poem based on a name. They either are given or select the name of a thing or a person. They then write this word vertically on a piece of paper and create a poem by using the letters of the word, coupled with the meaning of the word, to compose each poetic line. Here are examples.

Woe	*Maybe*
Anger	*Another woman would not*
Regret	*Understand, but she is*
	Really
	Amazing

Another activity is called the "How does it end?" activity. The teacher has students read the first part of a short story, preferably something that builds suspense but is not very long, and then asks them to complete the story. For example, I use an English translation of a German short story by Kurt Kusenberg called "Odd Tippling."[11] In this story a hiking traveler stops at a tavern to have a glass of wine. After ordering the first glass, the town mayor shows up and tells the traveler he has to pay a fortune for the wine. The traveler is surprised and argues with the mayor, but to no avail. Frightened and confused, the traveler decides to order a second and then a third glass, and to his amazement, he discovers that the third glass had created a totally new situation, that he was no longer in debt but rather owned the tavern and inn. Surprised, the traveler decides to have a fourth glass of wine.

I cut the end of the story off, and having students read all but the ending, I give a homework assignment, to write their own ending to the story, telling what happens to the traveler after ordering the fourth glass of wine. During the next class I have students read each others' endings, as well as write up a group ending to the story. After having students read their group ending to the class, we read the author's ending, sometimes amazed at how close some individuals and groups came to matching the author's ending, as well as appreciating the creative, and sometimes more interesting, endings of the students.

Another play activity aims at challenging students to communicate descriptions of people in writing. Students are divided into pairs and are given a picture that has lots of people in it. Each pair is asked to select one person in the picture to describe. After describing the person's physical appearance, the pairs exchange their pictures and written descriptions. The objective is to identify the person in the picture who the students described.

Newsletter Writing

Some classes (or schools/institutes) engage students in publishing their own newsletter. Such newsletters come out once a semester or every few months, and students can take on a variety of roles. The teacher can solicit or ask volunteer students to write columns for the newsletter on local cultural events, trips they took, and news about class members and teachers. Likewise, the newsletter can include students' creative writing, for example, short stories, poetry, or an editorial. They might also include announcements, test schedules, and other procedural-type news. Teachers usually try to have as many students as possible contribute their writing and participate in the production of the newsletter. As teachers and students who have taken the effort to publish their own newsletter will tell you, participants can gain a great sense of accomplishment and pride and learn lessons about writing with a purpose and to an audience, in this case one that they know will read and appreciate their efforts.

Pen Pals

Another way to provide a genuine writing experience for students is through pen pals.[12] There are a number of pen-pal organizations, and it is possible for teachers to establish their own pen-pal connections. For example, I established a pen-pal alliance between students in a Hungarian high school and native English-speaking students in a rural Pennsylvania school. It is also possible to establish pen-pal relations between EFL/ESL students in different countries (for instance, between EFL students in Brazil and Korea). Based on my experience with pen pals, I suggest that a one-to-one assignment of pen pals be made. For example, Andrea (an EFL student in Hungary) might be matched with Yoko (a Japanese ESL student in the United States).

Once the connection is established, one class needs to initiate a letter. If the students are fairly low level, a short generic letter can be written by the whole class and sent to each pen pal. Students can study letter format, including how and where to write the date and examples of ways to open and close letters. Basic get-acquainted questions can be included, such as "What's your name?" "How old are you?" "How many brothers and sisters do you have?" and "What do you like to do?" Of course, students can introduce their own questions, which the teacher can help them with as a group or individually.

Specific days for writing to pen pals (e.g., once every two months) can be set aside in the schedule. Students can bring letters they got from their pen pals to class and voluntarily read them to classmates, pass them around for others to read, or put them on an overhead for the class to read together. Class time can be spent writing back to their pen pals, and spontaneous lessons on grammar, punctuation, spelling, and more can result.

Dialogue Journal Writing

A dialogue journal is a written conversation between two or more people.[13] Through the use of notebooks or computers, these people write back and forth to each other on a regular basis, on topics of their choice. Quite often the teacher and each student in the class write back and forth, and there are benefits to such a one-to-one exchange. It is possible to get to know the students, better understand their language problems, and create a personal way to motivate each student. It can also teach students that we write to an audience, that we think about the reader as we write.

If it is impossible for the teacher to write to each student, an alternative is to respond to close-knit groups. Each student still writes to the teacher, but the teacher's response is in a single entry to the entire group.[14] Here is an example.

Dear Everybody,

It's always a delight to read your journal entries! Mario, I really enjoyed hearing about your trip to the zoo! How did you get the monkey to pose like that? Could I see other pictures you took? Andrea, your weekend sounded very frustrating! Everything went wrong, huh? How could you have forgotten to take sunscreen! Is your back still red? I hope you are over the pain. As I have similar skin—that is, I burn easily—I know what you are going through.

Carlos, I don't agree with your idea about memorizing word lists. This takes more time than it's worth. I suggest you keep a vocabulary notebook. Each day add three new words. Write down example sentences with the words in them. You can also draw sketches to illustrate them and can include different forms of the word. For example, if the word is a noun, also include the adjective and adverb forms of the word if they exist. You might also include your own definition of the word.

Mohammed, your interest in cultural-adjustment processes really captures my interest. I'm happy you liked the documentary we viewed in class on the stages of cultural adjustment. Do you have any interesting stories about adjustment to other cultures? In fact, I would be pleased to read any of your group's cultural-adjustment stories!

Yoko, how about you! I miss reading your journal entries! I hope that you are feeling better and ready to correspond with me again!

Enjoy!

Your teacher

Although a teacher-student dialogue exchange has benefits, there are also problems. First, as experienced teachers know, writing to each student or even to groups of students can be an extraordinary amount of work for the teacher, even impossible if the teacher has a large class. Second, the students know that the teacher cannot necessarily relate to their view of the world. Students quite often write about the teacher's interests and will not consider discussing what genuinely interests themselves. Third, and closely related to the second problem, is the problem of status. Some teachers want to really reach students. But even when the teacher tries hard to establish a special rapport, some EFL/ESL students will resist. This is especially true for students who are from places (such as many Asian countries) where the culturally based rules demand that students place the teacher on a hierarchical level above the student. In brief, it would be impolite for the students to complain, criticize, or openly write about a topic that could cause the teacher to lose face or that could upset their harmonious relationship.

Considering these factors, an alternative is to have students communicate with each other through journals. This is what Karen Bromley does with "buddy journals," which she uses to connect immigrant and American children in sharing language and literacy.[15] Likewise, this is what Colette and John Green do with "secret friend journals" in which they create a gamelike mystery for the students by keeping the students' names a secret.[16] With both "buddy" and "secret" journals, students can feel free to establish rapport based on shared interests, problems, and tastes without worrying about status or about pleasing the teacher or taking his or her time.

What Problems Do Some EFL/ESL Teachers Have as Writing Teachers?

Problems some EFL/ESL teachers face include the following.

The "teaching the less-proficient writer" problem. Some students use ineffective writing strategies, and the teacher is faced with showing these students how to write.

The "I can't write English" problem. Some students have negative attitudes about writing or lack confidence in themselves as writers. The teacher is faced with changing their attitudes and building confidence.

The "teacher response" problem. Students do not always understand or pay attention to the content of the teacher's response to their written work. Teachers need to explore different ways for students to get feedback on their writing.

The "Teaching the Less-Proficient Writer" Problem

To teach less-proficient writers, it helps to identify how they process writing differently from the proficient writer.[17] Unlike proficient writers, less-proficient writers tend to jump right into the writing task without using prewriting strategies to generate ideas and organize thoughts. In addition, rather than quickly getting organized thoughts onto paper, they might take much time to write down their ideas, as well as focus primarily on surface level aspects of writing, struggling with form over meaning.

The Composing Behaviors of EFL/ESL Writers

Proficient Writers	*Less-Proficient Writers*
• Think about the task. Use a variety of prewriting strategies.	• Start off confused, without using prewriting strategies.
• Have a sense of audience. Will consider audience while composing.	• Have vague or little awareness of audience.
• Once organized, get ideas onto paper quickly.	• Take much time to get ideas onto paper.
• At drafting stage, pay attention to meaning over form.	• Work primarily at the sentence level, struggling with form.
• Concerned with higher levels of meaning along with surface level.	• Concerned with vocabulary choice and sentence structure.
• Will revise at all levels (word, sentence, paragraph, entire text).	• Will revise primarily at the word and sentence level. Revise surface level items (spelling, grammar, punctuation, etc.).
• Will revise by adding, deleting, reordering ideas.	• Are bothered by confusion over revision. Tend to avoid adding, deleting, and reordering ideas.
• Generate several drafts, each with some revision.	• Revise primarily only the first draft.

Unlike proficient writers, less-proficient writers will revise primarily at the word and sentence level, using the revision process to edit grammar, syntax, spelling, and punctuation. Their revisions do not usually show many additions, deletions, substitutions, or reordering of ideas, and when revision is done, it occurs primarily on the first draft. Perhaps this is because there is often confusion associated with revision, and unlike proficient writers, less-proficient writers seem to lack patience to work through the confusion in the process of clarifying meaning.

Understanding the writing behaviors of proficient and less-proficient writers is a start. The question then becomes how teachers can provide opportunities for less-proficient writers to improve their writing skills. We need to give less-proficient writers more of everything—"more time; more opportunity to talk, listen, read, and write; more instruction and practice in generating, organizing, and revising ideas; more attention to the rhetorical options available to them; and more emphasis on editing for linguistic form and style."[18] In short, we need to do more than simply take less-proficient students through a process of producing a piece of writing. We also need to give our full attention to them, to show them how to plan a piece of writing through prewriting activities (discussed earlier in this chapter), how to draft and revise (discussed later in this chapter, under "The 'Teaching Response' Problem"), and how to read their writing as an editor.

We can also create interesting and real writing challenges for them, ones that include a real audience. One main reason less-proficient writers lack audience awareness could be because of the nature of the writing activities they are given. Students often recognize a writing activity as simply a "mundane school sponsored writing assignment."[19] Some students simply do not respond well to such artificial assignments. Such students might respond differently to a real audience, such as a pen pal, a secret journal reader, or newsletter readers.

The "I Can't Write English" Problem[20]

Some students simply do not like to write. In fact, I get some highly emotionally charged responses when I ask students how they feel about writing: "I really don't like to write. It's boring"; "Writing is so difficult. I always feel my English is terrible. It make me sad." Such negative attitudes are problematic in EFL/ESL writing classrooms. When students believe they cannot write, or have a defeatist attitude toward writing, they disengage themselves from the writing process.

It is important for us, as teachers, to identify students who have negative attitudes toward writing. To do this, we "need to be researchers who observe, listen, and learn from students."[21] Talking to students informally about writing, listening to stories about their writing experiences and their views of themselves as writers, not only offers us knowledge about the student as writer but can make students more aware of themselves and their attitudes, possibly leading to change.

In addition, to explore ways to give students a more positive perspective about their writing, we can demystify the writing process. We can point out that no one's writing is perfect, that writing is often hard work, and that the point of writing is to express our ideas. To demystify the process, we can lead students through prewriting, drafting, and revising activities, such as the ones discussed earlier in this chapter, and we can join them. We can let students read our drafts and revisions, including those that are partially developed. By doing this, students can see that writing is indeed a process of development that takes time and effort.

Another way to provide students with a more positive perspective about their writing and themselves as writers is to ask them to put together a portfolio of their best writing. When students can see their best work together in one place, they often feel very good about themselves, even proud of their efforts. And we can reward students for doing their best to develop a piece of writing. One way to reward students is to have class members read each others' portfolios and recommend a piece of writing for a class "publication." When students see their writing in print, along with other writers, they quite often are delighted and make such comments as "It's a wonderful feeling!"[22]

The "Teacher Response" Problem

Writing teachers often spend many hours reading and marking students' papers, offering revision suggestions and feedback on language errors. We correct, circle, underline, and write notes like "preposition problem." But students quite often do not pay attention to our comments and corrections. When what we do does not seem to work, or when we simply want to explore new ways of responding to students' work, we can try out alternative ways to respond to students' writing. In this section, I offer some of the ways that EFL/ESL writing teachers have responded to students' writing.

Writing teachers need to recognize if they treat an initial draft as if it were a final draft, applying a prescriptive, grammar-focused stance. As this fails to consider the developmental nature of the composing process, a grammar-focused teacher can consider responding to student drafts in ways that are appropriate to the development of a piece of writing. One way to do this is to require students to hand in two or three drafts of their writing. The teacher can then respond to each draft of writing in dissimilar ways.[23] For example, on some students' early drafts, the teacher can comment on how the students can revise their work, using such remarks as "Did your topic change here? You need to add a transition." "What are ways to capture the reader's attention at the start of your essay?" and "I like the content of the five points. But try reordering them. See if you like the change." On a later draft, the teacher can respond to surface-level errors, such as grammatical, spelling, punctuation, and syntactical errors.[24] It is worth pointing out that students say they appreciate and gain something from the teacher's responses, especially if these responses are clear in their intent.[25]

In addition to written responses, teachers can work with students on developing their written work through one-to-one conferences. Teachers and students often point out the value of such conferences, especially when the teacher and student focus on specific aspects of the student's writing and the student has chances to negotiate meaning.[26] One way to provide focus is have the student prepare for the conference by writing down questions, comments, and explanations before the conference. The teacher can also prepare by reading the student's draft before the conference while taking side notes on problems (e.g., with revision) that can be addressed during the conference. A way to encourage students to negotiate meaning is to let the student begin the conference (rather than the teacher) by describing what he or she wants to accomplish in the piece of writing and noticeable problems in doing this. As the student talks, the teacher can paraphrase, thus providing a recognized version of what the student has said and a way for the student to reflect and discover new things in his or her writing. If the student does not react well to a paraphrasing approach, which is the case for some students, another way to engage the student in negotiation is through collaboration. For example, the teacher and student can take turns generating ways to revise the student's paper. The teacher might suggest the student rewrite the essay in first person, the student might suggest writing a new conclusion, the teacher might suggest that the student use the final paragraph to begin the essay, and so on. At any point in this turn-taking process, the student should feel free to ask questions, add details, and explore additional ideas.

Peer response groups offer another way for students to get feedback on their writing. Here is a set of procedures for conducting a peer-group response session.[27]

1. Provide students with guidelines.
2. Model appropriate responses to students' drafts.
3. Group students.
4. Have students photocopy essay drafts for group members.
5. Have students read each others' drafts. Have them write on the draft or complete a peer review sheet.
6. Have students discuss their peers' drafts.

Guidelines include advice for the draft reader and the author. "Do not quarrel with other readers' reactions," "Describe your reactions as you read the paper," and "Be specific by pointing to a particular item in the paper" provide necessary advice to the reader. Advice to the writer includes "If you want comments on a specific part of your paper, ask," "Listen carefully," "Do not argue, reject, or justify," and "Remember that comments from readers are only suggestions. This is your paper, and you make the final decisions about how to write it."

Providing a model can also help clarify what the students are expected to do. Some teachers show example drafts with specific written comments on an overhead projector, as well as have the whole class read and respond to the same draft of an essay. Peer response sheets are also useful. As these sheets include questions about specific aspects of the essay, using these sheets can provide a way for readers to give relevant feedback to writers.[28] I provide an example of a sheet I have used with university freshman ESL writers (Peer Review Sheet). Although readers do not have to complete every item, I encourage them to do this, if for no other reason than to provide another option.

Peer Review Sheet
After reading the paper, complete the following sentences.

1. I think the best part of your paper is
2. You could reorganize your ideas by
3. I think you could change or omit
4. I do not understand
5. You could add
6. You are good at

I also provide another peer review sheet I have used (Student-to-Student Writing Conferences). This one includes more specific tasks for the readers. (See page 242.)

Teacher Self-development Tasks

Talk Tasks

1. What do writing experts mean when they say "writing is a recursive process of creating meaning"? Ask other teachers this question.
2. What activities do I suggest writing teachers use with beginning writers? Meet with another teacher. Add an additional three activities that a teacher might use to teach beginners.
3. Study the list of prewriting activities. Which have you used, or which would you like to use? Find out what prewriting activities other teachers have used.
4. Study the kinds of activities I suggest teachers use to provide a genuine writing experience for students. Which have you used, or which would you like to use? Find out what activities other teachers use or would like to use.

Student-to-Student Writing Conferences

1. Pair up with a classmate. Take turns reading your own piece of writing aloud. Feel free to stop in the middle of reading to make fast changes or take notes.
2. Exchange papers. Each read the others' writing silently.
3. Taking turns, each reader should summarize the others' writing in the following way:
   a. Tell quickly what you found to be the main idea, main feeling, or center of gravity.
   b. Summarize the piece into a single sentence.
   c. Choose one word from the writing that best summarizes it.
4. Each reader should write down answers to these questions:
   a. Does the writer capture your attention? Why?
   b. Are the ideas well organized? How does the writer organize the ideas in the piece of writing?
   c. Are there words that seem powerful? Which words? Are there words that seem weak or repeated too often?
   d. Does the writer use transitions to go from one idea to the next idea? Can you identify them? Can the writer identify them for you?
   e. Does the piece of writing have paragraph development?
   f. Is there anything else to say about the piece of writing?

Observation and Talk Tasks

1. Interview a writing teacher. Find out what his or her beliefs are about teaching students to write. Then observe his or her class. Are this teacher's beliefs reflected in the classroom writing activities?
2. Ask a writing teacher if you can observe his or her class. Take detailed descriptive notes that focus on the activities the teacher has students do in class. After the class, consider what you saw this teacher do that you would like to do in your own teaching.
3. Locate an EFL or ESL student. Ask this student to describe how he or she composes. It might help to ask, "How do you write an

essay from beginning to end?" Keep the student talking by paraphrasing what he or she says, adding comments like "Very interesting! Tell me more!" and showing interest with facial and other nonverbal expressions. After talking with the student, consider what he or she told you. Does he or she consider the audience? Pay attention to expressing meaning in early drafts? Reorganize, delete, and add? Generate several drafts? Does the student see writing as a developmental process? Interpret what the student said. Would you classify him or her as a proficient writer? What advice (if any) would you give to this writer?

Journal Writing Tasks

1. Write about your own experiences in learning to write. Did your teachers treat writing as a process of development? Why or why not?
2. Reflect on how you compose. Do you do the kinds of things writing experts say proficient writers do?
3. Write about your observation and interviewing experiences from doing the observation and talk tasks.

Recommended Teacher Resources

Readings for Writing Teachers

Johnson, D., and D. Roen. eds. 1989. *Richness in Writing: Empowering ESL Students.* White Plains, N.Y.: Longman.

Leki, I. 1992. *Understanding ESL Writers: A Guide for Teachers.* Portsmouth, N.H.: Boynton/Cook Publishers.

Nelson, G., and J. Murphy. 1992. "An L2 Writing Group: Task and Social Dimensions." *Journal of Second Language Writing* 1:171–90.

Raimes, A. 1991. "Out of the Woods: Emerging Traditions in the Teaching of Writing." *TESOL Quarterly* 25:407–30.

Tannacito, D. J. 1995. *A Guide to Writing in English as a Second or Foreign Language: An Annotated Bibliography of Research and Pedagogy.* Alexandria, Va.: TESOL.

White, R.V., ed. 1995. *New Ways in Teaching Writing.* Alexandria, Va.: TESOL.

EFL/ESL Writing Texts

Bates, L. 1993. *Transitions: An Interactive Reading, Writing, and Grammar Text.* New York: St. Martin's Press. (Advanced)

Blot, D., and D. M. Davidson. 1995. *Starting Lines: Beginning Writing.* Boston: Heinle and Heinle. (Beginner)

Brown, H. D., D. S. Cohen, and J. O'Day. 1991. *Challenges: A Process Approach to Academic English.* Englewood Cliffs, N.J.: Prentice Hall. (Advanced)

Phinney, M. 1994. *Process Your Thoughts—Writing with Computers.* Boston: Heinle and Heinle. (Intermediate)

Reid, J. M. 1987. *Basic Writing.* Englewood Cliffs, N.J.: Prentice Hall. (Beginner)

Scarcella, R. C. 1993. *Power through the Written Word.* Boston: Heinle and Heinle. (Intermediate)

Notes

1. A number of EFL/ESL writing researchers have addressed the recursive process that writers go through to create meaning. Among these researchers are Richards (1990), Raimes (1985), and Zamel (1982, 1983).

2. Olshtain (1991), Raimes (1983), and White (1981, 1995) describe and illustrate a number of activities for beginning EFL/ESL writers.

3. I discovered this listing activity in Olshtain 1991.

4. A number of EFL/ESL writing professionals agree that learning to write includes developing an effective nonlinear process. These professionals include Kroll (1991), Raimes (1985), Silva (1990), and Zamel (1982, 1987).

5. "Strategic questioning" is discussed in Richards 1990.

6. "Freewriting" was originally discussed by Elbow (1973).

7. These prewriting strategies are discussed in Kroll (1991), Oluwadiya (1992), Richards (1990), and Scarcella and Oxford (1992). The "Sketching" and "Exploring the Senses" activities are created out of my own experience as a writing teacher.

8. I created the "Exploring the Senses" prewriting activity while studying "Neurolinguistic Programming" (NLP). Although NLP is controversial because knowledge of it can be used to manipulate and control others, it does offer a way to guide people through hypnotic trance states that can, in regards to prewriting, offer writers new ways to

understand their own experience. Introductory books include Bandler and Grinder's *Patterns of the Hypnotic Techniques of Milton H. Erickson* (1975) and *Frogs into Princes* (1979) and Lankton's *Practical Magic* (1980).

9. These three ways to generate drafts are discussed in Scarcella and Oxford 1992.

10. The idea for "Name Poems" and the example poems are from Egbert and McColloch 1992.

11. "Odd Tippling" can be found in Lewis and Jungman's 1986 collection, *On Being Foreign: Culture Shock in Short Fiction.*

12. I would like to thank Mark Peters, an experienced foreign language teacher, for his ideas on the use of pen pals in language teaching.

13. A number of teachers have written about the use of dialogue journals, including Dolly (1990), Green and Green (1993), Lindfors (1988), Peyton and Reed (1990), Peyton (1993), Staton (1987), and Staton, Shuy, and Kreeft (1982).

14. Rinvolucri (1995) also explains how the teacher can write to groups rather than to each student.

15. See Bromley 1995.

16. Green and Green (1993) outline procedures for establishing and maintaining secret friend journals.

17. The characteristics I assign to less-proficient (and proficient) writers are based on research done by Lapp (1984), Raimes (1985), and Zamel (1982, 1983), as well as on my own experience. These characteristics are tentative and meant to be heuristic in nature, as it would be a mistake to overgeneralize patterns of writing behavior based on our limited knowledge.

18. See Raimes 1985, 248.

19. See Raimes 1985, 251.

20. Many of the ideas in this section on the affective side of the writing process are also expressed by Thomas (1993), whose work I admire.

21. See Thomas 1993, 15.

22. Holmes and Moulton (1994) provide a rich description of what publishing students' work means to the ESL students.

23. The idea of treating writing from a developmental point of view and responding to writing in ways appropriate to the development of the piece of writing is most convincingly made by Zamel (1985).

24. Mahili (1994), a writing teacher in Greece, explains and illustrates how she responds to different drafts of students' writing.

25. Based on her research on student reactions to teacher response on multiple drafts of compositions, Ferris (1995) discovered that stu-

dents appreciate feedback and generally find it useful. However, she also found that students cannot always understand the teacher's comments, and she suggests that teachers need to be more intentional in their comments to students. Reid (1994) makes this point also and encourages teachers to make use of their roles as writing experts as they provide explicit feedback.

26. In their research, Goldstein and Conrad (1990) discovered the impact of negotiation during writing conferences. They found that students who are actively involved in the negotiation of their intended meaning in their essays make revisions that result in improvements in their revised drafts.

27. Nelson and Murphy (1992/93) provide a set of procedures they use to set up peer conferencing groups, as well as guidelines for students. The procedures and guidelines I illustrate are based on my experience as a writing teacher and on those given by Nelson and Murphy.

28. Nelson and Murphy (1992/93) point out that low-intermediate ESL students are able to identify macrolevel problems with organization, development, and topic sentences but are less able to identify sentence-level and intersentential features, such as parallel structure and repetition of words. They suggest teachers teach students how to identify these things. Likewise, Mangelsdorf (1992) found that more advanced students were able to give useful advice at the drafting stage of the essay but were less able to give advice on later stages of development.

Appendixes

A Selected Assortment of Professional Journals

Applied Psycholinguistics

Published quarterly, this journal includes articles on the psychological processes involved in language acquisition, comprehension, and language impairment. Write to: Cambridge University Press, 32 East 57th St., New York, NY 10022, USA.

College ESL

Published quarterly, this journal focuses on theory and practice in teaching ESL at the college level, especially to urban immigrant and refugee adults in college and precollege settings. Write to: Editor, College ESL, Instructional Resource Center, The City University of New York, 535 East 80th Street, New York, NY 10021, USA.

ELT Journal

Published quarterly by Oxford University Press in association with the British Council, this English language teaching journal maintains an international scope. Practical articles are written by experienced EFL/ESL teachers and teacher educators. Write to: Editor, ELT Journal, 2 Smyrna Road, London NW6 4LU, England.

English for Specific Purposes

Published three times each year by the Pergamon Press, this journal publishes articles that address language teaching and learning within specific contexts. Write to: Pergamon Press, English for Specific Purposes, Maxwell House, Fairview Park, Elmsford, NY 10523, USA; or Headington Hill Hall, Oxford OX3 OBW, England.

English Teaching Forum

Published quarterly by the United States Information Agency (USIA), this journal publishes mostly practical articles on teaching EFL/ESL. A popular journal among EFL teachers, it is available through the United States embassy in most countries; or write to: Superintendent of Documents, U.S. Government Printing Office, Washington, DC 20547, USA.

Foreign Language Annals

Published six times each year by the American Council on the Teaching of Foreign Languages (ACTFL), this journal seeks to serve the interests of teachers, administrators, and researchers in foreign language teaching. Write to: ACTFL, 6 Executive Blvd., Upper Level, Yonkers, NY 10701, USA.

Guidelines

Published biannually, this journal focuses on practical ideas and suggestions for EFL/ESL teachers. Write to: The Editor, Guidelines, SEAMEO Regional Language Centre, 30 Orange Grove Road, Singapore 1025, Republic of Singapore.

Hands-on English

Published six times a year, this periodical is specifically for teachers and tutors who want practical ideas for teaching ESL to adults. Write to: Hands-on English, P.O. Box 256, Crete, Nebraska 68333, USA.

International Review of Applied Linguistics

Published quarterly, this review publishes articles on all aspects of language teaching and includes theoretical and practical articles on teaching and learning a variety of different languages (not just English). Write to: Julius Groos Verlag, Pastfach 102423, D-6900 Heidelberg, Germany.

JALT Journal

Published semiannually by the Japan Association of Language Teachers, this journal publishes research-oriented articles on teaching and learning EFL. Write to: JALT Central Office, Shamboru Dai-2 Kawasaki #305, 1-3-17 Kaizuka, Kawasaki-ku, Kawasaki-shi 210, Japan.

Journal of Second Language Writing

Published three times a year, this journal publishes articles on topics related to teaching writing in the EFL/ESL classroom, especially theoretically grounded research reports on implications for teaching. Write to: Ablex Publishing Corporation, 355 Chestnut Street, Norwood, NJ 07648-9975, USA.

Language Learning

Published quarterly by the University of Michigan, this highly academic journal publishes articles in applied linguistics and language learning. Write to: Language Learning, 178 Henry S. Frieze Bldg., 105 South State St., Ann Arbor, MI 48109-1285, USA.

PASAA

Published annually by Chulalongkorn University, this journal includes research and practical articles on teaching and learning foreign languages, mostly Thai and English. Write to: PASAA Business Manager, Chulalongkorn University Language Institute, Prem Purachatra Building, Chulalongkorn University, Phyathai Road, Bangkok 10330, Thailand.

Prospect

Published three times each year by the National Centre for English Language Teaching and Research, this journal has articles on applied linguistics and teaching concerns related to the adult ESL field. Write to: Sales and Marketing Manager, NCELTR, Macquarie University, Sydney, NSW 2109, Australia.

RELC Journal

Published semiannually by the Southeast Asian Ministers of Education Organization (SEAMEO), this journal reviews current research on teaching English in southeast Asia and has articles on theory and teaching practices and materials. Write to: RELC Journal, SEAMO Regional Language Centre, RELC Building, 30 Orange Grove Road, Singapore 1025, Republic of Singapore.

Studies in Second Language Acquisition

Published quarterly by Cambridge University Press, this journal publishes articles related to second language acquisition and foreign language learning and teaching. Write to: Cambridge University Press, 32 East 57th Street, New York, NY 10022, USA.

TESOL Journal

Published quarterly by TESOL, this journal is popular among classroom teachers and includes articles on classroom research done by EFL/ESL teachers, practical applications of this research to teaching, materials development, and teacher development. Write to: TESOL, 1600 Cameron St., Suite 300, Alexandria, VA 22314-2751, USA.

TESOL Quarterly

Published quarterly by TESOL, this journal represents contemporary thinking in the field and includes original research, reviews of research, and practical applications of theory and research to teaching EFL/ESL. Write to: TESOL, 1600 Cameron St., Suite 300, Alexandria, VA 22314-2751, USA.

TESL Reporter

Published quarterly, this journal has short practical articles on teaching and learning EFL/ESL. Write to: TESL Reporter, Brigham Young University-Hawaii, Box 1830, Laie, HI 96762-1294, USA.

TESL Talk

Published quarterly by the Canadian Ministry of Citizenship and Culture, this journal has thematic issues related to ESL learners. Write to: Citizens Development Branch, Ministry of Citizenship and Culture, 77 Bloor St., 5th Floor, Toronto, Ontario M7A 2RG, Canada.

Appendix B

Publishers of EFL/ESL Resources

This appendix includes an alphabetical listing of selected publishers of EFL/ESL resources. For each publisher, there is a brief summary of the types of resources offered, followed by addresses, telephone numbers, and fax numbers of offices throughout the world where further information and publication catalogs may be requested.

Academic and Professional Book Centre

Located at the City University of Hong Kong, this center supplies research reports, papers, and manuscripts on practical aspects of language learning and teaching, such as in second language writing, culture, motivation, teachers' instructional decisions, and professional development.

Academic and Professional Book Centre
City University of Hong Kong
83 Tat Chee Avenue, Kowloon, Hong Kong

Addison-Wesley/Longman

Addison-Wesley, which also represents Longman Publishing, offers EFL/ESL textbooks, audio cassettes, videos, and computer software that can be used to teach children, young people, and adults. Their materials cover a wide variety of possible courses or skill areas, including conversation, listening, reading, writing, and vocabulary, as well as business and TOEFL preparation. Teacher resources include books on methodology, linguistics, and self-development.

Addison-Wesley Publishing Company
World Language Division
10 Bank Street
White Plains, NY 10606-1951 USA
Tel: 1-800-266-8855

Great Britain and Africa:
Addison-Wesley Publishing
Finchampstead Road
Wokingham, Berkshire
RG11 2NZ
United Kingdom
Tel: (44) 734 794 000

Asia:
Addison-Wesley Publishers Japan Ltd.
Nichibo Building, 1-2-2 Sarugakucho
Chiyoda-ku, Tokyo 101 Japan
Tel: (81) 33 291 4581

Alta Book Center

This book center distributes a wide selection of ESL texts, audio and video materials, computer software, and professional books from major publishing companies throughout the United States. Their large inventory includes materials for all ages and language skills.

Alta Book Center
14 Adrian Court
Burlingame, CA 94010 USA
Tel: 1-800-258-2375 (Canada and USA)
(415) 692-1285 (USA and International)

Berty Segal, Inc.

Berty Segal focuses on communicative/cooperative learning books and other materials, including materials used to teach TPR (Total Physical Response), the natural approach, whole language, and LEA (Language Experience Approach).

Berty Segal, Inc.
1749 Eucalyptus
Brea, CA 92621 USA
Tel: (714) 529-5359

Cambridge University Press

Cambridge is well known for its collection of books for teacher training and development, methodology, linguistics, and culture. In addition, student textbooks and videos are available in the Cambridge adult and college series, from beginning through advanced English ability levels, covering listening/speaking, grammar, pronunciation, reading/writing, TOEFL preparation, and English for specific purposes.

Cambridge University Press
ESL Marketing Department
40 West 20th Street
New York, NY 10011–4211 USA
Tel: 1-800-872-7423

Outside North America:
Cambridge University Press
ELT Marketing Department
The Edinburgh Building,
Shaftesbury Rd., Cambridge
CB2 2RU England
Tel: (0223) 312393

Council on Foreign Relations Press

This unique press publishes the magazine *Foreign Affairs,* as well as timely books about international affairs in countries and regions throughout the world, including southeast Asia, Europe, and Latin America. Up-to-date cultural, political, and economic information supplies EFL/ESL teachers with relevant background understanding of their students' worlds.

Council on Foreign Relations Press
58 East 68th Street
New York, NY 10021 USA
Tel: 1-800-488-2665

ERIC Clearinghouse on Languages and Linguistics

ERIC is an operation of the Center for Applied Linguistics providing a variety of resources for the EFL/ESL teacher. For example, two-page ERIC "Digests" are helpful summaries of current topics of interest, such as the use of dialogue journals in language teaching, technology in the foreign language classroom, and teacher supervision. "Minibibs" are annotated bibliographies on such topics as second language learning styles and strategies, cooperative learning approaches, and teaching literature in the foreign language classroom. Other useful publications include "Language in Education" monographs and research reports.

ERIC Clearinghouse on Languages and Linguistics
User Services Coordinator
1118 22nd Street, NW
Washington, DC 20037 USA
Tel: (202) 429-9292

Georgetown University Press

This press publishes books on languages and linguistics. Their GURT series (Georgetown University Round Table on Languages and Linguistics) anthologizes the major presentations at the annual GURT conference, many of which are applicable to EFL/ESL classroom theory and practice.

Georgetown University Press
P.O. Box 4866
Hampden Station
Baltimore, MD 21211-4866 USA
Tel: (410) 516-6995

Heinle and Heinle

Heinle and Heinle publishes EFL/ESL course materials, including books and video, computer software, multimedia, and text/audio packages. Secondary and adult curriculum offerings cover reading, writing, speaking, listening, vocabulary building, cultural understanding, and more. Teacher development books include titles on classroom resources, learner strategies, methodology, and second language acquisition.

Heinle and Heinle Publishers
Sales Service Department
20 Park Plaza
Boston, MA 02116-4507 USA
Tel: 1-800-278-2574
(617) 451-1940

Asia:
International Thomson Publishing
Block 211, Henderson Rd. #08-03
Singapore 0315 Republic of Singapore
Tel: 65 272-6496

United Kingdom, Europe, and the Middle East
Nelson ELT
Berkshire House
168-173 High Hollbourn
London WC1 V7AA United Kingdom
Tel: 44 71 4971422

Intercultural Press

Intercultural Press specializes in the publication of books and educational materials on cross-cultural awareness. A variety of videos and simulation games focus on cross-cultural communication. The press also markets easy-to-understand books on specific cultures and countries.

Intercultural Press, Inc.
PO Box 700
Yarmouth, ME 04096 USA
Tel: (207) 846-5168

Multilingual Matters

This publishing company focuses on cultural resources and teacher education books in areas including translation guides, second/foreign language learning, bilingual/minority education and issues, cross-cultural education, and sociolinguistics.

Multilingual Matters
c/o Taylor and Francis Inc.

United Kingdom and World:
Plymbridge Distributors Ltd

1900 Frost Road, Suite 101
Bristol, PA 19007-1598 USA
Tel: 1-800-821-8312

Plymbridge House, Estover Road
Plymouth PL6 7PZ United King-
dom
Tel: 0752-695745

Oxford University Press

Oxford publishes a wide variety of student books, cassettes, and videos for young children to adults, covering all language skills. Oxford also publishes resources for English for specific purposes, business and technology, and TOEFL preparation; an extensive catalog of professional books in areas of teaching methodology and applied linguistics; and relevant professional journals, including *ELT Journal* and *Applied Linguistics International.*

Oxford University Press
2001 Evans Rd.
Cary, NC 27513 USA
Tel: 1-800-445-9714

International:
Oxford University Press
ELT Sales Department
Walton St.
Oxford OX2 6DP England
Tel: (0865) 56767

Prentice Hall/Regents

Prentice Hall/Regents offers a large collection of books, audio cassettes, interactive videos/software, and reference works for EFL/ESL students of all ages. For teacher development, they offer professional materials on teaching methodology, classroom techniques, translation, and teacher resources.

Prentice Hall/Regents
One Lake Street
Upper Saddle River, NJ 07458 USA
Tel: 1-800-375-2375

Pro Lingua

Pro Lingua publishes a mix of student and teacher resources for EFL/ESL classrooms, including card games, radio dramas, readers on special topics, cross-cultural activities, and more.

Pro Lingua Associates
15 Elm Street
Brattleboro, VT 95301 USA
Tel: 1-800-366-4775

Australia and New Zealand:
Antipodean Educational Enter-
prises
PO Box 445, Cammeray
NSW 2062 Australia
Tel: 61-2-906-2257

RELC (Regional English Language Centre, Southeast Asia)

Located in Singapore, RELC publishes the Anthology Series of academic papers, the Monograph Series on linguistics and language
learning, and the Occasional Papers, reprints of useful language-
learning articles and materials. All these publications are selected
for their high interest and practical use for teachers and researchers
of EFL/ESL. Example titles include "Patterns of Classroom Interaction in Southeast Asia," "Cultural Components of Reading," and
"Classroom Aids: A Practical Guide for Language Teachers." Also
available is the *RELC Journal.*

The Publications Officer
SEAMEO Regional Language Centre
30 Orange Grove Road
Singapore 1025 Republic of Singapore
Tel: 7379044

TESOL (Teachers of English to Speakers of Other Languages)

TESOL publishes for the purpose of strengthening effective teaching and learning of English around the world. TESOL books, audiotapes, videos, and information packages are available in a variety of
areas, including testing, program self-study, ESL/EFL job search,
and books on teaching all skill areas. Also available are professional
journals, including the *TESOL Quarterly* and the *TESOL Journal.*

TESOL
1600 Cameron Street, Suite 300
Alexandria, VA 22314-2751 USA
Tel: (703) 836-0774

TOEFL Publications

TOEFL Publications produces the TOEFL (Test of English as a Foreign Language) exam. Full-length sample tests and TOEFL preparation kits (with audio cassettes) are also available. These resources can be used for self-study, tutorial, and classroom purposes and are especially designed to help nonnative English-speaking students become familiar with current versions of the test.

TOEFL
P.O. Box 6161
Princeton, NJ 08541–6161 USA
Tel: (609) 771–7243

The University of Michigan Press

The University of Michigan Press publishes quality, innovative EFL/ESL materials for all language ability levels and skill areas. Materials also available for instruction.

The University of Michigan Press
P.O. Box 1104
Ann Arbor, MI 48106–1104 USA
Tel: (313) 764–4392

Asia and the Pacific:
Lee and Cassidy International
Pte. Ltd, 1 Farrer Road #07–05
Singapore 1026
Republic of Singapore
Tel: (65) 468–6242

Bibliography

Adams, M. 1990. *Beginning to Read*. Cambridge: MIT Press.

Adler, P. S. 1987. "Culture Shock and the Cross-cultural Learning Experience." In *Toward Internationalism*, ed. L. F. Luce and E. C. Smith, 24-35. Cambridge, Mass.: Newbury House.

Allen, M. 1985. *Teaching English with Video*. White Plains, N.Y.: Longman.

Allen, P., M. Frohlich, and N. Spada. 1984. "The Communicative Orientation of Language Teaching: An Observation Scheme." In *On TESOL '83*, ed. J. Handscombe, R. A. Orem, and B. P. Taylor, 231-52. Washington, D.C.: TESOL.

Allen, V. F. 1983. *Techniques in Teaching Vocabulary*. New York: Oxford University Press.

Allwright, D., and K. M. Bailey. 1991. *Focus on the Language Classroom: An Introduction to Classroom Research for Language Teachers*. Cambridge: Cambridge University Press.

Alpert, R., and R. Haber. 1960. "Anxiety in Academic Achievement Situations." *Journal of Abnormal and Social Psychology* 61:207-15.

Altman, H. B. 1981. "What is Second Language Teaching?" In *The Second Language Classroom*, ed. J. E. Alatis, H. B. Altman, and P. M. Alatis, 5-19. New York: Oxford University Press.

Anderson, A., and T. Lynch. 1988. *Listening*. Oxford: Oxford University Press.

Anderson, J. A. 1988. "Cognitive Styles and Multicultural Populations." *Journal of Teacher Education* 39:2-9.

Anderson, N. J. 1993. "Pump It Up." In *New Ways in Teaching Reading*, ed. R. R. Day, 188-89. Alexandria, Va.: TESOL.

Arcario, P. 1994. "Post-observation Conferences in TESOL Teacher Education Programs." Ph.D. diss., Teachers College, Columbia University.

Asher, J. 1982. *Learning Another Language through Actions: The Complete Teacher's Guidebook*. Los Gatos, Calif.: Sky Oaks Productions.

Atkinson, J. M., and J. Heritage, eds. 1984. *Structures of Social Action: Studies in Conversation Analysis*. Cambridge: Cambridge University Press.

Bailey, K. M. 1990. "Diary Studies in Teacher Education Programs." In *Sec-*

ond Language Teacher Education, ed. J. C. Richards and D. Nunan, 215-26. New York: Cambridge University Press.

Bailey, K. M., and L. Savage, eds. 1994. *New Ways in Teaching Speaking.* Alexandria, Va.: TESOL.

Bandler, R., and J. Grinder. 1975. *Patterns of the Hypnotic Techniques of Milton H. Erickson.* Cupertino, Calif.: Meta Publications.

———. 1979. *Frogs into Princes.* Moah, Utah: Real People Press.

Barnlund, D. C. 1975. *Public and Private Self in Japan and the United States.* Yarmouth, Maine: Intercultural Press.

Barns, D. 1975. *From Communication to Curriculum.* Harmondsworth: Penguin.

Bartlett, L. 1990. "Teacher Development through Reflective Teaching." In *Second Language Teacher Education,* ed. J. C. Richards and D. Nunan, 202-14. New York: Cambridge University Press.

Baudoin, E. M., E. S. Bober, M. A. Clarke, B. K. Dobson, and S. Silberstein. 1988. *Reader's Choice: Second Edition.* Ann Arbor, Mich.: University of Michigan Press.

Bernhardt, E. B., ed. 1991. *Reading Development in a Second Language: Empirical and Classroom Perspectives.* Norwood, N.J.: Ablex Publishing.

Bowen, D. J., H. Madsen, and A. Hilferty. 1985. *TESOL: Techniques and Procedures.* Rowley, Mass.: Newbury House.

Breen, M., and C. N. Candlin. 1980. "The Essentials of Communicative Curriculum in Language Teaching." *Applied Linguistics* 1 (2): 89-112.

Breyer, P. P. 1995. *Grammar Work.* Englewood Cliffs, N.J.: Prentice Hall.

Brindley, G. 1989. "The Role of Needs Analysis in Adult ESL Programme Design." In *The Second Language Curriculum,* ed. R. K. Johnson, 63-78. Cambridge: Cambridge University Press.

Brinton, D. M. 1991. "The Use of Media in Language Teaching." In *Teaching English as a Second or Foreign Language,* ed. M. Celce-Murcia, 454-72. Boston: Heinle and Heinle.

Brislin, R. W., K. Cushner, C. Cherrie, and M. Yong. 1986. *Intercultural Interactions: A Practical Guide.* Beverly Hills: Sage Publications.

Brock, C. A. 1986. "The Effects of Referential Questions on ESL Classroom Discourse." *TESOL Quarterly* 20:47-59.

Bromley, K. 1995. "Buddy Journals for ESL and Native-English-speaking Students." *TESOL Journal* 4 (3): 7-11.

Brophy, J. E., and T. L. Good. 1986. "Teacher Behavior and Student Achievement." In *Handbook of Research on Teaching,* ed. M. C. Wittrock, 328-75. New York: Macmillan.

Brown, G., and G. Yule. 1983. *Teaching the Spoken Language: An Approach Based on the Analysis of Conversational English.* Cambridge: Cambridge University Press.

Brown, H. D. 1987. *Principles of Language Learning and Teaching.* Englewood Cliffs, N.J.: Prentice Hall.

———. 1991. *Breaking the Language Barrier.* Yarmouth, Maine: Intercultural Press.

Bueffel, E. G., and C. T. Hammett, producers. 1982. *It's Toddler Time.* Long Branch, N.J.: Kimbo Educational. Record.

Bullough, R. V., and K. Baughman. 1993. "Continuity and Change in Teacher Development: First-year Teacher after Five Years." *Journal of Teacher Education* 44 (2): 86–93.

Bygate, M. 1987. *Speaking.* Oxford: Oxford University Press.

Calderhead, J., ed. 1988. *Teachers' Professional Learning.* London: Falmer Press.

Canale, M., and M. Swain. 1980. "Theoretical Bases of Communicative Approaches to Second Language Teaching and Testing." *Applied Linguistics* 1 (1): 1–47.

Carrell, P. L. 1987. "Content and Formal Schemata in ESL Reading." *TESOL Quarterly* 21:461–81.

Carrell, P. L., J. Devine, and D. Eskey, eds. 1988. *Interactive Approaches to Second Language Reading.* New York: Cambridge University Press.

Carrell, P. L., and J. Eisterhold. 1983. "Schema Theory and ESL Reading Pedagogy." *TESOL Quarterly* 17:553–73.

Carruthers, R. 1987. "Teaching Pronunciation." In *Methodology in TESOL,* ed. M. H. Long and J. C. Richards, 191–200. Rowley, Mass.: Newbury House.

Celce-Murcia, M. 1987. "Teaching Pronunciation as Communication." In *Current Perspectives on Pronunciation,* ed. J. Morley, 1–12. Alexandria, Va.: TESOL.

Celce-Murcia, M., and J. M. Goodwin. 1991. "Teaching Pronunciation." In *Teaching English as a Second Language,* ed. M. Celce-Murcia, 136–53. Boston: Heinle and Heinle.

Chan, M. 1994. "Pronunciation Warm-Up." In *New Ways in Teaching Speaking,* ed. K. M. Bailey and L. Savage, 199–201. Alexandria, Va.: TESOL.

Chaudron, C. 1988. *Second Language Classrooms: Research on Teaching and Learning.* New York: Cambridge University Press.

Chaudron, C., and J. C. Richards. 1986. "The Effect of Discourse Markers on the Comprehension of Lectures." *Applied Linguistics* 7 (2): 113-27.

Clarke, M. A. 1982. "On Bandwagons, Tyranny, and Common Sense." *TESOL Quarterly* 16:437-48.

Curran, C. 1976. *Counseling-learning in Second Languages.* Apple River, Ill.: Apple River Press.

————. 1978. *Understanding: A Necessary Ingredient in Human Belonging.* Apple River, Ill.: Apple River Press.

Dale, P., and L. Poms. 1995. *English Pronunciation for International Students.* Englewood Cliffs, N.J.: Prentice Hall.

Day, R. R., ed. 1993. *New Ways in Teaching Reading.* Alexandria, Va.: TESOL.

Doi, T. 1973. *The Anatomy of Dependence.* Tokyo: Kodansha International.

Dolly, M. R. 1990. "Adult ESL Students' Management of Dialogue Journal Conversation." *TESOL Quarterly* 24:317-21.

Edge, J. 1992. *Cooperative Development.* Essex: Longman.

Egbert, J. L., and M. McCulloch. 1992. "Language Play, Language Learning: Writing Activities for Second Language Exploration." *English Teaching Forum* 30 (4): 8-11.

Elbow, P. 1973. *Writing without Teachers.* New York: Oxford University Press.

Eskey, D. 1986. "Theoretical Foundations." In *Teaching Second Language Reading for Academic Purposes,* ed. F. Dubin, D. Eskey, and W. Grabe, 3-23. Reading, Mass.: Addison-Wesley.

————. 1988. "Holding in the Bottom: An Interactive Approach to the Language Problems of Second Language Readers." In *Interactive Approaches to Second Language Reading,* ed. P. Carrell, J. Devine, and D. Eskey, 93-100. New York: Cambridge University Press.

Fanselow, J. F. N. d. "A Reading Class Observation Guide." Unpublished. Department of Languages, Literature, and Social Studies in Education. Teachers College, Columbia University.

————. 1977a. "Beyond Rashomon: Conceptualizing and Observing the Teaching Act." *TESOL Quarterly* 11:17-41.

————. 1977b. "The Treatment of Learner Error in Oral Work." *Foreign Language Annals* 10:583-93.

————. 1980. "'It's too damn tight'—Media in ESOL Classrooms: Structural Features in Technical/Subtechnical English." *TESOL Quarterly* 14:141-54.

————. 1987. *Breaking Rules: Generating and Exploring Alternatives in Language Teaching.* White Plains, N.Y.: Longman.

———. 1988. "'Let's See': Contrasting Conversations about Teaching." *TESOL Quarterly* 22:113-30.

———. 1992. *Contrasting Conversations: Activities for Exploring Our Beliefs and Teaching Practices.* White Plains, N. Y.: Longman.

Farrell, T. S. C. 1993. "Anxiety: The Hidden Variable in the Korean EFL Classroom." *Language Teaching* 1 (1): 16-18.

Ferguson, C. 1975. "Toward a Characterization of English Foreigner Talk." *Anthropological Linguistics* 17:1-14.

Ferris, D. 1995. "Student Reactions to Teacher Response in Multiple-draft Composition Classrooms." *TESOL Quarterly* 29:33-53.

Fieg, J. P. 1989. *A Common Core: Thais and Americans.* Yarmouth, Maine: Intercultural Press.

Folse, K. S. 1990. *English Structure Practices.* Ann Arbor, Mich.: University of Michigan Press.

———. 1994. "Minimal Pairs." In *New Ways in Teaching Speaking,* ed. K. M. Bailey and L. Savage, 205-6. Alexandria, Va.: TESOL.

Forest, T. 1992. "Shooting Your Class: The Videodrama Approach to Language Acquisition." In *Video in Second Language Teaching,* ed. S. Stempleski and P. Arcario, 79-92. Alexandria, Va.: TESOL.

Frake, C. 1980. *Language and Cultural Description.* Stanford, Calif.: Stanford University Press.

Freeman, D., and J. C. Richards. 1993. "Conceptions of Teaching and the Education of Second Language Teachers." *TESOL Quarterly* 27:193-216.

Fuchs, M. 1992. *Longman Dictionary of American English Workbook.* White Plains, N.Y.: Longman.

Fuller, F. F. 1969. "Concerns of Teachers: A Developmental Characterization." *American Educational Research Journal* 6:207-26.

Fuller, F. F., and O. H. Bown. 1975. "Becoming a Teacher." In *Teacher Education: The Seventy-fourth Yearbook of the National Society for the Study of Education,* ed. K. Ryan, 25-51. Chicago: National Society for the Study of Education.

Garber, C. A., and G. Holmes. 1981. "Video-aided Written/Oral Assignments." *Foreign Language Annals* 14:325-31.

Gebhard, J. G. 1985. "Teaching Reading through Assumptions about Learning." *English Teaching Forum* 23 (3): 16-20.

———. 1987. "Successful Comprehension: What Teachers Can Do before Students Read." *English Teaching Forum* 25 (2): 21-23.

———. 1990a. "Freeing the Teacher: A Supervisory Process." *Foreign Language Annals* 23:517-25.

———. 1990b. "Interaction in a Teaching Practicum." In *Second Language*

Teacher Education, ed. J. C. Richards and D. Nunan, 118–31. New York: Cambridge University Press.

———. 1991. "Seeing Teaching Differently: The Teacher as Observer." *Language Teacher* 15 (5): 17–20.

———. 1992. "Awareness of Teaching: Approaches, Benefits, Tasks." *English Teaching Forum* 30 (4): 2–7.

Gebhard, J. G., S. Gaitan, and R. Oprandy. 1987. "Beyond Prescription: The Student Teacher as Investigator." *Foreign Language Annals* 20:227–32.

Gebhard, J. G., and A. Ueda-Motonaga. 1992. "The Power of Observation: 'Make a Wish, Make a Dream, Imagine All the Possibilities.'" In *Collaborative Language Learning and Teaching,* ed. D. Nunan, 179–91. Cambridge: Cambridge University Press.

Gibson, R. 1975. "The Strip Story: A Catalyst for Communication." *TESOL Quarterly* 9:149–54.

Gilbert, J. N.d. "Nonverbal Tools for Teaching Pronunciation." University of California, Davis. Photocopy.

———. 1987. "Pronunciation and Listening Comprehension." In *Current Perspectives on Pronunciation,* ed. J. Morley, 29–40. Alexandria, Va.: TESOL.

———. 1994. "Intonation: A Navigation Guide for the Listener." In *Pronunciation Pedagogy and Theory: New Views, New Directions,* ed. J. Morley, 36–48. Alexandria, Va.: TESOL.

Goldstein, L. M., and S. M. Conrad. 1990. "Student Input and Negotiation of Meaning in ESL Writing Conferences." *TESOL Quarterly* 24:443–60.

Good, T. L., and J. E. Brophy. 1987. *Looking into Classrooms.* New York: Harper and Row.

Grabe, W. 1991. "Current Developments in Second Language Reading Research." *TESOL Journal* 25:375–406.

Green, C., and J. M. Green. 1993. "Secret Friend Journals." *TESOL Journal* 2 (3): 20–23.

Greenfield, R. 1994. "Minimal Pairs with Street Names." In *New Ways in Teaching Speaking,* ed. K. M. Bailey and L. Savage, 218–19. Alexandria, Va.: TESOL.

Grellet, F. 1981. *Developing Reading Skills: A Practical Guide to Reading Comprehension Exercises.* New York: Cambridge University Press.

Hairston, M. 1982. "The Winds of Change: Thomas Khun and the Revolution in the Teaching of Writing." *College Composition and Communication* 33 (1): 76–88.

Hall, E. T. 1966. *The Silent Language.* New York: Anchor Books.

Harsch, K. 1994. "Paraphrasing Races." In *New Ways in Teaching Speaking,* ed. K. M. Bailey and L. Savage, 97–98. Alexandria, Va.: TESOL.

Heinze, R. I. 1982. *Tham khwan: How to Contain the Essence of Life.* Kent Ridge: Singapore University Press.

Helgesen, M. 1993. "Creating Active, Effective-Listeners." *Language Teacher* 17 (8): 13–14.

Hoffer, B. L. 1984. "English Sociokinesics." *Die Neueren Sprachen* 83:544–54.

Holmes, V. L., and M. R. Moulton. 1994. " 'I Am Amazine to See My Write in Print': Publishing from ESL Students' Perspective." *TESOL Journal* 3 (4): 14–16.

Johnson, K. E. 1992. "Learning to Teach: Instructional Actions and Decisions of Preservice ESL Teachers." *TESOL Quarterly* 26:507–34.

Kajornboon, B. 1989. "Video in the Language Class." *PASAA* 19 (1): 41–52.

Kitao, K. 1986. "Using Authentic Video Materials in the Language Classroom." *Cross-Currents* 12 (2): 17–28.

Klippel, F. 1984. *Keep Talking: Communicative Fluency Activities for Language Teaching.* Cambridge: Cambridge University Press.

Kluge, D. E. 1993. "Your Turn at the Mike." In *New Ways in Teaching Reading,* ed. R. R. Day, 9–11. Alexandria, Va.: TESOL.

Krashen, S. 1982. *Principles and Practice in Second Language Acquisition.* Oxford: Pergamon.

———. 1985. *The Input Hypothesis: Issues and Implications.* White Plains, N.Y.: Longman.

Krashen, S., and T. Terrell. 1983. *The Natural Approach: Language Acquisition in the Classroom.* Oxford: Pergamon Press.

Kroll, B. 1991. "Teaching Writing in the ESL Context." In *Teaching English as a Second or Foreign Language,* ed. M. Celce-Murcia, 245–63. Boston: Heinle and Heinle.

Kusenberg, K. 1986. "Odd Tippling." In *On Being Foreign: Culture Shock in Short Fiction,* ed. T. Lewis and R. Jungman, 51–53. Yarmouth, Maine: Intercultural Press.

Lankton, S. 1980. *Practical Magic: A Translation of Basic Neuro-linguistic Programming into Clinical Psychotherapy.* Cupertino, Calif.: Meta Publications.

Lapp, R. E. 1984. "The Process Approach to Writing: Toward a Curriculum for International Students." Working paper, ESL Department, University of Hawaii at Manoa.

Larimer, R., and S. Vaughn. 1993. *Real Conversations: Beginning Listening and Speaking Activities.* Boston: Heinle and Heinle.

Larsen-Freeman, D. 1986. *Techniques and Principles in Language Teaching.* New York: Oxford University Press.

Lee, W. R. 1979. *Language Teaching Games and Contests.* Oxford: Oxford University Press.

Lewis, T. J., and R. E. Jungman, eds. 1986. *On Being Foreign: Culture Shock in Short Fiction.* Yarmouth, Maine: Intercultural Press.

Lieberman, A. 1992. Foreword to *Contrasting Conversations: Activities for Exploring Our Beliefs and Teaching Practices,* by J. Fanselow. White Plains, N.Y.: Longman.

Lindfors, J. W. 1988. "From 'talking together' to 'being together in talk.'" *Language Arts* 65 (2): 135–41.

Littlewood, W. 1981. *Communicative Language Teaching.* Cambridge: Cambridge University Press.

Lonergan, J. 1984. *Video in Language Teaching.* Cambridge: Cambridge University Press.

Long, M. L. 1977. "Teacher Feedback on Learner Error: Mapping Cognitions." In *On TESOL 77,* ed. H. D. Brown, C. Yorio, and R. H. Crymes, 278–94. Alexandria, Va.: TESOL.

Long, M. L., and C. Sato. 1983. "Classroom Foreigner Talk Discourse: Forms and Functions of Teachers' Questions." In *Classroom-Oriented Research in Second Language Acquisition,* ed. H. Seliger and M. Long, 268–86. Rowley, Mass.: Newbury House.

Lorayne, H., and J. Lucas. 1974. *The Memory Book.* New York: Dorset Press.

Lortie, D. C. 1975. *Schoolteacher: A Sociological Study.* Chicago: University of Chicago Press.

Mahili, I. 1994. "Responding to Student Writing." *English Teaching Forum* 32 (4): 24–27.

Maley, A., and A. Duff. 1982. *Drama Techniques in Language Learning.* New York: Cambridge University Press.

Mangelsdorf, K. 1992. "Peer Reviews in the ESL Composition Classroom: What Do the Students Think?" *ELT Journal* 46:274–84.

Marshall, T. 1989. *The Whole World Guide to Language Learning.* Yarmouth, Maine: Intercultural Press.

Maurice, K., K. Vanikieti, and S. Keyuravong. 1989. "Putting Up a Reading Board and Cutting Down the Boredom." *English Teaching Forum* 27 (2): 29–31.

McCarthy, M., and R. Carter. 1995. "Spoken Grammar: What Is It and How Can We Teach It?" *ELT Journal* 49:207–18.

McCoy, L. R. 1979. "Means to Overcome the Anxieties of Second Language Learners." *Foreign Language Annals* 12 (3): 185–89.

McKay, I. S. 1993. *Beginning Interactive Grammar.* Boston: Heinle and Heinle.

McKay, S. L. 1992. *Teaching English Overseas: An Introduction.* New York: Oxford University Press.

McLaughlin, B. 1990. "Restructuring." *Applied Linguistics* 11:113–28.

Melamed, L., and D. Barndt. 1977. "Exercises Focusing on Non-verbal Communication." *TESL Talk* 8 (4): 31–38.

Melvin, B. S., and D. F. Stout. 1987. "Motivating Language Learners through Authentic Materials." In *Interactive Language Teaching,* ed. W. Rivers, 44–56. New York: Cambridge University Press.

Moore, C. G. 1992. *Heart Talk.* Bangkok: White Lotus.

Morain, G. 1987. "Kinesics across Cultures." In *Culture Bound,* ed. J. M. Valdes, 64–76. New York: Cambridge University Press.

Morley, J. 1979. *Improving Spoken English: An Intensive Personalized Program in Perception, Pronunciation, Practice in Context.* Ann Arbor, Mich.: University of Michigan Press.

———. 1991a. "Listening Comprehension in Second/Foreign Language Instruction." In *Teaching English as a Second or Foreign Language,* ed. M. Celce-Murcia, 81–106. Boston: Heinle and Heinle.

———. 1991b. "The Pronunciation Component in Teaching English to Speakers of Other Languages." *TESOL Quarterly* 25:481–520.

———, ed. 1987. *Current Perspectives on Pronunciation.* Alexandria, Va.: TESOL.

———, ed. 1994. *Pronunciation Pedagogy and Theory: New Views, New Directions.* Alexandria, Va.: TESOL.

Moskowitz, G. 1978. *Caring and Sharing in the Foreign Language Classroom.* Rowley, Mass.: Newbury House.

Nash, R. J., and D. A. Shiman. 1974. "The English Teacher as Questioner." *English Journal* 63:38–44.

Nation, P., ed. 1994. *New Ways in Teaching Vocabulary.* Alexandria, Va.: TESOL.

Nelson, G. L., and J. M. Murphy. 1992–93. "Writing Groups and the Less Proficient ESL Student." *TESOL Journal* 2 (2): 23–25.

Nicholson, P., and R. Sakuno. 1982. *Explain Yourself! An English Conversation Book for Japan.* Kyoto: PAL.

Nunan, D. 1988. *The Learner-centered Curriculum.* New York: Cambridge University Press.

———. 1991. *Language Teaching Methodology: A Textbook for Teachers.* Englewood Cliffs, N.J.: Prentice Hall.

———.1992. "The Teacher as Decision-maker." In *Perspectives on Second Language Teacher Education,* ed. J. Flowerdew, M. Brock, and S. Hsia, 135–65. Hong Kong: City Polytechnic of Hong Kong.

———. 1993. "EFL Global Views: Challenges in EFL Classrooms." *TESOL Matters* 3 (3): 7.

Nydell, M. K. 1987. *Understanding Arabs: A Guide for Westerners.* Yarmouth, Maine: Intercultural Press.

Ogami, N., producer. 1988. *Cold Water: Intercultural Adjustment and Values of Foreign Students and Scholars at an American University.* Yarmouth, Maine: Intercultural Press. Videotape.

Olshtain, E. 1991. "Functional Tasks for Mastering the Mechanics of Writing and Going Just Beyond." In *Teaching English as a Second or Foreign Language,* ed. M. Celce-Murcia, 235–44. Boston: Heinle and Heinle.

Oluwadiya, A. 1992. "Some Prewriting Techniques for Student Writers." *English Teaching Forum* 30 (4): 12–15.

Orion, G. F. 1988. *Pronouncing American English: Sounds, Stress, and Intonation.* Boston: Heinle and Heinle.

Oxford, R. 1990. *Language Learning Strategies: What Every Teacher Should Know.* Boston: Heinle and Heinle.

Papalia, A. 1987. "Interaction of Reader and Text." In *Interactive Language Teaching,* ed. W. M. Rivers, 70–82. New York: Cambridge University Press.

Parry, K. J. 1987. "Reading in a Second Culture." In *Research in Reading in English as a Second Language,* ed. J. Devine, P. L. Carrell, and D. Eskey, 59–70. Alexandria, Va.: TESOL.

Pearson-Hamatani, E. P. 1993. "Without a Dictionary." In *New Ways in Teaching Reading,* ed. R. R. Day, 217–18. Alexandria, Va.: TESOL.

Pennington, M. C. 1989. "Teaching Pronunciation from the Top Down." *RELC Journal* 20 (1): 20–38.

———, ed. 1995. *New Ways in Teaching Grammar.* Alexandria, Va.: TESOL.

Pennington, M. C., and J. C. Richards. 1986. "Pronunciation Revisited." *TESOL Quarterly* 20:207–25.

Peyton, J. K. 1993. "Dialogue Journals: Interactive Writing to Develop Language and Literacy." *ERIC Digest,* April.

Peyton, J. K., and L. Reed 1990. *Dialogue Journal Writing with Nonnative English Speakers: A Handbook for Teachers.* Alexandria, Va.: TESOL.

Porter, D., and J. Roberts. 1987. "Authentic Listening Activities." In

Methodology in TESOL, ed. M. L. Long and J. C. Richards, 177–87. Rowley, Mass.: Newbury House.

Prodromou, L. 1991. "The Good Language Teacher." *English Teaching Forum* 24 (2): 2-7.

Raimes, A. 1983. *Techniques in Teaching Writing.* New York: Oxford University Press.

———.1985. "What Unskilled ESL Students Do as They Write: A Classroom Study of Composing." *TESOL Quarterly* 19:229-58.

Rardin, J. P., D. D. Tranel, P. L. Tirone, and B. D. Green. 1988. *Education in a New Dimension: The Counseling-learning Approach to Community Language Learning.* East Dubuque, Ill.: Counseling Learning Publications.

Rathet, I. 1994. "English by Drawing: Making the Language Lab a Center of Active Learning." *TESOL Journal* 3 (3): 22-25.

Rayner, K., and A. Pollastek. 1989. *The Psychology of Reading.* Englewood Cliffs, N.J.: Prentice Hall.

Reid, J. M. 1987. "The Learning Style Preferences of ESL Students." *TESOL Quarterly* 21:87-111.

———.1994. "Responding to ESL Students' Texts: The Myths of Appropriation." *TESOL Quarterly* 28:273-92.

———.1995. *Learning Styles in the ESL/EFL Classroom.* Boston: Heinle and Heinle.

Richards, J. C. 1987. "The Dilemma of Teacher Education in TESOL." *TESOL Quarterly* 21:209-26.

———.1990. *The Language Teaching Matrix.* New York: Cambridge University Press.

———. 1993. "Beyond the Text Book: The Role of Commercial Materials in Language Teaching." *RELC Journal* 24 (1): 1-14.

Richards, J. C., J. Hull, and S. Proctor. 1990. *Interchange: English for International Communication.* New York: Cambridge University Press.

Richards, J. C., and C. Lockhart. 1994. *Language Teaching in Focus: Reflective Teaching in Second Language Classrooms.* New York: Cambridge University Press.

Richards, J. C., and T. Rodgers. 1986. *Approaches and Methods in Language Teaching.* New York: Cambridge University Press.

Rinvolucri, M. 1984. *Grammar Games.* Cambridge: Cambridge University Press.

———. 1995. "Language Students as Letter Writers." *ELT Journal* 49:152-59.

Rivers, W., ed. 1987. *Interactive Language Teaching*. New York: Cambridge University Press.

Rosen, S. 1982. *My Voice Will Go with You: The Teaching Tales of Milton H. Erickson*. New York: W. W. Norton.

Rowe, M. 1974. "Wait-time and Rewards as Instructional Variables, Their Influence on Language, Logic and Fate Control: Part 1—Wait-time." *Journal of Research in Science Teaching* 11 (2): 81-94.

———. 1986. "Wait Time: Slowing Down May Be a Way of Speeding Up." *Journal of Teacher Education* 37 (1): 43-50.

Rubin, J., and I. Thompson. 1994. *How to Be a More Successful Language Learner*. Boston: Heinle and Heinle.

Sainz, M. J. 1993. "Good Evening, and Welcome to This Edition of the News." *TESOL Journal* 3 (1): 41-42.

Scarcella, R. C., and R. L. Oxford. 1992. *The Tapestry of Language Learning: The Individual in the Communicative Classroom*. Boston: Heinle and Heinle.

Schenkein, J., ed. 1978. *Studies in the Organization of Conversational Interaction*. New York: Academic Press.

Schmitt, N., and D. Schmitt. 1995. "Vocabulary Notebooks: Theoretical Underpinnings and Practical Suggestions." *ELT Journal* 49:133-43.

Schoenberg, I. E. 1989. *Talk about Values*. White Plains, N.Y.: Longman.

Scovel, T. 1978. "The Effect of Affect on Foreign Language Learning: A Review of Anxiety Research." *Language Learning* 28:129-42.

Segal, B. 1983. *Teaching English through Action*. Brea, Calif.: Berty Segal.

Segal, B., and H. Sloane, producers. 1984. *TPR and the Natural Approach: The Joy of Acquiring Language*. Brea, Calif.: Berty Segal. Videotape.

Shanefield, L. 1993. "Eight Steps to an ESOL Collection." In *New Ways in Teaching Reading,* ed. R. R. Day, 22-24. Alexandria, Va.: TESOL.

Silva, T. 1990. "Second Language Composition Instruction: Developments, Issues, and Directions." In *Second Language Writing: Research Insights for the Classroom,* ed. B. Kroll, 11-23. New York: Cambridge University Press.

Smith, F. 1994. *Understanding Reading*. New York: Holt, Rinehart, and Winston.

Stanwyck, D., and P. Abdellal. 1984. "Attitudes toward Cheating Behavior in the ESL Classroom." Paper presented at the annual conference of the National Association for Foreign Student Affairs, Nashville, Tenn.

Staton, J. 1987. "New Research on Dialogue Journals." *Dialogue* 4 (1): 1-24.

Staton, J., R. Shuy, and J. Kreeft. 1982. *Analysis of Dialogue Journal Writ-*

ing as a Communicative Event. Washington, D.C.: Center of Applied Linguistics.

Steffensen, M. S., C. Joag-Dev, and R. C. Anderson. 1979. "A Cross-cultural Perspective on Reading Comprehension." *Reading Research Quarterly* 15:10-29.

Stempleski, S. 1992. "Teaching Communication Skills with Authentic Video." In *Video in Second Language Teaching,* ed. S. Stempleski and P. Arcario, 7-24. Alexandria, Va.: TESOL.

Stenton, A., coordinating ed. 1983. *Longman Dictionary of American English.* White Plains, N.Y.: Longman.

Stevick, E. W. 1978. "Control, Initiative, and the Whole Learner." In *Collected Papers in Teaching English as a Second Language and Bilingual Education,* ed. R. L. Light and A. H. Osman, 34-45. New York: NYS ESOL BEA.

———. 1980. *Teaching Languages: A Way and Ways.* Rowley, Mass.: Newbury House.

———. 1982. "My Understanding of Teaching Languages: A Way and Ways." Paper presented at the TESOL Convention, Honolulu, Hawaii.

Storti, C. 1989. *The Art of Crossing Cultures.* Yarmouth, Maine: Intercultural Press.

Swaffar, J. 1988. "Readers, Texts, and Second Languages: The Interactive Processes." *Modern Language Journal* 72 (1): 123-49.

Tambiah, S. J. 1970. *Buddhism and the Spirit Cults in North-east Thailand.* Cambridge: Cambridge University Press.

Tanka, J. 1993. "Teaching Listening in the Language Lab: One Program's Experience." *TESOL Journal* 3 (1): 15-17.

Thomas, J. 1993. "Countering the 'I Can't Write English' Syndrome." *TESOL Journal* 2 (3): 12-15.

Tudor, I. 1993. "Teacher Roles in the Learner-centered Classroom." *ELT Journal* 47:22-30.

Ur, P. 1984. *Teaching Listening Comprehension.* New York: Cambridge University Press.

Via, R. 1987. "'The Magic If' of Theater: Enhancing Language Learning through Drama." In *Interactive Language Teaching,* ed. W. M. Rivers, 110-23. New York: Cambridge University Press.

Wallace, C. 1992. *Reading.* Oxford: Oxford University Press.

Wallace, M. J. 1991. *Training Foreign Language Teachers: A Reflective Approach.* New York: Cambridge University Press.

Wallender, D. 1977. "Excerpts from a Volunteer's Journal." *The Bridge,* fall.

Wardhaugh, R. 1985. *How Conversation Works.* Oxford: Blackwell.

Watson, M. O. 1974. "Conflicts and Directions in Proxemic Research." In *Nonverbal Communication,* ed. S. Weitz, 230-41. New York: Oxford University Press.

West, M. 1960. *Teaching English in Difficult Circumstances.* London: Longman.

White, D., producer. 1978. *Action Songs for Indoor Days.* Los Angeles: Tom Thumb Records. Record.

White, R. V. 1981. "Approaches to Teaching Writing." *Guidelines* 6 (1): 1-11.

———,ed. 1995. *New Ways in Teaching Writing.* Alexandria, Va.: TESOL.

Wright, A. 1989. *Pictures for Language Learning.* Cambridge: Cambridge University Press.

Wright, A., D. Betteridge, and M. Buckly. 1994. *Games for Language Learning.* Cambridge: Cambridge University Press.

Wright, T. 1987. *Roles of Teachers and Learners.* Oxford: Oxford University Press.

Wylie, L., and R. Stafford. 1977. *Beaux Gestes: A Guide to French Body Talk.* Cambridge, Mass.: Undergraduate Press.

Yorkey, R. 1984. *Springboards: Interacting in English.* Reading, Mass.: Addison-Wesley.

Zamel, V. 1982. "Writing: The Process of Discovering Meaning." *TESOL Quarterly* 16:195-209.

———. 1983. "The Composing Processes of Advanced ESL Students: Six Case Studies." *TESOL Quarterly* 17:165-90.

———. 1985. "Responding to Student Writing." *TESOL Quarterly* 19:79-191.

———. 1987. "Recent Research on Writing Pedagogy." *TESOL Quarterly* 21:697-715.

Zukowski-Faust, J., and M. K. O'Brien. 1991. *Grammar One.* Boston: Heinle and Heinle.

Index